Watts: The Aftermath

Watts: The Aftermath

An Inside View of the Ghetto
by The People of Watts

*Edited, with an introduction, notes, and a
concluding chapter by Paul Bullock*

Grove Press, Inc., New York

To my wife, Connie

Acknowledgments

Perhaps the most difficult burden borne by any writer is the acknowledgment of his debts to others. If he is thorough and honest in his identification of the many persons and organizations that have guided, inspired, influenced, and assisted him in the complex process of preparing or editing a book, the list would probably become a book in itself. There is always the additional danger that one will blindly overlook the contribution of someone who deserves recognition. As I put down a partial list of my debts, let me first apologize to the many whom I have omitted for reasons that range from absent-mindedness to discretion.

First, and perhaps most obviously, I acknowledge the opportunity and the unfailing support given to me over the past three years by the Institute of Industrial Relations at UCLA, and particularly by a friend and colleague who is also the Institute's Associate Director in charge of research—Dr. Irving Bernstein. The biggest single debt, in a sense, is owed to the Institute secretarial staff who assumed the thankless but indispensable chore of transcribing the tapes (which, as often as not, were just barely audible) and typing the manuscript in its several versions: notably my conscientious secretaries during that period, Mrs. Kathleen Greene and Miss Barbara Stempel. At some very critical junctures in the progress of the work, they had efficient help from other members of the Institute staff: Miss Joan Gusten, Miss Dina Lebow, and Miss Shirley Matthews. Of course, as I emphasize once again in the Introduction, the value of the editorial assistance given me by Mrs. Felicitas Hinman has been inestimable.

Next, I am indebted, to a degree which can only be inadequately expressed, to many persons who counseled me along the way as the book gradually took shape. The members of a reading committee appointed by the Institute—Dr. John Horton of the Sociology Department, Professor Leon Letwin of the School of Law, and Dr. Bernstein of the Political Science Department and the IIR, all of UCLA—offered helpful comments on an earlier draft, which resulted (I trust) in a measurable improvement in the quality. Another colleague of mine at the Institute—Fred H. Schmidt—has consistently been generous and thoughtful in appraising some aspects of the book and offering very incisive observations about the problems discussed. The several Graduate Research Assistants at the Institute, each of whom ferreted out information and checked factual statements as the writing proceeded, have contributed much to this work, and only the requirements of space and the fallibility of my memory prevent me from naming each one individually. Above all, I am grateful to Miss Lynne Shifflett, now a faculty member of the University of Wisconsin's School for Workers, for the criticisms, suggestions, and counsel she has provided over such a long period. Her wisdom and insight have saved me from egregious errors and many other pitfalls, and her contribution is of such magnitude that she has almost been a collaborator.

I should merely add, in closing this acknowledgment, that the conclusions and interpretations in the pages of this book are entirely my own, as editor, and that my friends and associates bear none of this responsibility.

The Authors*

Tracy Adkins
William Armstead
Mary Baines
T. Baker
Donnie Bradley
S. Collins
Antonette Culpepper
James Currie
Gary Davis
Sylvia Evans
F. Harper
W. Henderson
Ardelphia Hickey

Osee Lily
Robert Mason
Ann Miller
Richard Morris
Ted Owens, Jr.
G. Sanders
Lynne C. Shifflett
M. Taylor
J. Thomas
Richard Townsend
Earnest Walker
Paul Williams
W. Willis, Jr.

*The names of persons contributing to Chapters V and VI, and to certain parts of Chapter II, have been omitted from the above list. In addition, the names of many other contributors were unavailable, for one reason or another.

Contents

Introduction 3

I Watts: Before the Riot 11

II The Riot 33

III After the Riot: Image and Reality 51

Some Contrasting Impressions of the Community (1966-67) 57
"Leadership" (1967-69) 61
"All Power to the People" (1966-69) 69

IV Employment and Economics 105

V The Police 133

VI Pot and Pills 155

VII The Schools 165

VIII Welfare 197

IX Watts: A View From The Outside 217

A Note on Language 275

The Contributors 278

My thoughts have brought me to the point where I am on the edge of a line that is so thin it is like the edge on a razor blade. So narrow and short where either side could find yourself falling off into a world where there is no identity for me, particularly because of my color. I am a light-brown complexion, but I consider myself belonging to the black race, the Afro-American, the man who is seeking his identity in this country. The man who wants to be equal, but yet in his own culture, in his own color, in his own race, to the man who has put himself on a pedestal above every other race, a man who wants to dominate the world.

What is my identity? I am a brown-skinned person, a man in my own sense of being a man, but there are those who doubt this, those who still call me boy, one who has not yet reached the "maturity of understanding" in trying to be assimilated into a structure that has already stomped him into the lowest depth of humanity. I know that now I feel like, as the song says, a runaway child; they say, you better go back home where you belong. But where is home? Where do I belong? I'm still running, I think that I am going to continue to run until I do find out where I belong. Is it here—is it in Africa—or is it in a section not yet discovered? Which culture is going to accept me as an individual? . . .

I think that now the black people are like the Israelites in the Bible. Just like the Jews rising up against a dominating Pharaoh who has placed them in bondage for so many years, they have now come to the edge of the Red Sea and Moses is standing there praying, waiting for the miracle where the river will part and everyone will cross and live in the promised land. The black people are saying: I want to be free, I am here, "Let my people go." I am a man; I am not some sub-creature. I am not some animal. I am a man, equal in every respect to you who is white in color. I was not placed here by God to serve you, but to be equal to you.

And not "equal" in the bourgeois sense of "I am black in color, but in mind I am white; I want to be like you." This is not me. This is a brainwashing process, and with all the thoughts portrayed by the medias of communication, the black man will become more white than he is black and lose more of his identity than that which he already has. These will be my thoughts upon returning [from Vietnam], if God is willing, when I will return to my people and join them in a common struggle to find their identity. When I go back home where I belong. That is where I am going.

James (1969)

Watts: The Aftermath

Introduction

This is not an "objective, academic" study of a community. It is subjective and, in some respects, partisan. The statistics are sparse and marginal; no sampling surveys were conducted; no mimeographed questionnaires were circulated. I make no claim to impersonality in my own approach to the problems discussed: many of the people whom the reader will meet in the pages of this book are my friends.

This is an effort to capture and convey the feelings of people— neither "leaders" nor "spokesmen"—who live in or close to that part of the Los Angeles Negro ghetto known as Watts. The violence of August, 1965, has given Watts a national identification which is often misleading, both geographically and culturally. The community of Watts, actually a loosely defined part of the city of Los Angeles (with a few unincorporated county tracts adjoining), covers only about two and one-half square miles in a riot "curfew" zone which extends for forty-six square miles. My own decision to focus principally on Watts is partly personal and partly philosophical, but has little to do with its accidental fame. My acquaintanceship with the people and the problems of the area began in mid-1964, a full year before the outburst which brought it into worldwide headlines. Without claiming any special omniscience, I can say that there is no other section of Los Angeles County, including the west side area in which I live, with which I am as familiar. I was a frequent visitor to Watts months before the "riot," not always to carry on research, but often to meet with friends.

There is, of course, a deeper reason for selecting Watts: it represents a microcosm of the strengths and weaknesses of ghetto living. To be sure, it is not a slum in the usual sense, and a visitor is often surprised and a bit nonplused by its reasonably decent appearance. Yet its small area probably contains more residents of public housing than does any other part of Los Angeles County, and a high proportion of its population is unemployed, underemployed, or on welfare. At the same time, its headline identification has brought it more publicity, and perhaps more programs, than any other poverty area of the County. The fact that it has received such attention is of some practical value to us as observers. It gives us an opportunity to evaluate the relative effectiveness of antipoverty programs in a "riot" area, and if the residents here fail to perceive tangible improvements in their lives, we can infer that the problem is exacerbated in those communities which have obtained a smaller proportion of funds.

Anyone, and especially the white outsider, faces difficult and complex problems whenever he attempts to discuss and interpret life in the black ghetto. Questions of terminology and semantics are among the most vexing. One's choice of words can, unconsciously perhaps, distort the image of an event or a community, or raise extraneous issues which cloud the main point. For instance, what term should one apply to the eruption of August, 1965? The conventional and familiar term is "riot," but many feel that this obscures or understates the broader social implications of the event. They would prefer to describe it as a "revolt," an "uprising," or an "insurrection."

Much depends, of course, on one's interpretation of the term "riot." If it is regarded as only an aimless or selfish act of disorder and violence, clearly the 1965 event in Los Angeles was considerably more than that. If, however, it is viewed more broadly as any mass defiance of law and constituted authority, whatever its motivation, the term "riot" unquestionably is meaningful. Since I am convinced that the violence of August, 1965, had both conventional *and* ideological significance, I shall use the more familiar term in its broader sense. Its social implications will, I hope, be evident in the comments and descriptions contained in the pages of this book.

I have made no attempt to describe the riot in detail; others have undertaken this task with skill and understanding. Certainly, however, the riot and its impact on the community cannot be ignored, and I have included some of the impressions and observations of riot participants as a means of illuminating their feelings about the police, merchants, and other groups involved in the ghetto. Primarily, this is an account of how people feel, and why they feel that way, in an area in which a major riot has occurred. The authors of this book are the people of Watts, speaking (I hope) frankly and sometimes ungrammatically about the problems they face every day. Their candor, in many respects, creates an unsettling problem for the editor, since some of the activities they describe are unlawful. Obviously, it is essential that their anonymity be protected, and I have striven to do so even though this makes it impossible to offer as much biographical data about them as I might wish. I have given information about individuals wherever this has been consistent with my obligation to protect them.

Before proceeding to the text itself, I am impelled to offer a few personal observations. I have said that this work is not scientific in a traditional sense, and I make no apology for that fact. In the past, I have supervised or participated in formal studies and surveys, and undoubtedly I shall do so again in the future. That approach, with its emphasis on statistics, mathematical probabilities, and sampling techniques, has substantial value, but also some drastic limitations and defects. The statistical form, conveying results filtered through the computer, sometimes gives a specious impression of accuracy and objectivity, when in fact the possibilities of human error are manifold. This is not, however, the primary objection to the formal method. The major limitation is inherent in the nature of social science as opposed to natural science.

Some social scientists have sought to expand the scientific content of their respective disciplines, but their efforts are always thwarted, at some point, by the fact that human beings cannot be "controlled." The scientist in his laboratory can be reasonably sure that the individual wills and characteristics of the materials he is studying will not influence the results of his investigation in a fashion which he cannot predict, but the economist or sociologist is never so fortunate. The people who are studied by the social scientist are themselves a part of the study or research process, and their awareness of their own role can easily affect the process itself.

Social research can provide us with a great deal of factual information, but its usefulness is severely limited when it encounters problems of causation and motivation. The social scientists can tell us whether boys are more likely to drop out of high school than girls, or at what age the dropping out is most likely to occur, but the conventional techniques are only partially and inadequately helpful in explaining the precise reasons why a given youngster drops out, or what combination of circumstances is most likely to reduce the dropout rate in a particular area. The figures on unemployment are available, though highly inadequate in areas like Watts, but they cannot always explain why one man is more employable than another.

If the conventional methods of social research are deficient even when applied to middle-class Americans, they are virtually useless in the low-income, black ghetto. The ghetto resident is suspicious of strangers wearing coats and ties, carrying notebooks, and asking personal questions. If the interview contains questions relating to welfare, unemployment compensation, school attendance, or anything that might possibly involve the law or bureaucratic regulations, the suspicion is heightened. The normal assumption is that the stranger seeks information for ulterior purposes, and that he is probably a policeman, welfare investigator, truant officer, dope peddler, politician, or the like. In many cases, the interviewer will not get beyond the front doorstep; the residents will be scurrying out the back door.

Such skepticism is pervasive in the ghetto, confirmed and strengthened by long experience. The resident has no reason to trust strangers. Some time ago, as I walked through the Jordan Downs housing project with a young friend one evening, we passed a group of teen-agers and one of them yelled to my friend: "Ernie, man, you been busted?" It was the second time that day that someone had mistaken me for "Irvine" (the local nickname for a cop), and I was a relatively familiar figure in Watts.

Nor is the ghetto resident completely reassured when the stranger is a Negro. He is well aware that Negro policemen, social workers, probation officers, bill collectors, and school officials operate in the area, and he is quick to detect variations in speech patterns, mannerisms, and so forth, which would suggest that the stranger does not really belong in the community.

When questioned by unfamiliar researchers or journalists, he may be either excessively cautious or excessively aggressive in his answers. The white interviewer will be told what—in the perceptive view of the interviewee—he expects or wants to hear, or what seems most likely to impress and shock him. The youngsters, in particular, soon discover that the more belligerent and militant response is sure to gain the greater share of attention. There can be little doubt that much genuine and deeply rooted feeling is reflected in such a response, and that many residents derive a profound emotional satisfaction from the opportunity to bait and annoy Mr. Charley. The increased militancy in the ghetto is fact, not fiction. Yet such replies cannot always be taken at face value. Many youngsters are masters of the "put-on," and there is often a gap between statement and performance.

These are the kinds of problems which create formidable difficulties for the conventional researcher. The partial solution, in my judgment, is to pursue the path already opened up by anthropologist Oscar Lewis and, in a somewhat different sense, by Claude Brown, whose remarkable and moving reconstruction of his own experiences in the Harlem ghetto provides an invaluable insight into the social and psychological forces at work therein.[1] Lewis probes deeply into the feelings of poor persons with whom he has established a personal tie and rapport, letting them tell their own stories in their own way. Clearly there is much subjectivity in such studies, partly because the observer is intimately associated with those being observed. At least the reader can be aware of its presence and give it whatever weight it seems to deserve, whereas in many of the more formal studies the value judgments or simple human mistakes are hidden from view.

One underlying purpose of these works—and of this one—is to give us a deeper insight into the motivations and the perceptions of people who live in poverty. These are people who have often been regarded as nonverbal or inarticulate, and resistant to any attempted exploration of their attitudes and feelings. This is a misconception, derived largely from the inability of most researchers to communicate with those of a far different background, and to establish the kind of mutual confidence which is a precondition to rapport. The residents of the poverty ghetto, most notably the youngsters, are frequently more incisive and perceptive in describing problems and motivations than are the supposedly more sophisticated members of society. Rationalization and self-deception are far more common in Beverly Hills or Malibu than in Watts; no one on the margin of hunger and deprivation can afford to kid himself. Such honesty and candor, I hasten to add, may coexist with a "hustler's" philosophy and a calculated use of charm and wile to gain one's ends. This is a phenomenon to which I shall return later.

---

[1] Some of Lewis's major works are *Five Families* (New York: New American Library) and *The Children of Sanchez* (New York: Random House, Vintage), studies of the Mexican lower-class culture; and *La Vida* (New York: Random House, Vintage), a study of Puerto Rican culture. Brown's autobiographical work is *Manchild in the Promised Land* (New York: New American Library, Signet).

I am concerned here with the way in which the people of Watts *perceive* their problems and the social institutions which affect them. Our behavior, after all, is determined by our perceptions, which are not always in accord with the objective facts. In the midst of the police incident which triggered the 1965 Los Angeles riot, the rumor spread throughout the area that the policemen had mistreated a pregnant woman. The reported pregnancy was nonexistent, but the black residents of south Los Angeles were prepared to believe the rumor because it was fully consistent with their experience. The persistent reports of progress in employment within the south central ghetto, since the riot, will be credited by the people only as this progress becomes visible to them as individuals. Until an improvement in police practices is directly observed in the neighborhood, the resident will retain his usual opinions of "Irvine."

For these and other reasons, I have decided to let the statements stand just as spoken or written. This book is not intended as a precise factual account of "Life in Watts," but rather as an expression of feelings and personal experiences. I can attest, on the basis of my own involvement in the community over the past four years, that in nearly every instance these observations are in accord with reality.

The mechanics of interviewing and organization may be of some interest to the reader. While in a few cases the statements were written, they were mainly taped in a series of discussions on the UCLA campus, or in the Watts community, starting in the summer of 1966 and ending in the early months of 1969. The participants were usually acquaintances of mine—about thirty in number—or their friends. Most of them are teen-agers or young adults, which is to be expected in a community in which most of the residents are below the age of twenty-five.

I tried to create an atmosphere in which everyone would be unhesitant about speaking frankly, a task made easier by the fact that we were already known to one another. I gave them my assurance that their frankness would not lead them into difficulty, such as reprisals from law enforcement agencies, school officials, or social workers, and that assurance has caused me to change or eliminate the real names of persons mentioned and to perform other editing to obscure their individual identities. Other than that, the tapes were edited only to reduce repetition or to clarify certain statements which might not otherwise be understood by the reader. Essentially, the original language has been left intact, and the reader who is confused by the many slang expressions should consult the appended glossary.[2] In the process of editing, I have had the invaluable assistance of Mrs. Felicitas Hinman, editor on the staff of the Institute of Industrial Relations, University of California, Los Angeles.

Each discussion was intended to focus on a particular subject, but inevitably the comments ranged widely. I have segregated the various statements according to category, e.g., schools, law enforcement, narcotics, etc., which required that I extract observations on, say, education, from a discussion initially focused on social welfare. This brings a certain discontinuity into the narrative, but I have resisted the temptation to edit more fully in preference to retaining the original language.

It is difficult, of course, to guarantee the "representativeness" of any group of interviewees. I know of no technique by which it could be demonstrated that a given statement accurately reflects the opinion or the experience of a "community" or a specified percentage thereof. There is much heterogeneity in Watts, and the reader will note both the similarities and divergences among the observations offered. I have deliberately retained some repetition because the same point made independently by different persons, especially if they differ on other subjects, may be of considerable significance.

In organizing the material, I have prepared an introduction to the subject matter of each chapter as a means of setting the scene for the reader. The first chapter, however, follows a somewhat different approach; it gives a historical view of the community, prepared from various sources. As the discussion proceeds from one point to another, I have also included transitional statements of my own which will provide background for what is to follow. I have reserved a systematic expression of my personal observations and thoughts for the concluding chapter, in which I have presented both my own views and some occasional comments of area residents which emerged from private conversations.

The most difficult question to confront, I think, is whether a white man can elicit candid responses from blacks who live in the ghetto, or can write meaningfully about their problems. I admit to nagging doubts about the answer to that question even as I put these words on paper. I can only say that my observations and judgments are based on considerably more than a casual or short-term or "academic" view of the community. If, as may well be possible, I have not been sufficiently close to the most militant and alienated

---

[2] See p. 274.

residents, I would emphasize that the criticisms and frustrations expressed by the more "moderate" thereby assume an even greater importance. Their apparent frankness in discussing the manifestations and effects of white racism can hardly be dismissed as the mouthings of a handful of "black nationalists."

One final word on my prejudices as an editor and a collaborator. I have said at the outset that this is, in a sense, a biased and partisan work. Without in any way seeking to romanticize the residents of a ghetto, I confess to a profound affection and admiration for the people who have written this book. Over the past three or four years, we have listened to jazz together, drunk together, gone to the beach together, played sports together, and participated in those many other experiences that friends share. The people of Watts are neither superhuman nor subhuman; they are a group of remarkable human beings, surviving and even developing in an environment which would crush the spirit of many of the rest of us. They have much to say, and I have tried to give them a forum. The reader must judge for himself whether I have succeeded or failed in capturing at least some fraction of the understanding and insight which I admire so deeply.

—PAUL BULLOCK

I

Watts: Before the Riot

Whatever may be the stereotypes created by national magazines and the other mass media, Watts is in no sense a completely unified and homogeneous community. The hostile delinquent, the aggressive nationalist, the "middle-class" homeowner, the college-bound youngster, the hustler, the conventional politician, the welfare recipient, the hard-core unemployed, and the hard-working employed are all represented, and only a journalist with a superficial view and a pressing deadline would dare to suggest that any one group symbolizes the "community." The one common bond is skin color, but even here we must recognize the presence of Mexican-Americans, now dwindling in number but still noticeable in some neighborhoods.

In the early days of Los Angeles, the area now known as Watts was part of a large ranch, El Rancho Tajuata.[1] When the original owner died, his estate was divided into many parcels to accommodate his heirs. In those days, land in California was easily acquired —legally and illegally—from its Mexican owners, and a number of Americans benefited.

Two subsequent building booms, the first in 1885-88 and the second in 1900-1910, hastened the growth of Tajuata, still an unincorporated area in the county of Los Angeles. Twenty-five-foot lots sold at a dollar down and a dollar a week. Land speculation, largely associated with the building of railroads and of Henry Huntington's Pacific Electric transportation system, eventually led to

---

[1] In the following historical discussion, the editor has drawn heavily from an unpublished historical essay on Watts, prepared by Franklyn Rabow, in the early part of 1965. At the time of writing, Mr. Rabow was a graduate student at UCLA. His study was initially commissioned by the editor as background for socio-economic analyses of the area.

further settlement of the area, close to the city but not in it. A major spur of the Pacific Electric tracks ran north and south through Tajuata, which was a junction for tracks running to Long Beach and San Pedro.

With the construction of the Pacific Electric railroad came the immigration of poor Mexican laborers, most of them employed by the railroad. By this time the heirs of the original owner had sold the land to subdividers. The PE decided to build a station on the old ranchland and acquired the necessary property from several Anglo subdividers, among whom was Julia A. Watts. The railroad men called it the Watts Station, and the growing settlement became known, unofficially, as Watts. Even then the cheap land and the corruption gave Watts something of a local reputation. One resident, a white American who had lived in Watts for many years, commented:

> "A dollar down and a dollar a week" became a by-word. This, with the politics and vice which abounded among the white inhabitants, caused Watts to be used as a joke in the theaters and on the streets. A spite deal sold the first land to the Negroes in the southern part of Watts. . . .[2]

Whatever the nature of this "spite deal" may have been, it is certain that some time before the first World War the southern edge of Watts became a Negro ghetto. Locally known as "Mudtown," this rustic community served as a port of entry for Negroes immigrating from the South. In his 1931 novel, *God Sends Sunday*,[3] the distinguished author Arna Bontemps described the early black settlements in Los Angeles:

> In those days, fifteen or twenty years ago, Negroes were not plentiful in the far West. Least of all were they to be seen in rural parts. A few of them, to be sure, had come as early as the historical gold rush with the forty-niners, working in personal service. Others had followed the conquest of the frontier. But the number had remained small until the great transcontinental railway lines established important terminals in Los Angeles and in San Francisco. Then the real immigration began. First, the railroad men, Pullman porters and dining car

---

[2] Quoted in "The Development of the Mexican People in the Community of Watts, California," a thesis by Clara Gertrude Smith, Department of Sociology, University of Southern California, April 17, 1933, p. 8.

[3] New York: Harcourt, Brace and Co., 1931, pp. 117, 119, 144, 162.

waiters, brought their families; hearing the rumors of attractive working conditions, their friends followed. Still the tendency was for them to remain in the larger centers and particularly in the location of the train yard.

The small group in Mudtown was exceptional. Here, removed from the influence of white folks, they did not acquire
the inhibitions of their city brothers. Mudtown was like a tiny
section of the deep south literally transplanted. . . .

The streets of Mudtown were three or four dusty wagon
paths. In the moist grass along the edges cows were staked. . . .
Ducks were sleeping in the weeds, and there was on the air a suggestion of pigs and slime holes. Tiny hoot-owls were sitting
bravely on fence posts while bats hovered overhead like shad-
ows. . . .

If early Mudtown was like a section of the South transplanted, it would not remain so for long. Mudtown was a part of Watts,
both geographically and commercially. As the population grew,
and as the Anglo and Mexican inhabitants of Watts moved toward
political self-determination, the Negro community became less isolated. Incorporated as a separate city in 1907, Watts was the scene
of unending political turmoil as the Anglos sought to maintain their
control of community affairs. When industrial development associated with World War I encouraged further immigration from the
South, mainly from Texas, Louisiana, and Mississippi, the black
newcomers settled either in Watts or in the Central Avenue ghetto to the north, closer to downtown. The expanding Watts ghetto, however, remained surrounded by Anglo communities, existing as a Negro island in an otherwise "lily white" and often hostile
sea. Indeed, until World War II, Watts itself retained its racially
heterogeneous character, its population divided about equally among
Anglos, Mexicans, and Negroes.

The internal politics of Watts became more troubled in the twenties. The Ku Klux Klan, already a force in the Compton area just to
the south, schemed to gain control of city government through the
use of recall petitions and devices to split the Negro community. Its
plans were thwarted by unwelcome publicity, but it remained active.[4] The political difficulties in the small town, coupled with water
shortages which could only be overcome through the Owens Valley

---

[4] Charlotta Bass, *Forty Years* (Los Angeles, 1960), pp. 56 - 57. Published by
Charlotta Bass.

Aqueduct project, led, in 1926, to the abandonment of cityhood and annexation to the city of Los Angeles.

Its absorption into Los Angeles, however, did not destroy Watts' identity as a community. Anyone familiar with Los Angeles knows that it is not one city but, rather, a series of distinct communities: one lives in Pacific Palisades, or San Pedro, or Eagle Rock, or Highland Park, or Bel Air, each technically a "neighborhood" within Los Angeles. Watts, of course, had a further claim to distinction: it contained a high proportion, though still a minority, of Negroes. Except for the Central Avenue area and a small middle-class Negro community along West Jefferson Boulevard to the north and west, Negroes in Los Angeles were to be found only in Watts, and, even then, mainly in the southern part of the community below 103rd Street. Northern Watts remained dominated by Anglos and Mexicans. Before World War II, the Mexican and Negro inhabitants were of lower economic status; in 1938, a writer commissioned by the Works Progress Administration (WPA) noted, somewhat snobbishly, that a low grade of labor was demanded by the manufacturing plants which had located on the eastern edge of Watts, and that this fact, plus the impact of the depression, had changed the character of the community. He also noted the mixture of good and poor dwellings in the area, a characteristic which remains in evidence today.[5]

During World War II, the population of Los Angeles boomed and Watts was no exception. Many of the immigrants were Negroes drawn by the lure of jobs in the war industries, and they encountered a critical housing problem when they entered this thoroughly segregated city. Tens of thousands moved into "Little Tokyo," vacated by the Japanese, but other thousands had to find accommodations in the traditionally segregated Central Avenue and Watts ghettos. Some of those who had decent jobs bought or built pleasant homes, many of which are still visible in the western part of Watts below 103rd Street and just east of Central Avenue. But many others moved into deteriorating or substandard housing, absentee owned, and several hundred more located in public housing projects built by the federal government in the Watts area.

The construction of the public housing projects, which became all-Negro though they were supposedly interracial, accelerated the ghettoization of the community. Three projects were built during

---

[5] William Burk, "Poor Housing in the Los Angeles Metropolitan Area." WPA Delinquency Prevention Project, L - 9304, March, 1938, no page numbers. Published by the U.S. Government.

the war, and a fourth, William Nickerson Jr. Gardens, was finished in 1955. The earliest—Hacienda Village (1942)—is the most attractive, with trees shading its single-story units. It was constructed as a permanent project, and its designers (Richard Neutra, Paul Williams, and Welton Becket) are now among the most prominent architects in California. Jordan Downs (September, 1944) and Imperial Courts (May, 1944) were semi-permanent projects for war workers, which were later converted into permanent units. Like Nickerson Gardens, they are massive and conventional two-story structures.

By 1946, Negroes represented almost two-thirds of the population of Watts, twice their proportion in 1940. Writing during the war, sociologist Lloyd H. Fisher noted the increasing tension in the community. Watts elementary schools were interracial both in teaching staff and student bodies, but the only high school (actually a combined junior and senior high), David Starr Jordan, was predominantly Negro because Anglo youngsters were encouraged to go elsewhere for their high school education. The nearby junior college in the all-white city of Compton discouraged Jordan High graduates from attending it. Fisher observed a lack of confidence in the police force, the absence of an interracial church, and a lack of leadership and organization within the community. In short, he detected all the major elements which were to explode into violence twenty years later.[6]

Nor was Fisher alone in his observations. In a book[7] on the Los Angeles Youth Project, published in 1949, Duane Robinson described the Watts area in terms which, in essence, were equally applicable fifteen years hence:

> This area is surrounded by strong Anglo-American communities which in the past have manifested discriminatory practices—even physical aggression. The Latin-American residents are disturbed by the rapidly growing Negro majority. The native Negroes are disturbed by the incoming "southern" Negroes, many of whom have imported and are supporting the approximately eighty churches in the area, ranging from magnificent edifices to tattered tents. Recreational and other facilities are hopelessly overwhelmed. There is no sizable building facility for recreation in the entire area.

---

[6] Lloyd H. Fisher, "The Problem of Violence," American Council on Race Relations, San Francisco, n.d., pp. 7 - 10.

[7] Duane Robinson, *Chance to Belong, Story of the Los Angeles Youth Project, 1943 - 1949* (New York: Woman's Press, 1949) pp. 38 - 39.

Even some bureaucrats and public officials seemed aware that something was amiss in Watts. In a report[8] on conditions of blight in the central area of the city of Los Angeles, the City Planning Commission, in 1947, concluded that Watts was

> an obsolescent area in which all the social and physical weaknesses of urban living are to be found. Some streets are unpaved, others have fine concrete roadways and ornaments; some structures seem about to fall apart, while next to them exist new, standard buildings. In some areas, a great number of twenty-five foot lots stand vacant, while in others six or more dwellings are crowded into a similar parcel. Recreational facilities in certain sections are few in number and limited in area. Schools are located in places where the maximum walking distance, rather than the minimum, is required of a great number of children. The shopping district on 103rd Street has little provision for off-street parking, and during busy hours the street is cluttered with double parked vehicles and is almost closed to traffic movement. Some of the worst interracial conflicts occurring in the past decade were in this area. The low rental pattern, the low assessed value of property, the high disease and delinquency rates, all reflect the blighted character of this district.

Clearly, every evidence of social pathology in Watts was a matter of public knowledge as early as 1947. But no action was forthcoming, or even suggested. After its incisive analysis of the problems in the area, the City Planning Commission offered no concrete plan for their alleviation. The conditions which breed riots had already emerged, conservatively speaking, a generation ago. In the light of such public indifference to deprivation and deterioration, the wonder is not that a riot eventually exploded in the area but, rather, that the residents were patient for so long.

The 1950's saw a few changes in Watts, but the movement of the community remained primarily the same, and was perhaps accelerated. In the first half of the decade, the Nickerson Gardens project was completed and both Jordan Downs and Imperial Courts were converted to permanent units, and by the decade's end over a third of the total population lived in public housing. Inevitably, the actual population density in the projects far exceeded the earlier projections, and the streets and yards swarmed with children. Large families were often crammed into relatively small quarters. The per-

---

[8] "Conditions of Blight, Central Area of the City of Los Angeles," Los Angeles Department of City Planning, 1947, unpaged.

centage of young people under the age of twenty-five rose to a little more than sixty per cent in 1960, and the proportion of homeowners dropped markedly as the projects expanded. The construction of a modern junior high school—Edwin Markham—improved the school system in a physical sense, but the dropout (or pushout) rate at Jordan High School was depressingly high. Anglos virtually disappeared, though a very few remain even today, and the Mexican-American percentage of total population dropped to less than eleven per cent, concentrated mostly in the eastern section.

As the community entered the 1960's, the forces of social and economic disorganization became stronger and more pervasive than ever. In a 1959 study, the Welfare Planning Council had noted that there was still no master plan for the Watts area, nor was there any current program of planning or activity even in regard to parks and schools. Its analysis has a familiar ring:[9]

> Preoccupation with earning a living for many persons in this area reduces their interest in preparation for or acceptance of leadership of youth groups. This condition, however, does not mean that there is no leadership; rather, it means that it is harder to locate and recruit. The continual immigration of persons from different sections of the country makes it difficult to stabilize and stimulate interests in long range projects or even in the immediate social problems as related to youth. Compounded upon these factors is that most of the residents in this area are employed outside the area which poses a transportation problem of taxing even more the inadequate public transportation system of the area. This hinders the chance of developing a strong feeling of community responsibility with so much of the residents' time spent outside the area.

As the summer of 1965 approached, the character of the Watts community had been fixed inexorably by the events of the previous two decades. The previously separated ghettos—Watts, Central Avenue, and West Jefferson—had now been amalgamated by the vast increase in black population and outflow of Anglos during the 1940's and 1950's, creating a massive, segregated area in the heart of the county which stretches from the western part of the city of Compton on the south to the lower part of downtown Los Angeles; and from Alameda Street on the east to the pleasant, middle-class (and occasionally integrated) Crenshaw-La Brea district on the west.

---

[9] "Watts Area Study, 1959," South Central Area Welfare Planning Council, Welfare Planning Council, Los Angeles Region, July - September, 1959, p. 7.

Alameda Street, still the site of the railroad tracks, remains an impenetrable "Berlin Wall," which has always separated the Negro ghetto from the lily-white and decidedly unfriendly communities of South Gate, Huntington Park, Lynwood, and Bell. Thus, the direction of the ghetto's expansion is predominantly westward, and it is now merging into, and possibly transforming, an area which has been largely Jewish in population.

In the postwar years, the development of Los Angeles' complex freeway system further compounded the isolation of those Negroes who remained in the poorest section of the ghetto. The Harbor Freeway, linking downtown Los Angeles with the coastal communities of Wilmington and San Pedro, bisects the huge central ghetto, leaving what are, in effect, two distinct Negro settlements. The area to the east of the freeway, which includes Watts, is predominantly poor, with a few middle-class enclaves, while the area to the west is predominantly middle-class, with a few low-income enclaves. In the hills above Crenshaw Boulevard, on the western edge of what was later defined as the riot "curfew zone," an integrated high-income community contains impressive homes, often with swimming pools, inhabited by Negro professionals and businessmen. In the West Adams area, an extension of the early West Jefferson middle-class ghetto, the neighborhoods differ from those in the Anglo areas only in the darkness of the residents' complexions.

Even the area east of the Harbor Freeway would not be adjudged a "slum" by those accustomed to the rat-infested tenements of Eastern cities. Single-family dwellings still predominate, though probably a third of the population of Watts itself (narrowly defined as the area between 92nd Street on the north and Imperial Highway on the south, Central Avenue on the west and Alameda Street on the east) still lives in public housing. At the corner of Central Avenue and 103rd Street, on the western edge of Watts, Will Rogers Park gives the visitor a favorable first impression, with its spacious lawns, baseball diamonds, tennis courts, swimming pool, and large gymnasium. However, programs at the park are limited, partly because its administrators are fearful of "incidents." About a mile further to the southeast, the famous Watts Towers, fashioned by Italian immigrant Simon Rodia out of steel, cement, and fragments of bottles, shells, and glassware, rise majestically on a small plot of land at the end of a street which leads into the abandoned PE right-of-way.

Then, as now, as the observer moves from one neighborhood

to another, he is invariably impressed by the diversity in the physical appearance of Watts. The neat, attractive, and well-maintained
houses on Zamora or Pace Avenue south of 103rd—many of them
owned by residents who came to Los Angeles during the 1940's—
would do credit to the most status-conscious suburb. Nearby are two
of the imposing public housing projects, Hacienda Village, to the
north, and Nickerson Gardens, to the south. The other two projects
provide living space for about 5,000 persons in other sections of
Watts. Elsewhere, shabby absentee-owned houses contrast sharply
with better-maintained residences on the same block or around the
corner, the latter attesting to the earnest but probably futile efforts
of the inhabitants to preserve some semblance of pride in their aging
homes. Just across Central Avenue, on 94th and 95th Streets, a
neighborhood of handsome homes attracts thousands of visitors
every December to its imaginative display of outdoor Christmas
decorations.

As one ventures into still other neighborhoods, new and more
mixed impressions come to the fore. Small and usually dilapidated
churches, of rare religious denominations, are everywhere, challenged in number only by the many liquor stores. The main business
center is along 103rd Street, with dozens of dingy stores offering
their wares at prices and terms well in excess of those charged in
Anglo neighborhoods. On the eve of the riot, the only new construction in sight was the still-unfinished Doctors' Building, the iron
framework being raised by an all-white crew of building craftsmen.
At the other end of 103rd, near Alameda, marijuana and pills of all
varieties are readily available on and off the campus of David Starr
Jordan High School. In a corner lot adjoining Jordan Downs project, the dropouts and delinquents of the "parking lot gang" terrify
the rest of the community.

Watts is characterized by one-parent households. It is a community of young people, the yards and streets filled with children,
the classrooms overflowing. The observer is impressed by their apparent health and handsomeness: the boys are muscular and live-
ly, the girls well-developed and neatly dressed. The older teen-agers
search desperately for "kicks," a respite from the boredom and frustration of a ghetto in which there is nothing to do. Many of the
youngsters carry their most prized possession—a "box" (radio)—
from which "soul" sounds blare incessantly. Thousands of them will
rarely see the world outside the ghetto, except perhaps in jail. The
whites they know are policemen, probation officers, merchants, and
teachers, and the relationship is often uneasy or hostile.

It is ironic that Watts should have achieved its major identity on the basis of a riot. Few other low-income communities of its size can boast of an equally impressive list of men whose cultural and professional achievements have left their mark on the entire nation. Simon Rodia's Towers remain a monument to the imagination and persistence of the eccentric immigrant, and the athletic field at Jordan High School is named for a distinguished alumnus, Dr. Glenn Seaborg, former chancellor of the University of California at Berkeley and now the Chairman of the Atomic Energy Commission. Dan A. Kimball, another product of the area who was to become Secretary of the Navy in the Truman Administration, is now the Chairman of the Board of Aerojet-General Corporation and sparked the establishment of Aerojet-General's Watts Manufacturing Company on El Segundo Boulevard immediately to the southwest of Watts. Rodia, Seaborg, and Kimball were of course members of the Caucasian community, now dwindled to a handful, but the list of distinguished Negroes is no less outstanding. Stan Sanders, a brilliant Jordan alumnus who became a Rhodes Scholar and a student at Yale Law School, returns to the community in the summertime to participate in special anti-poverty programs; Charles Mingus, bassist and composer, is only one of many superlative musicians who emerged from the community; Baltimore Scott, a former Jordan High and Occidental College student-body president, gains increasing prominence in administrative and organizational activities in California; and Budd Schulberg's Writers Workshop, a post-riot enterprise, enlists and develops talent in many forms of literary expression.

In 1964 and 1965, William Armstead and Richard Townsend, juniors at Jordan High School, were potential members of this distinguished group. Bright, thoughtful, and articulate, even in their mid-teens, they excelled both athletically and scholastically. Both come from families which had migrated from the deep South, though both had spent the major part of their lives in the Watts area. Armstead, in fact, was born in Los Angeles, while Townsend was born in Birmingham and raised in Selma, Alabama. Townsend, short but muscular, was a baseball, football, and track star, winning the All-City 100-yard-dash championship in 1965. Armstead was a top student at Jordan, excelling in mathematics and the social sciences and humanities. When he graduated in 1966, he received more awards and scholarship offers than any other male student in his class.

Though their educational motivation and their achievements stamped them as "middle class" in the eyes of many outsiders, and their views appeared "moderate" at that time, they shared a common conviction with the militant youngsters who now comprise organizations like the Sons of Watts: that a primary need in the community is pride and self-respect. As early as 1964, Armstead and Townsend, and other Jordan students, had formed the Student Committee for Improvement in Watts (SCFIW). With the help of a young woman teacher, they initiated various community improvement projects, including renovation of deteriorated buildings, cleanup work in yards and alleys, and summer parades and festivals. Their plans for a second festival in the summer of 1965 were upset by the riot, but the spontaneous activities they had undertaken were subsequently carried on by other organizations, usually with substantial governmental funding.

Viewing the SCFIW experience from the vantage point of late 1968 (both Armstead and Townsend were then student activists and leaders in the Black Students' organizations on their respective campuses), Townsend saw it as a stage through which they had passed in the development of black awareness. "We kept talking about community pride. And I think if you look at the way things are now, it's the same thing. Like, we were able to see what it really was, and we were talking like [the way the militants talk today], only we didn't say *Black* pride, we said *community* pride. I think, on the whole, the activities of SCFIW, like showing people that things are not what they should be and that they could be otherwise, aroused questions in people's minds."

Though they had lived in the Watts area for almost all of their sixteen years and had experienced poverty (Townsend, an only child, resided with his mother in Jordan Downs housing project, while Armstead lived with his family in a small house on Watts' south side), they did not fit the stereotype of the deprived ghetto youngster. Fully at ease in non-ghetto surroundings and equally versed in the standard language of the American intellectual and the slang of the ghetto, by 1966 they had managed to achieve considerable recognition outside Watts. In their mid-teens, they would each summer enroll in a school somewhere outside the ghetto, putting them in touch with youngsters of different ethnic and cultural backgrounds. Their academic and athletic records brought them a variety of choices for higher education: in the fall of 1966, Armstead entered Antioch College in Ohio and Townsend enrolled at the University of California at Santa Cruz. Like Stan Sanders, they are politically and socially conscious, and deeply involved in the black community's struggle for power and independence.

Townsend explains that his interest in learning and education was triggered by a change in residence during his childhood; he temporarily attended a middle-class elementary school in Los Angeles, where for the first time he was pressured to achieve and compete. Other than that, there is little in the background of either Armstead or Townsend which would make them atypical. Yet, in their ventures outside the ghetto, they were often dismayed by expressions of disbelief when they explained that they were natives of Watts.

In 1964, about one year before the riot, Armstead and Townsend prepared a special report on "Watts: Its Problems and Possible Solutions," later published as an appendix to *Hard-Core Unemployment and Poverty in Los Angeles.*[10] Theirs was probably the only *inside* view of Watts available prior to August, 1965, providing a picture of the community as seen by two teen-agers. Their viewpoints are thus uninfluenced by the notoriety and the newsworthiness achieved by Watts since the riot.

They had access to none of the documentary materials cited earlier in this chapter. Yet the reader will note the remarkable similarity between their comments as teen-agers and the conclusions expressed almost two decades earlier by Lloyd Fisher, Duane Robinson, and the City Planning Commission, and by the Welfare Planning Council in 1959, on the basis of formal studies. The following are comments on community conditions, spending habits, and social and educational problems in the ghetto, taken from their 1964 report.

> The area in which the community of Watts is located is often referred to as a "port of entry" for Negroes coming into Los Angeles or Southern California. Generally these Negroes will find themselves settling in one of the housing projects for a short stay. The ones who are financially able and prefer not to live in one of the housing projects will rent either in a single family house or in some kind of apartment house. The average stay in the community in the dwellings mentioned is from 2 to 3 years. Many stay just long enough so that they can get situated, and then move. Thousands of people move into the community of Watts each year with the intention to stay no longer than they have to. These masses of people, mainly Negroes from the South, are attracted to Watts for a number of reasons:
> (1) Since the rental fee in the housing projects is generally

---

[10] Report of the UCLA Institute of Industrial Relations to the Area Redevelopment Administration, U.S. Department of Commerce, December, 1964. Published in September, 1965.

pretty inexpensive, these migrants, for the most part of the low-
income bracket, are apt to make their initial stop here.

(2) Since Watts is one of the Negro ghettos of Los Angeles,
the migrants are usually confident of finding at least a few
familiar faces. They feel that in a city as large as Los Angeles
it is better to be certain that one has friends beforehand, in
order that they may become acquainted with the city quicker
and without so much confusion and difficulty.

(3) Watts' geographical situation is a relatively important
factor in the attraction of the migrants mentioned. Watts is
located in a rather centralized position in regard to obtaining
transportation. It is also centrally located relative to downtown, or the core of Los Angeles, as compared to many other
communities of Los Angeles.

(4) There also seems to be a certain feeling that a number of people have that Watts, in a sense, is at the bottom of
the social and economic ladder. Many migrants have the feeling that they are starting at the bottom and working themselves up when they move into the community.

Many kinds of housing as well as community problems
are created because of this ever increasing problem of migration
and mobility. Although many problems are caused by the migrants, a number of them have their roots right here in the community. These latter problems are created chiefly because of
the negligence on the part of the community residents. They
do not realize the importance of a person's feeling that he is
a part of a community. Possibly if the residents of the community realized this importance and acted accordingly, the mobility rate wouldn't be so high. . . .

The majority of people that do have jobs have the low-paying ones. These are the blue-collar workers in the semiskilled and
unskilled professions and the white-collar workers, working
mainly in the clerical field. For many of these workers who find
it so hard to remain in one home for any length of time, repos-
session of property is common. They usually have large families to take care of and their income is generally barely enough
to adequately support a small family. In a number of cases
this results in discouragement, discontent, and misunderstand-
ings within the family. The outcome of all this depression is
cited as another major problem: broken homes. This problem
of broken homes contributes to a number of community problems, a few of them being high mobility rate, high and fast rate
of depreciation of property values, and lack or loss of self and
community pride.

The problems contributing to broken homes combine to

play an important part in lack of community pride. Community pride, as mentioned here, engulfs three main areas: cleanliness, mental attitude, and the physical condition of the community. People steadily moving in and out of the community don't get an opportunity to develop any kind of community pride. In order to really have this pride, one must realize and understand the problems of the community. Unfortunately there aren't very many people in the Watts area who have taken their responsibility of attempting to understand the problems of the community. There is an even smaller number who attempt to do anything about the problems. The main aspect in the area of mental attitude in community pride is self-respect. Having community pride is merely having respect for other members of the community and acknowledging one's civic responsibilities to the community. A person cannot very easily have respect for others when he hasn't any self-respect to begin with. This aspect of self-respect also is an important part of the area of cleanliness.

The majority of the residents of the community of Watts notice the terrible physical condition of a large portion of the area and comment on it, but that's all![11] There aren't enough people in the area who have shown their interest in the physical conditions of the community by doing something constructive for the betterment of the community. The physical condition of most of the dilapidated buildings in this area is due to absentee landlords and owners.

Negroes spend entirely too much money for liquor and churches. It might seem peculiar for us to associate churches with liquor in terms of money, but the fact remains that too much is spent for church real estate by the residents of Watts. These churches are built because of a so-called preacher who decides to make it a business venture. These churches are usually used by these so-called preachers as a stepping stone to wealth. They are misused, and something should be done, soon if not sooner. An enormous amount is also spent on liquor and automobiles. . . .

In the ghetto of Watts there exists a social problem "en masse" of [an] inferiority [complex]. This overwhelming feeling of inferiority is produced in the community by both external and internal sources, and persons living both in and out of Watts.

External sources of inferiority feeling in Watts are developed by lack of enlightenment on the financial and social prob-

---

[11] It should be emphasized that public services, like street maintenance and trash collection, are traditionally inferior in the black ghettos.—*Ed.*

lems existing, by those not living in Watts. When a person
not living in Watts is not exposed to the reasons for conditions in Watts, he makes a predetermined decision that the
condition exists because of sheer neglect on behalf of the community. This situation causes employers, business leaders,
and often political leaders to lose interest in giving a helping
hand to the community. After all, what politician wants to
perform for a community that he has determined is a neglect-
ful ghetto?

The problem here is lack of supplementary educational
programs and facilities. It is a lack of sustained educational-
cultural programs. About eight years ago the primary problem
for the community was a lack of things to do for the busy hands
of youth. This problem was solved by devising extensive athletic
programs within the community; this developed the athletic
resources. Now there is a bigger and much more severe problem
facing the community. There must be something other than
athletics to occupy the time of those that do not care to delve
into athletic competition and those unable to participate. This
problem of idle hands ties in with another very evident problem,
crime.

It has often been stated that the number one motive for
juvenile crime is not necessity, but sheer lack of anything else
to do. Therefore it can safely be concluded that if there was more
for the idle hands to do, there would be less juvenile crime, resulting in less upset in the life of ghetto individuals.

Exterior sources are not always the creators of problems
in the community of Watts. While reading of how the external situations cause problems in Watts, one must take into
consideration the fact that many problems stem from internal sources.

Since a high percentage of Watts residents, as compared
to the county average, are migrants from other regions of the
nation, many of the people in Watts use the fact of unfamil-
iarity with the situation as a motive for social negligence. How
many times have these writers heard migrants in Watts say,
"I just got here an' I ain't got no reason to respect Watts." How
many times have they heard, "It was like this when I got here
an' it ain't gonna change." All of this internal strife is so indirectly caused by external sources that it will be classified as
an internal source of social problems.

Cultural depression, lack of pride, resulting in mass feelings of inferiority, all together make an excellent setting for
the role that the many social problems play in the lives of the
people in Watts. The role is one of acute seriousness. The social problems in the community of Watts are ones that should

be, can be and will be remedied with the help of people living
and serving both inside and outside Watts.

Lack of pride is one of the most severe problems in Watts.
. . . Pride includes community cleanliness and participation in
community functions. When one has no pride in a community, there is certainly no reason and no desire to keep it clean
or participate in its vital functions, political or otherwise.
Thus the job of keeping the community clean, participating
in and carrying out its vital functions, is left to rest on the shoulders of a few individuals.

Definitely not all people who take part in the functions are
dishonest and out for the sole purpose of self profit; but when
the number of people participating is so limited, this leaves
the proceedings in Watts easy prey for a diluted form of car-
petbagging.

This giving of top positions to people who couldn't care
less about the situation in Watts provides nourishment for
the ghetto's vicious circle, which only magnifies the situation
of poor pride and social deprivation to an unbearable degree.

In 1963, the California Legislature enacted an "open housing"
law roughly comparable to a statute passed years earlier in the State
of New York and still in effect. The Rumford Act, as it is generally
known, prohibits discrimination in the sale or rental of many types
of housing. The California Real Estate Association immediately
mounted a campaign to secure its repeal, and in November, 1964,
the voters of California approved (by a two-to-one margin) a constitutional amendment which, in effect, protected the "right" of
all property owners to discriminate. Although the California Supreme Court has since invalidated Proposition 14, thereby restoring
the Rumford Act to full legal status, its future remains in considerable doubt. Richard Townsend here describes how the residents
of Watts reacted to the overwhelming passage of the discriminatory Proposition 14.

Townsend: I can sum up [the community's attitude toward integra-
tion] by discussing my opinions on NO ON 14, the housing proposition. I think it indicates the general feeling of people in Watts concerning especially integration into and dispersion through Los
Angeles. The people of Watts, by and large, very few knew a great
deal about NO ON 14, and what it exactly is; very few got out and
really pushed the issue, very few got out and knocked on doors, although many people did put the stickers on their bumpers. It wasn't
an extremely important political or economic issue, as it was in other

places, because the people in Watts really couldn't afford to move
any place, but it was important from the psychological or personal
viewpoint, especially when it [open housing] was voted down. . . .
The attitude of the people in Watts [was] "I didn't really want to
move there, but it's just the idea of you didn't want me anyway; it
was like a bar you put there, that we didn't want to cross it, but you
put it there, so that's pretty mean, it indicates how you feel about me.
So, for that reason, I feel a certain way about you." Taking the kids I
know at school, they aren't hostile towards white kids, as such, as
an entire group; there are, however, little personal hostilities and
fears that arouse in any group that hasn't been exposed to anything
different or new, but you find if you take a group of Negro kids and
put them with a group of white kids for any length of time, a certain amount of identification will grow, and I found this in every
case I've ever been in; there just wasn't this unceasing hostility
or the group so parageneous [*sic*] they couldn't get together at all.
I'd say this is basically true of . . . roughly seventy per cent [of Jordan High School students]; most of the kids feel this way: "It [inte-
gration] isn't really that important, I'm not going to rack my brains
out if it can happen; we'll let it, we won't block it, it's like 'don't put
the bar up there before it even happens,'" and that's how I sum
up the attitude toward integration. O.K., fine, nobody knocks your
head out to do it, but just don't knock your head out to stop it. This
anti-segregation is not extremely pro-integration, but it's just like
a real neutral attitude, generally speaking.

[As we have noted, the racial character of the population of
Watts changed over the years, with the impact of World War II finally transforming it from a multiracial community to a black ghetto. Some of the adults recall the earlier days, when whites lived nearby, but segregation was still the rule in everything else. The color of
one's skin determined status and acceptance, just as it does today.
The vicious doctrine of "white superiority" even penetrated the thinking of Negroes, undermining their self-confidence and self-respect.
If the highest virtue was to *be* white, the next highest was to *appear*
white. The children were asked, in effect, to reject themselves and
their parents, and to assume a false identity. This was and is, perhaps, the worst crime perpetrated by white racism.

Mrs. Hitchcock and Mrs. Williams, both residents of the Watts
area, here discuss their lives before and after coming to Watts. Each
has been a victim of the color consciousness which infects and dis-
torts the perceptions of blacks and whites alike. Mrs. Hitchcock,

who is relatively light-skinned, was an early arrival, coming to Watts at about the time it abandoned cityhood and merged into Los Angeles. Mrs. Williams, darker-skinned, was a latecomer by comparison, arriving from rural Louisiana in 1956. Mrs. Hitchcock movingly relates her mother's, and her own, experiences with the "color problem," while Mrs. Williams's encounters with the problem are described later, in another context. Their brief reminiscences speak for themselves.]

Mrs. Hitchcock: I was raised in Watts, California, with exception of two years. I was born in a Catholic hospital [in Northern California], May, 1925. I was often told by Mother the unhealthy situation she had experienced in this hospital. The nurses expressed [that] my mother looked white. I looked reddish, my father's mother looked white, Grandmother's husband looked black, and my father they couldn't decide what color he looked like. The nurses would question my mother, "What nationality are you? Your baby is red." Mother answered, "I am American."

After eighteen months my brother was born in Venice, California, at Mother's parent home. Mother did not care for another hospital "color" remarks.

We moved in Watts October, 1927, in a newly built Spanish house. Only Negroes' families moved in the tracts. The white families were moving out. One middle-aged white woman remained on our street until she died, 1940. I learned early from this white woman a mild form of bigotry. She claimed she liked "colored people" only if they were personally clean and lived a good moral life. She hated my grandmother. She would not visit us if Grandmother was home from her job. Grandmother hated her in return.

Grandmother would upbraided Mother for having "poor trash" in the house. Grandmother had been a secondary-school teacher in Georgia. The old white woman lacked formal education. Mother put up with the situation for years because she had compassion for both. If Mother liked you for yourself, you were welcomed in her home.

Five colored families had gone to Compton Avenue Elementary School during the time I attended. We were subjected to separation from the Mexican, Greek, whites', and what nots' activities. I vividly remembered one good white teacher by the name of Mrs. _____, a third-grade teacher. She insisted that I and another colored girl be May Day princesses. She later became a Doctor in education. She was ahead of her times as far as I was concerned. My friend and I had to endure the oiling of our skin and ironing out of the hair, the poor parents trying to make us looked white. We were dressed in pastel colors like the white girls. I became very mean that May Day with the other girls. I wouldn't sit quietly. My parents couldn't understand these moods. I wasn't grateful at all. I was mad—angered. I was and will always be like this. Those strange feelings of not knowing which way or what I am as far as "color" is concerned. The hospital nurses—"your baby is red."

My activities through the Colored church helped me more than anything during my early childhood. I changed at age eleven from a nearly all-white Catholic church to a pro-Colored church. To work with my own people was a delight. To be able to participate in programs and activities was a thrill. I found I didn't have to be shy and mean anymore. I found I liked *all* people. The old, wise church members guided me into many worthy community activities. I often sent a cable, or had telephoned or visited these dear members. I loved them dearly. Through these beautiful people I found myself when I was a mere lonely "color" child.

Mrs. Williams: I was born in Natchitoches Parish, in Louisiana. I went to school in a house. It wasn't a school, it was a house. Somebody had moved out and they had school in it. And I went from there to this school near Route 2; then I went to the [Parish] high school, it was a white school but they had built another school for the white childrens and they let the Colored folks have the [old] school, and that was the high school.

I was born in January of 1925 and my mother died when I were nine, and I was going to school, before my mother passed, with my older sister, and she honestly taught me, because I didn't know anything about my mother too much. But my older sister really taught me how to piece quilts, I can do anything anybody else can do. If anything break down I can fix it, and I was a good housewife, I try to be a good mother to my kids, I would try to be a nice wife to my husband, but something went wrong and we're not together but I'm still with my five kids, but I had ten boys and five died and five lived.

I was married when I was twelve. I had four babies born dead, and one baby was two months and four days old when he died. Everybody was born in Louisiana but Don [the youngest, now five years old]. I came to California in December of 1956, right to Watts. My husband came here in September of 1956, and stayed with his uncle on 110th Street. I came by car, with the kids, two months after.

The only thing that was different about Watts [when I got here], they had more lights. Watts was like my home town, [but] in the country you don't have but a few lights, maybe every two or three miles you see a light. Up in the town they have lights just like they do in Los Angeles. But Watts is not as good as my home town.

It's some of the people in Watts. If you got a good way they'll try to change your way to bad. There's a mighty few people what encourage you to do the things that are right. Everybody you meet, almost, is gonna tell you something wrong, and if you're weak you'll fall for it. So that's why I believe that most of these childrens that is in trouble, some grown people has swayed these childrens. I never believe that their mother would teach these childrens to stray, but it's somebody that they don't even know, it's somebody that is taken for a friend, that is talkin' against the mother and father with these children.

The difference in Louisiana was, on Monday morning we didn't know nothing to do but go to the fields. We picked corn all day, or picked cotton all day, or dig potatoes all day; well, when you got all done workin' there was nothin' else to do but go home. The town was a pretty good piece away. If you worked for the white man, he give you fifty cents a hundred for a hundred pounds of cotton. Well, all right, maybe Friday you will make $10 or $15 or $20, *maybe*. Well, you have to go downtown to get paid off, at his office. Then, maybe some time, one of 'em talkin' loud or somethin' like that, the rest of 'em wouldn't get paid, but we'd have to go back there Monday and get the money, so many times I have went downtown on Monday just to get $15 that I had made, and that's all I know today. And that's still all I know to do, I don't know nothin' to do but just stay home and look after my children; a good time, I don't know what that is.

Maybe I would go back there, and maybe I wouldn't. It just depends; you see, me and my husband is not together and everybody down there is *his* folks, so I will be afeared around all his people. Because I wouldn't know what time they might want to gang up on me or somethin'. So I feel that I am more safe here than I am there, and I am on the County here and I couldn't get on the County if I were there. It would take a long time, I would have to become a citizen [of Louisiana] all over again before I could get County aid.

Let's see, my husband got hurt [a back injury] in October of 1957 and they take me on the County in 1960. My husband and me were still together then, but he couldn't work because of the injury. We went from '57 to '60 without [a regular source of] food and all the relatives and friends helped me until '60. We had a friend, he had a little old place and he even put up a secondhand store, and I run the store for about two months, and I made better than $40 a week, and he would give me every penny I would make. They got clothing from a rummage sale and give it to me because I didn't have anything, and my next-door neighbor, she bought a fifty-foot water hose and she put one to her hot water heater, and she hooked one to her cold water and that's how I got water. For quite some time I didn't have anything to sleep on but she gave me two blankets and somebody else gave me a quilt, and somebody else gave me a bedspread and somebody else give me some clothes for the children. And I haven't seen those people since. When I got on the County, I called about thirty-seven peoples that helped me, and said I'd try to pay them back, and they said they couldn't take my money because I wasn't gettin' too much. They said they was helpin' me because I was in need.

The *Sentinel* [leading Negro newspaper in Los Angeles] helped me. They ran a story, but they didn't have my phone, they didn't have my address or things in the newspaper, they just said a family in the Watts area, with the four children standing with their back to the wall. Their daddy had three slipped discs and a ball on his spine, the mother with a bad heart. That's the way they stated it, and that's the way it was.

I just get the $110.50 [welfare money] every two weeks, no more. I cash the check at the bank the first of the month, because I get my food stamps. They don't charge me anything when I get my food stamps. Now, on the sixteenth, if I cash it in town at the pawn shop, he will charge me $1.75, and so I give it to him. But if I cash it at the bank, I think it'll be thirty cents.

I've been trading with Benjamin [a local pawn dealer] ever since '61. I bought a automatic Frigidaire washing machine, I bought a TV, and I bought a set of wedding rings from Benjamin. . . . Benjamin is a very good man, you can get anything you want there. If you go to Benjamin and get $3, you got to pay him $6 [in repayment]. I had as high as $15 from Benjamin, and when I give him the money back, I had to give him $30.[12]

Benjamin recommended me to _____ [another store], and I got about $277 in clothes for the kids there. The clothes all fell apart, they were so cheap, and they said they would make it good. But they never did because the riot hit and the store was burned.

---

[12] A youngster argues that he can get money for less, but the interest he suggests is still phenomenally high.

The Riot

It goes without saying that the massive riot of August, 1965, remains the most significant event in the lives of the people of Watts. Although the actual curfew zone covered more than forty-six square miles in the heart of Los Angeles County, headlines and history have already identified it for all time as the area of the "Watts riot." Some of the most spectacular damage, it is true, did occur along 103rd Street, the main commercial center of Watts, since dubbed "Charcoal Alley." Yet it is equally true that much of the burning and looting took place elsewhere in the south central ghetto, on Central Avenue, Broadway, Florence, Vermont, and even Western Avenues—many miles to the west of Watts itself. Significantly, all of the damage was done *within* the ghetto; lily-white communities like South Gate and Huntington Park, Inglewood and Gardena, were untouched, though some of them are literally within a stone's throw of Watts.

The police action that triggered the four days of destruction seemed almost routine at the time. The arrest of the two Frye brothers on a drunk-driving charge, about a half-mile west of Watts on a hot Wednesday evening, had elements of ineptitude and misunderstanding, but it rated only a brief item on the third page of the *Los Angeles Times* the next morning. Though there was some violence following that incident, the next day appeared calm and tranquil, until darkness fell. I journeyed to Watts in the afternoon to keep an appointment, driving down 103rd Street to Wilmington Avenue, where the office of the Watts Labor Community Action Committee was then located. No expectation of imminent violence was in my mind, though rumors were spreading that the police had assaulted a pregnant woman the night before. A few hours later, after my return to the west side, the first reports of renewed and intensified activity in the area were broadcast. The volcano had erupted.

Friday was "Watts day." For the first time, 103rd Street was struck en masse, and the buildings housing stores became infernos. The small department stores, clothing stores, pawn shops, liquor stores, and many grocery stores were special targets, but there was never a completely consistent pattern. The relatively new Safeway store on Imperial and the Shop Rite store on Central went up in flames, but the infamous Giant Food Market on 103rd, whose white owner had an unenviable reputation in the community, was amazingly unscathed. (Apparently he had mobilized his own private army of employees.) On the other hand, the three ABC markets in the south central area were undamaged, though they were, and are, white-owned; their reputation for fairness, service, and cleanliness is good. It is probably accurate to say that with a very few fortuitous exceptions like the one noted above, the stores with especially unfavorable reputations in the area were uniformly hit, but beyond this it is difficult to generalize.

One may, of course, argue a different case, depending on one's ideological viewpoint. The conservatives suggest, on the basis of almost no evidence, that the "rioting" is either the work of criminals or malcontents or the result of a "conspiracy" by radical and militant groups. The militants sometimes respond that the "riot" is really a justified protest against police brutality, commercial exploitation, and general subjugation of the ghetto by white outsiders. My own reflections lead me to the conclusion that the conservative position is totally wrong and that the militant view is vastly oversimplified.

Perhaps a simple but critical point should be made first. The basic middle-class rules of morality become meaningless whenever "law and order" in the accepted sense have become inoperative. In no way is this a racial or cultural phenomenon as my own experience in the American army during World War II will attest. In those days of rigid segregation, my battalion in the 102nd Infantry Division was lily white and, essentially, a pretty representative cross-section of the dominant racial and cultural groups in America. Yet, as we proceeded through Germany in the wartime years of 1944 and 1945, we looted and stole and, sometimes, raped. Even the most moral and moralistic among us felt no guilt about taking "souvenirs" from the closets and drawers of houses in which we were bivouacked, including items of some value. The High Command issued directives that the looting must stop, particularly in the light of criticisms directed against the Russians for the same practice, but they had little effect in my outfit.

A particularly apt example comes to mind. Two of my closest buddies were devoutly religious, extremely moral young men, who were among the very few soldiers to respect the established rule against fraternization with *fräuleins* while it was in effect. One day, in the near-destroyed town of Krefeld, the three of us stumbled upon a large safe in the ruins of a bombed-out factory building. Without hesitation, my buddies proceeded to round up all usable tools and force open the door to the safe. To our amazement, they discovered the equivalent of several hundred dollars in negotiable Dutch currency, which was promptly removed and later sent home over a period of time. (I had wandered away before the safe was opened and the loot liberated, thereby invalidating my claim to a full share.) The prize was so embarassingly ample that it became necessary to fabricate a plausible and acceptable explanation. The explanation decided upon, if any question should arise, was that the money had been won through gambling. I do not know whether an explanation was ever demanded, but, if so, it would have had a most suspicious ring. My buddies were perhaps the only two persons in the platoon (possibly in the battalion) who *never* gambled, as a matter of principle.

I could multiply this example many times over. These same buddies, for instance, regularly collected items of German photographic equipment which we often encountered in houses, buildings, and stores, and put together a most impressive picture-taking and picture-developing operation. All of us, at one time or another, "liberated" liquor, articles of clothing, guns, watches, silverware, radios, and anything else that we valued and could carry. We felt especially justified in these practices because we were taking from the Germans, who had systematically looted and pillaged throughout Europe and murdered millions of innocent people. We reasoned that the Germans were the last people on earth who had any right to complain if we recaptured, individually or collectively, some of the material possessions which they had reaped directly or indirectly through the brutal, if efficient, workings of the Nazi system. Furthermore, some of us thought that the Germans (even the Nazis) would be on top again in a few years, suffering none of the burdens which they had imposed on others. Our "looting" was actually a small and inadequate punishment.

I hope that the analogy between our "white" behavior during

World War II and the "black" reasoning during the riot is now some-what clear to the reader. A riot certainly has many of the aspects of a war, and in the case of a black-white confrontation, the "enemy" is relatively easy to define. The whites, especially the white mer-chants, are seen as exploiters and parasites, and the decades of bru-tality, discrimination, and repression directed by whites against blacks become highly relevant. If stores are burned and goods are looted, this must be measured against the *systematic* exploitation of blacks by whites throughout a long and painful history. I do not claim an ability to penetrate the mind of a black "rioter" while in the act of "rioting," but surely some of my own reasoning in our confrontation with the Germans must be identical to his. The con-ditions and circumstances are remarkably parallel.

This attempted explanation undoubtedly overstates the degree of conscious reasoning exercised by a potential rioter. Once the spark has been ignited, even from accidental or spontaneous combustion, the conflagration gathers a force and momentum of its own. At a certain point, it is no longer necessary or even possible to reason in specific terms: it simply becomes clear that the goods will be taken by someone, and "it might as well be me." This, after all, is an old American principle, fully consistent with the moral bases of the capitalistic system. Is not the entire system based upon the relent-less and single-minded pursuit of one's own self-interest?

An incident during the riot will illustrate the point clearly. A young friend of mine had ventured into a Watts store to secure a new broom for his mother. Having made his selection, he left the premises and headed back toward his pad. A couple of blocks away he encountered a policeman, who eyed him incredulously. "For Christ's sake," the cop said, "why don't you pick up something worthwhile?" My friend turned around, returned to 103rd Street, and did precisely that.

In retrospect, perhaps the most astonishing thing about the 1965 violence is that so little of it, relatively, was directed against white civilians. Indeed, the official records tell us that not a single white person was killed by a black, but that thirty-one blacks lost their lives. In view of the reports of widespread sniping and attacks on whites in certain stages of the riot, the statistics seem almost incredible. We are forced to one or more of three conclusions: (1) The published figures do not tell the whole story; (2) the accounts of sniping and black violence directed against persons were exag-gerated for one reason or another; (3) the snipers and attackers were woefully inaccurate in aim or inefficient in execution, or per-

haps did not intend murder. The reminiscences of the three teen-
agers in this chapter, plus the news reports, confirm that some whites
were assaulted and injured, but we are told that no fatalities resulted.

This is all the more remarkable in the light of the location of
Watts in relation to the white communities to the east and to the
west of it. Imperial Highway, which forms the southern boundary
of Watts where "Mudtown" once stood, is one of those unique east-
west roads which almost spans the entire width of Los Angeles County. Across Alameda and along Imperial lie lily-white cities like South
Gate, Lynwood, Bell, and another vast Anglo region, and a few
miles to the west are Inglewood, Gardena, Westchester, and more
Anglo territory. Each day, especially at peak traffic hours, thousands of whites traverse Imperial Highway on their way to work,
home, the beach, or Disneyland. If the riot reflected a militant or
antiwhite conspiracy, it was poorly executed indeed.

There is, in fact, no evidence that the riot was organized or
planned in any way. It is probable that in certain cases, small bands
of teen-agers or young adults moved from one store to another, or
from one area to another, after the rioting had started, but their
organization was spontaneous and informal and had no ideological
meaning. The resentments expressed against white-controlled stores
and police practices have provided the basis for the suggestion that
the riot was actually an uprising which reflected frustration and
social protest. Without doubt, this was a powerful motivation behind much of the riot activity, but to many of the teen-age participants, the riot was primarily an exciting incident which destroyed
the boredom of hot summer days and offered an unexpected opportunity to obtain a few of those possessions which TV commer-
cials identify to them as essential parts of the "American way of
life."

In the following section some of the residents, mainly teen-agers,
reminisce about their actions and experiences during the riot, and
provide a bit of insight into attitudes toward the police, the merchants, and whites in general. Mike is the youngest; born in the
East but a long-time resident of Watts, he is quick-witted and articulate. Despite a sharp mind, he had not gotten along well in school,
had been in frequent difficulty with school officials and the law,
and had dropped out (or been kicked out). Henry is Mike's buddy,
though somewhat older. Born in Louisiana, he has been in Watts
since 1956, living first in a private home near Mike's place and later
moving into a housing project with his mother and four brothers.
He graduated from high school in the mid-sixties, and is intelligent

and alert. At the time of the riot his record was clean, but he sub-sequently got into trouble, along with his buddy, in an incident involving a car. Mel is somewhat younger than Henry, a product of Mississippi, but again a long-time Watts resident. He disliked school and dropped out in the eleventh grade. Highly verbal, he has a flair for drama and music, but is handicapped by a weakness in reading and by a "record" which resulted from hustling.

For obvious reasons, the names of persons referred to in the following section, in most instances, have been changed.

Mike: Let me see, first night when it got started. Henry and I were on our way home from a party they were having in my older sister's house; they was having an anniversary party that night. Me and Henry got off the bus down on 108th and Avalon, and we just saw a whole lot of people starting to run; I thought maybe somebody was fighting or something like that, or there had been an accident, so Henry and I went down to investigate. I saw a lot of police. I saw cars turned over on the street, and bricks, bottles, and a whole lot of glass lying around. I looked at Henry . . . and started laugh-ing. So we decided to go on down further. I looked around, a whole big crew of policemen just ran by us. They were running opposite directions; I didn't know what was happening. I just turned back to Henry, and we thought we'd come home before we got killed. You know, "Wow," and I'd got down on 109th and Avalon, about 112th and Avalon, and so we decided we'd then just go along home, and we passed by another group of policemen, and they stopped us. They asked us where we was going. Henry told him we were on our way home, and he asked us where we live, and we respond-ed and told him, and he told us where were we going and where were we coming from. Of course, Henry and I were scared, so I said, "We just got off work. . . ." We took a couple more steps, and he grabbed me by my shoulders, and I turned around and asked him what was wrong with him, and he swung at me with his night stick, but he missed. And I grabbed his arm and knocked his arm down, and I was going to hit him. Then a whole police gang got around him, and they had us circled. We just stood there, and he says, "Where did you say you was going?" I say, "I'm going along," and he says, "Let me see you get along". . . . He swung at me again, and he hit me on the leg. Then immediately I knew what was he talk-ing about, you know.

We started running, and we got down by the corner. We were

going to be smart, so I called him a name, and we took off again. We were in an open field, and we looked around, and a whole bunch of lights were flashing over that way, and we paused for a moment, then we looked back over there again, and there were nine or ten police cars behind us. So me and Henry started running again, and all of a sudden we thought, "here is the law." We thought somebody was shooting at us, and they got to ricocheting kind of close. I finally realized that we was being shot at, so me and Henry, we hit the dirt and we were crawling across this big old open field. They was shining a big old spotlight, trying to find us, so we made it over near the railroad tracks, and about that time, a train was coming, and I say, "Henry, man, let's hop on this train and get away from here," so I hopped on the train. We were leaving, you know. I looked around and said, "Come on, Henry, man, get on, man, get on." The train was increasing its speed quite a bit. I just got on, and I didn't see Henry. I looked around and Henry was laying there against the fence. So I got off the train; I say, "Come on, Henry." Henry was limping a little, and we got down on Central and Lanzit Avenue. . . . Right there you can just look up the creek . . . over near 103rd Street . . . and I looked up and I just saw a fire; the air was just full of smoke, and I glanced over and I saw a large fire over toward where I live at; I just saw things burning, burning, burning. Everywhere I looked, I saw a fire.

And I got all scared, and Henry was living around the corner from me at the time. So we took all the back streets and all the dark streets to the pad, and when I got home, I just sat down and looked at TV, and still I didn't feel, I didn't know, it was a riot. This was the first night [probably Thursday], and I finally . . . figured in the pad that there was a riot outside. At the last minute I suddenly realized that that was where I just came from. So my mother, she tried to encourage me to stay in the pad where I wouldn't get into no trouble, and all that, but you know me. She got to telling me about the looting; there wasn't nobody saying nothing about it. . . . So I got back out in the street again and participated and threw a few rocks, and looted a little case and stuff like that, and . . . I was on the street till they called out the National Guard, and that's when I decided to go back to the pad, 'cause the National Guard they weren't jiving.

Mel: I was, so happened to be, on 114th the night that this happened, all this occurred. I was over at my girl friend's house. At the time, we were all in the house watching television, and after we were watching television, we heard over the news that there was a riot in Watts, that peoples were burning up and looting. We had overheard the sirens outside, all the calling, hollering, and screaming, and peoples hollering "Whitey, kill Whitey,"and all this different stuff, so my girl friend's mother wouldn't let me out of the house. My girl friend's sister's boy friend was over, so myself and him and his brother, we tried to get out the house; we tried to sneak out the house. We finally sneaked out after everyone had went to bed that night.

So, across over on Imperial and Central, over a gas station called United gas station, there was a liquor store called Rocket. Peoples started running from the project, from across Imperial over, getting, just taking what they want, anything, all kinds of liquor, just from the store. This upset my mind, you know; I never seen anything like this. But at first I was really frightened, because I had heard about riots in other countries, but never a riot in America. Never had I realized what a riot really was. So I went in the store, and I was panicky. Everybody was knocking down, peoples grabbing stuff, grabbing wine, bottles, beer; stuff was all over the floor; people were just taking what they want.

Little kids was all out on the streets. Peoples were shooting guns, and the sky was just black, like the world was going to come to an end. People was running out, and there was this one lady, she was hollering, "Stop, you peoples don't know what you're doin'," and all this different stuff. It was in the afternoon, and people were coming from work, I guess. They was white people, Caucasian people coming from work, and they would have to take this route to get to Bellflower or South Gate, down Central and Avalon. And this was just horrible because colored peoples over there they just took advantage of them. They even detoured the buses through the projects, and why they do this, I do not know, because I was giving it up. They was just telling them, "Come on, you can do anything you want" . . . and it was horrible; I just didn't think stuff like that would exist, and I heard of wars and all this. . . .

People was turnin' over people's cars. . . . They ran over to the gas station, on Imperial; they took over the man's gas station, United. They started takin' gas out of the pump, putting 'em in Coca-Cola bottles, and beer bottles, and anything they could, big jugs, and scratchin' a match, and puttin' it to it, and throwin' it to a car, and blowin' it up, taking alcohol and making cocktail bombs out of 'em, whatever you want to call 'em, and just catch a car on fire in a matter of seconds, and peoples just lost their whole car, and some people even lost their lives in the car because they couldn't get out. . . .[1]

I saw cars with kids, this is what made me want to stop, because I saw little kids, seven or eight years old, Caucasian kids, in the cars flying down the street. Their fathers, their mothers, were driving; they had big holes in their heads, and all the windows were broken out of their cars. Peoples were hollering; every time a car would come by, everybody would jump over the fence and run at it, and it would look like a torch or something, like someone putting you in a room and just throwin' down on you with bottles, and bricks, and cans, anything they had, sticks. I saw one boy run after a car and had a big two by four in his hand, and the man came out, he was shooting a gun. He was just starting to shoot; the boy, he hit him across the head with the two by four and five or six other ones just beat him to death, beat him so bad, they beat all the clothes off of him. He was beaten badly. They tore all his clothes off him, the skin all off his back, all off the side of his face. It was just horrible.

I will be truthful with you. About two or three days after the thing happened, everybody was getting what they could get; I figure, well, I might as well get all what I could get. So people started talking about they coming down 103rd; they was burning up 103rd. They said the whole 103rd was on fire. This I could not believe. They said they was running into the pawn shop, getting guns, rifles, and machetes, all this other thing; so myself and a friend of mine and my brother-in-law we went to walking down 103rd; we saw these peoples running with suits in their hands; I never owned a suit in my life, and this just excited me. And when I got there, everybody was running with stuff, tape recorders, and record players; people were— even little kids—pushing washing machines down the street. And the first thing I saw was a stamp machine, a government stamp machine, and I thought about all the dimes that was in that stamp machine, and I pulled the stamp machine off the wall in the liquor store. And by the time I tore it off, all the dimes fell on the floor, there wasn't any dimes left because everybody else beat me to these dimes. Everybody pushed me out of the way, so I didn't get but

---

[1] The official records of the riot do not list any deaths of Caucasians, other than two policemen accidentally killed by fellow officers and a fireman killed by a falling wall. However, it is certain that many whites were assaulted and some seriously hurt.

maybe thirty, forty cents worth of dimes. So I saw a chance to get me a couple record players; I took those and then went over to Shop Rite market and got a little stuff.

We went over there, and the supply houses, they had boxes and boxes of beans in the back. They had beans, all kinds of canned goods, anything you wanted, just like a free for all; everybody could get what they wanted. . . . It wasn't on fire at the time, but . . . what made it so bad, the people who were throwing [Molotov cocktail] bombs, they would give you a limited time to be in there and tell you to get out. If you don't get out, they would throw them in there, and you would be caught. So I was in there, had a basket, just shopping for what I wanted. I was taking bread, sardines, crackers, everything my hand got on. I put it in the basket and rolled it down the street. I had bunches of greens, all in the basket; I had everything, and I got to my mother's car, put it all in the car, driving home; the police, they couldn't do nothing. The police couldn't . . . it seemed like the world was just out of hand.

The police were standing around looking, but they couldn't do nothing about it, and it was just like a Vietnam hand-to-hand combat war with rifles. On one side of the street were officers, on the other side was the citizens, and they were shooting at one another just like Dodge City, Tombstone Territory, anything you want to call it. They were shooting back at one another. . . .

Then this incident happened where this lady was coming through the project. She was a Caucasian lady and must have been about, I would say, about twelve or one o'clock at night, and this was on a Friday, I think it was. And she had a purse sitting beside her as she was coming through, and she had to stop for a red light. I opened the door, and I said, "Give me that purse," you know, like that, and it frightened her. She panicked, and I grabbed the purse, and I slammed the door, and I started running. By the time I started running, there were about ten other dudes behind me, and her money was in the purse. When I opened the purse up, I found a little chump change, which was about thirty or forty cents, and three packages of Pall Mall cigarettes, which I do not smoke. That is all.

This boy was a Western Union; he was on one of those little Honda 55's. He was coming by, I guess he didn't see that trash can, because a friend of mine took this trash can and knocked him off his bicycle, and I jumped on his Honda and started riding it around the project, started hollering, "Ride!" People start taking hose pipe, sticking them through the windows of their houses, running hot, scalding water out through the hose pipe. They put . . . hot water on Caucasian people there as they come by. . . . Peoples is all up on top of the project, sniping at the policemen, and they couldn't do nothing. A helicopter was coming down, and they was shooting at the helicopter.

It was just horrible. If I could do it all over again, I don't think I would do anything, because after I looked at the television and looked at everything, looked at how the smoke was smoking, it looked like the world was coming to an end; I was sitting out in my front yard wondering what tomorrow was going to hold. And that Saturday, that whole weekend, people just took what they want; they just ran all the white peoples away from Watts as far as they could; just tore it up, just drank it; wine, the winos had so much wine till they couldn't drink; the dope addicts had so much dope, they couldn't smoke it all, they couldn't take it all. The hypes had all they could have, and it was just a free for all, for everybody. And at the time, myself, I didn't have enough because I was scared. I was really scared.

Chuck: This is the way it happened to me. I got home around midnight, and at the time . . . Snick [SNCC—Student Nonviolent Coordinating Committee] had this house about three doors down from our house, and it was ran mostly by a Caucasian. Negroes were involved in the program, but the Caucasians would travel in during the day and leave during the night, but yet and still the Negroes that was working with this group would sort of hang around, would stay at the house, taking care of the house. This girl and I and three more of her friends were riding down Imperial Highway. They [the SNCC group] had this little teen-ager, named Eddie, he was in a car. They was coming across this canal. There around a corner was a taxi, and the driver that was killed, hit all in the head with bricks and stuff thrown. People got to calling Eddie "Whitey-lover." So finally . . . they rushed back to the house. People on my street were getting panicky, running all out of the house, hollering at "Whitey". . . . People started hollering, "Get out, Whitey, get out, Whitey." So all of a sudden, they [SNCC members] jumped in their car and split; we never hear anything else from them. . . . We never saw them again.

So, the next morning, Eddie and his sister, my next-door neighbor, we was going down 103rd; she was going down there to shop; people just standing around, standing around the street . . . like it was to watch a parade or something, walking back and forth, police down at the other end. All of a sudden, this big noise, people get this hollering and screaming going on. But it was a funny thing, on one side of the tracks they would do something over here, and the police from this end come over here, and this police go down there, and in the meantime while the police is transferring, they'd start hitting the buildings in between. Finally, the whole of 103rd was just up in flames. I stayed a while on 103rd, just to look; in other words, just to see could I see anything I wanted, like everybody, free.

I got off in this pawn shop, when the window was broken. . . . I got scared, broke another window . . . and finally . . . came to the door. . . . The police car was screaming and going on, and meanwhile . . . this man, he grabbed a box in the pawn shop. . . . He got to cut on it, he cuts it up, and I'm standing around, waiting, and hoping he gets money out, so I'd get a little bit. He cuts, he cuts, and cuts, and came to a little box in it, up in the center of it. He opened the box, and there aren't nothing but watches in the box; I am disappointed.

I went out to the back, you know, the room with the radios . . . tried to find something that I liked. Finally, I got AM-FM; it was black, short wave, AM-FM, and a guy sees me as I walked to the door; he snatched it out of my hand, so I turned around and go back and get another one. I went back home, put that down, because if they catch you with it, they are going to take it back, but I figure I will get that off my hands. During that time, the whole street was empty, just like it's dead down 103rd Street. This lady next door to me, her grandfather's friend had a big truck. So I jumped on the truck, went down to 103rd; she started loading up TV, washing machines. National Guard's coming back across the tracks on Santa Ana, on Graham. The National Guard stopped the truck, told everybody to get out back and front . . . so the man still sitting behind his wheel, and everybody else is out. . . .

So going home, my mother tells me to stay in the house, but I just find excuses to get out. Let's see, yeah, it was Eddie . . . at the time, he needed a battery for his car. Safeway had these Delco batteries, exactly the kind he wanted, so we get in the truck, and we split down to Safeway. When the riot broke out, we just broke and . . . put it all on the truck. We get back to the pad. We split that up. It was night. In the meanwhile, we went down to 103rd Street. Martin Luther King[2] is coming down on a truck with PA system: "My black brothers, why don't you go home?" People just ignore him, start throwing stuff at him. Along 103rd, everything

---

[2] It was undoubtedly another "civil rights" leader.

was just burned, ashes. . . . National Guards were there, so they
had those signs, TURN OR GET SHOT, and the brother of a friend
of mine was killed just by disobeying one of those signs.

Mel: That Sunday . . . when everything had cooled off, and the
National Guards had arrived. And I had this radio, this FM, I had
looted out of the store, my personal self, and we was sitting off in
the project . . . over by Bob's liquor store on 103rd, they said everybody . . . had to make a curfew at eight o'clock. We didn't believe
this curfew. So we's sitting down drinking up wine. Everybody
got something else; they got wine, whisky, beer, and everything;
everybody sitting out at the project socializing, talking about what
they looted, what they stole, and all this. So this man comes over,
this colored dude comes over with a tape recorder; he gets to talking about what's our names, you know, and all this stuff. We had
a fifth of corn whisky. He asked us all our names. We gave him all
phony names. He said, "I know this is phony." I said, "If you know
it, why do you want to ask?" He was supposed to have been a newspaper reporter, or something . . . tennis shoes, levis; he had a tape
recorder. I thought he was losing his mind, you know.

All of a sudden, we heard shots, five minutes to eight, just boom,
boom, boom, boom. I just grabbed my radio. I had to go over to
my friend's house to stay all night, because I couldn't get out, and
I saw everybody at Bob's liquor store. National Guard had one of
those big, old 21 BM's,[3] whatever you want to call it, just sitting
it up on the air, just blow out a whole light pole . . . with one shot,
blowed the whole light out and people standing like fools, standing over there on the property shooting at him with little, old .45's
and the Guards had great big machine guns, and tearing the brick
walls up, tearing the whole wall up with three or four shots. . . .

Let me tell you, and this is the truth. I saw a 1964 or '65 Dodge
with a Caucasian, it got stopped on Wilmington right at 105th. . . .
They stopped him early in the morning, Monday, must be about
6:30 or 7:30 in the morning, and they opened the trunk of that man's
car. He had rifles for an army; he had rifles; he had machine guns;
they opened up the back of his seat, he had so many bullets that
he could start anything he wanted. He was over there selling that
stuff to them colored peoples. That is the truth, and the National
Guard catch him, held him there until the police came. . . . White
people, they did a hell of a lot in the riot.

---

[3] The speaker probably is referring to a 20 mm. gun.

Mike: I saw one incident where two Caucasians were driving an old model car, and they stopped at a red light, and they spotted these police, and they took off, but the police caught them; I would say [they were] about our age. They found guns in the car that had been fired recently. . . . They came over from South Gate, Lynwood, Bellflower, Huntington Park.

I saw another incident that I thought was pretty cold. I had figured the world was coming to an end, so I decided to go to church that night, and we was going down Alameda, the only way we can come down and go where the church was is to come down Alameda to Imperial from where we live and . . . we were coming down Imperial, and right there by the corner of Mona and Imperial, there is a liquor store. We was riding alongside of a sheriff's car at the time. And after that, we were coming to a light, and for some reason, I don't know why, I just decided I would pull behind the sheriff's car instead of pulling up next to it, for the lane was free; we stopped at a light, and something just told me to pull up behind them, and as soon as I pulled up behind, three or four shotguns came out the window, boom, boom, boom, out at the store, where people were off in there looting. Before I knew how to start beating it, I just saw the shotgun for a minute and closed my eyes, and I looked back up, I saw the sheriff's car taking off right quick. As it pulled off, I saw this man coming; I saw him come staggering out the liquor store, and he fell dead, dead.

We was walking down from 107th and Graham, from the Teen Post, on Friday night, and at this time, the police was riding four deep with shotguns hanging out the window. They stopped us; they stopped us all at once and told us to put our hands against the wall, and we had this truant officer with us named Jim. He was supposed to have been a probation officer. They made *him* get up beside the wall, and we was all up beside the wall till Ricky said—this one boy name Ricky—he said, "What did we do? We didn't do nothing." So the police kicked him, then took his jacket, took this big stick he had out and poked Ricky with it. He told Ricky, "You are getting smart." Ricky didn't say nothing; Ricky just couldn't say nothing; he had all the wind out of him. Then he [the cop] came over to me, and he started talking to me; he said, "You want to get smart?" I said, "No, sir. I ain't said nothing, sir," just like that. So he went where Henry was; he put his knee up on Henry's butt and told Henry to straighten up and kick, open his legs up, you know, and I thought he was beating on his behind, myself, so I started laughing. So he came back to me and asked me what was funny. I told him, "Nothing." He grabbed me in the back of my neck, and he slugged me down; he told me, and he told all of us, to go. He told all of us to get on home where we was going. He said, "You are going to walk down the street; you are not going to look back, and you aren't going to think no nasty names in your mind to call us, are you?" And I said, "No, sir, we are going on home." So we were going home.

So this SA [Spanish-American, or Mexican-American] Johnny Garcia, he was walking down the street, and he was walking minding his own business; the police flashed a light in his face and told him to stop, and he was walking and looking at him. He told him to come here, and the Mexican fellow was walking over, blocking the light out of his eyes. By the time he got up on him, the police hit him, wham, wham, slapped him upside and pushed him, told him to get on, just like that. We felt like running; we all started running and started laughing about it, and later we got together, we called ourselves camouflaged police that night. We started throwing bricks and bottles; that was what started us; that's what really started us. Like we get dog dukey, put it in a bottle, throw it on them, messing them up, that was what we did after they did that. We weren't thinking about it at first, you know.

A Teen-Ager: Another night . . . the police and some National Guard had camped in the Teen Post when the Teen Post was at the Art Center, so all that night we was gonna go and get them, and we ran around, trying to find some gasoline. There was a big old truck and we wanted to set the truck on fire, and the National Guard overheard us, but anyway we got ourselves together to set the Teen Post on fire to burn them up in there with it. . . . The truck caught on fire; this dude burned the truck, but the Teen Post wouldn't burn. . . .

Some residents react to the question of whether there was some sort of pattern to the rioting, and why the stores in nearby Caucasian areas were not hit.

Sam: I never did myself go out for that "brothers" talk, that "black power" talk, until after the riot; that is when I really got involved in it; that's when everyone really got involved in it. They started reading this literature and started getting interested.

Sam, Chuck, and *Bill*:   No, there was no pattern, just as it went. . . . The bus drivers let you ride free on the buses. . . . They stole most of the buses from the bus company and took them way out in the country in Compton and hid 'em. It was something else. . . .

They sound like they are unbelievable, but everything is true. I never in my life experienced things like this till I came to California.

I hope there will never be another riot. A lot of people think there is going to be another riot, but I don't think there will ever be another riot in Watts, because if there will be another riot, I feel there will be a nuclear war between Caucasians and Colored people.

[White areas weren't hit] because for the simple reason . . . the merchants that owns the stores in Watts, they would take money out of [the community] this is where they get . . . their hustle. This is how they work. They would come in and open up a business here, and they would charge you $20 for a pair of shoes. You can go to Huntington Park or anywhere else and get it for $8.01 or so. Go to Kinney's and get it even for $7.98. They felt that they would just go in and take these suckers. . . . They call them [the merchants] the blue-eyed devils. We gonna take these devils' business so he can't make it no more. That is why everybody did that; that's why. A lot of people owed them for the rest of their lives, see what I mean, and they said we are going to destroy these records; they won't find no records so I won't owe them a damn thing, and get away with it.

Sam: I was in Mississippi until I was ten years old. I could see how the black man could live in the state of Mississippi, Georgia, Arkansas, anywhere else you want, for $2.50 a week. They can go over to the store and buy a can of beer, salt meat, a loaf of bread or more for a dollar. When you come here, there's bread here, 41¢ a loaf. How's a man going to live in Los Angeles, 41¢ a loaf? When you are . . . living in the [housing] project, you go to stores, these prices are jacked up so high till if a lady got eight or nine kids and living in a project, she might as well give it up. . . .

Al and *Sam*:   I noticed that when I was around a Negro neighborhood . . . the food is jacked up sky high, but you go to the white man's neighborhood, like you go to Baldwin Hills, somewhere like that, you can get it real cheap. . . .

I think . . . taxes are higher in Watts. We went over to Compton and bought cigarettes for 25¢ a pack; we get back over here, cigarettes cost 40¢ a pack. You know why? Because there is a difference in the community. It is where you live, is what you pay. A business . . . in a Negro area . . . is taxed to death.

Sam, Chuck and *Bill*:   See, in this community the Jews and the Mexicans usually own the liquor stores, and Chinese own some of the food stores. They will go back home, and think, "Well, we got the Negroes over there." They know you got to buy the stores' stuff to survive off of. . . . You can go to Hollywood and buy soda water from any store. You can buy some cheaper than you can in Watts. What they got here in Watts is jacked up so high that people in Hollywood wouldn't dare drive those prices up so high.

I think Watts is definitely better off without Martin's. [One of the stores that was burned in the riot.] For furniture, jewelry, clothes, you always pay more in Watts. Like, you go up there and get a watch, they say they have diamonds in it. You take the watch, it cost you two or three hundred in Watts; it's not even worth $75. Then they had this layaway plan: they'd charge you for layaway.

Mrs. Williams: You know, I once got some clothes for my children at _____. [A store which was burned.] The clothes fell to pieces, but they are still trying to collect $25 from me. The records were burned in the fire, but they still harass me with bills. I went to the man [at Neighborhood Legal Service, an OEO-funded agency to help poor people with legal problems] and told him I only owed about $15, which I would pay. He phoned them and they said they would accept the $15. I sent a money order for the exact amount to the man at Legal Service, so he could send it in and know I was paying the bill. The store got my money, but they are still sending me bills for more money.[4]

You can go down there [to 103rd Street], you are going there to buy a belt, you pay three or four dollars for that belt, but you can go downtown and get a belt for $1.79. . . . I'll tell you why people shop in Watts; they don't have no way of getting rides to the stores [in other areas].

Chuck: You could go down to _____ loan company, and say, "I am going to pawn this $200 watch," and throw it up there on the table; the man grabbed it and looked at it. "This ain't no $200 watch, what's wrong with you? Who sold you this watch for $200?" And looked at him like he is a fool, and . . . he looked all over to see [if] diamond is in it; if the diamond is in it, he don't know if there is any diamond in it. He is looking all in the back of it, checking in it, and tearing it all up. "I will give you $15 cash money, that's all I can lend, that's it." And the man has been trading there ever since 1900. That don't mean a thing. "Mr. _____," he said, "I can't give you no more than that." They'll rob you for this money. It's just

---

[4] The editor can verify the truth of these statements.

like a pack of wolves. . . . They will con you out of every dime you got, every dime.

Sam and *Chuck*:   Most people don't know what it's like in Watts. They [Caucasians outside Watts] never experienced poverty in their lives; they never seen ignorance; they never seen disease like there is in Watts; they never seen crime like there is in Watts; they never really known what poorness is; they never really experienced anything bad in their lives. . . . And they figure, especially in Washington or downtown at the City Hall. . . the south Los Angeles is a bad place. . . . "There is a bunch of colored peoples out there; they are no good," this and that. They put all this in the people's head in Beverly Hills, and Malibu, and we go out there looking for jobs, and we couldn't get hired.

One day . . . someone brought up the subject about looking at the paper for jobs. So we all got together, six or seven of us, looking through the paper for jobs. So three of us hit on the same job, on Washington. . . . We were supposed to be selling these magazines. The first question the man asked, after he looked over our application and everything, he said, "Oh, I see. You young men are from the south central area." I said, "Yes, we are from Watts," like this. He looked as though he was objecting to us, like we was no good. He just told us, "Well, I will see what I can do, I will call you if I need you." That was the only reply we got from this man. . . . That's the only reply we got from any Caucasian person that we went to get hired from. . . . I know one person that had gotten a job, but he's Mexican-American.

After the Riot: Image and Reality

The riot transformed the face of 103rd Street, the business center of Watts. The newly dubbed "Charcoal Alley" was now filled with the rubble of burned buildings, smashed windows, and strewn merchandise. Empty lots gaped where some of the major stores had been, and virtually no rebuilding took place. But at least one other change had occurred as a result: Watts had finally achieved an international reputation. In a superficial sense, the 1965 riot had given Watts an identity and a touch of glamour. For weeks after the uprising, 103rd Street was choked with cars transporting curious sightseers. The foreign visitor to Los Angeles was now more likely to tour Watts than MGM or Forest Lawn. The special investigations and reports, surveys, publications, lectures, conferences, and programs virtually defy enumeration.

As the months passed, other changes became evident. The mention of Watts in a proposal for a government contract or grant had a magic effect, as funds began to pour into special programs and facilities in the area. Expenditures were actually scanty in proportion to the size of the problem confronted, but they were much greater than all previous public spending. The State of California promptly opened a multiservice center in the community, staffed with representatives of the Department of Employment, the Fair Employment Practices Commission, the Division of Vocational Rehabilitation, and other agencies. John McCone, chairman of the Governor's riot investigating commission, assisted in the establishment of an "indigenous" training operation patterned after Reverend Leon Sullivan's successful Opportunities Industrialization Center in Philadelphia; the Los Angeles OIC, however, floundered in internal dissension until late 1967, and trained relatively few residents. Only later, under new leadership, did it gain some momentum, but then it collapsed completely in early 1969.

The Westminster Neighborhood Association, originally a Presbyterian settlement house which had received major antipoverty funds, obtained additional money for special training, job development, and community action programs. Its Operation Job Power, a summertime project in 1967, boomeranged when charges of financial irregularities appeared. The charges were ultimately dismissed, but the program, which employed local residents in home maintenance and cleaning services, catering, telephone answering, gardening, and other enterprises designed to teach them business principles and stimulate community employment, lost its funding.

Considerably more fortunate was the Watts Labor Community Action Committee, a cooperative effort launched early in 1965 by a combination of Watts area residents, trade union representatives, and UCLA staff members. Already in operation at the time of the riot, WLCAC picked up momentum in 1966 when a dynamic UAW shop steward, a long-time resident of the area, assumed the chairmanship and sparked a campaign for a full-scale county hospital in South Los Angeles. The hospital proposal was subsequently approved by the County Board of Supervisors, with completion tentatively planned for 1970. Beginning in the summer of 1966 and continuing through 1968, WLCAC secured substantial federal and private funds for the construction of "vest-pocket" neighborhood parks and senior citizens' centers, a small chicken farm, agricultural plots, a service station which could also be used as a training facility for auto maintenance, a consumer education program, basic education and training, and a number of other activities. In the summer of 1967, the organization conceived and administered a massive project to transport several hundred Watts youngsters to Camp Roberts, a partially deactivated military installation in northern California, for a vacation combined with work experience. The project generally received high praise, though some complaints were heard from participants. The organization now operates a summer camp and training facility for youngsters at a site leased from the city and located in the northern part of the county. WLCAC buildings are scattered along Central Avenue on the west side of Watts, and its program is easily the most "visible" within the community.

The vocational training facilities have also multiplied. Two skills centers, funded under the Manpower Development and Training Act of 1962, one immediately to the west of Watts and another several miles to the south, offer training in mechanical and clerical occupations. The most imaginative project, however, is the Transportation Opportunity Program (TOP), administered by the Teamsters Union in cooperation with the UCLA Institute of Industrial Relations. In addition to providing training in truck driving, auto maintenance, and driver education, the union also assures the placement of the trainees in full-time jobs. Unlike some other programs, it welcomes applications from the "hard core" and offers remedial education and special counseling wherever required. The major training facility is located several miles from Watts, but an intake office served the Watts area in 1968.

Some physical improvements along 103rd Street are now in evidence. The modern Doctors' Building has been completed and houses government agencies like the Employment Service, as well as medical offices and a pharmacy. Across the street, the Department of Public Social Services (the county welfare agency) has constructed new offices, and the Concentrated Employment Project (CEP) now has a facility there. At the other end of the street, a new multipurpose health clinic has been built by the University of Southern California Medical School on the site where the "parking lot gang" had formerly terrorized the community. A number of improvements have been made at Jordan High School, located at the far eastern end of the street. In 1968, a few prefabricated model homes were put on display. Yet most of the empty lots remain, and little private capital has ventured back into the area.

There is much discussion of a possible "urban renewal" project in the Watts area, and a number of alternative plans are in the offing. The Southern Pacific Railroad, which owns a considerable amount of land, has submitted tentative proposals for large-scale industrial development. The city's Community Redevelopment Agency has indicated an interest in several plans, including the possible construction of a commercial mall along 103rd Street. Perhaps to the surprise of many of the planners, the residents were not favorably impressed by existing blueprints for industrial location, and vocally insisted upon their right to full participation in the planning process. The record of the city administration was viewed so negatively in Washington that Los Angeles was not even designated to receive funds under the initial Model Cities program. WLCAC subsequently received a grant to develop a plan for the south central area.

Elsewhere in the community little apparently has changed since the 1965 riot. There are several new organizations, some of which have a strong "nationalistic" orientation, but they seem to have no leverage in their confrontation with the major social institutions. There are special educational programs and new facilities at the schools, but the basic educational pattern remains the same (some noteworthy events in late 1968 and early 1969 will be discussed later). There have been new community relations programs in the police department since the death of the unpopular Chief Parker, but the behavior of the patrolman on the local beat has not markedly changed. There are job referral and development projects, both public and private, but they appear to serve primarily the already qualified or near-qualified. The public welfare policies are essentially the same as they were at the time of the riot, and a state administration, unsympathetic to the welfare program, is pressing for cutbacks. Despite some worthy programs, most of the "hard core" youngsters are still on the streets.

There is, of course, competition among colleges, apprenticeship programs, and businesses to enlist the top graduates from Jordan High School. But the "average" youngster is seldom so fortunate. *If* he manages not to offend the teachers and administrators, and *if* he remains out of the clutches of the law, he may survive until the graduation ceremony, but his prospects are uncertain. He is impatient for a job and an income, but he may not be "career-minded." Deferring the gratification of his present needs, in the interest of a distant and amorphous future goal, is foreign to his experience and his thinking. Ultimately, he may be more inclined to adjust to the possibilities of the moment than to pioneer in unexplored and ill-defined territory.

It is easier to generalize about young people in the ghetto from a distance than from a closer vantage point. Despite the community of feelings and interests which segregation imposes, they remain diverse and distinct personalities. Labels such as "militant," "middle class," "motivated," and "moderate" are convenient, but misleading and undependable. Like those who reside elsewhere in the city, the residents of Watts resist easy categorization. The "Black Muslims," for instance, may be regarded in one sense as militant, but their rigid moral and behavioral code is puritanical and conservative to a degree which would put the Anglo middle-class American to shame. Their objective of creating independent profit-making enterprises for ghetto residents is hardly revolutionary; indeed, it is the essence of capitalism. Even the "hustler" is functioning according to time-honored "American" principles, though the middle class will not recognize it. Many of the "militants" are not re-

belling against the dominant economic system; they merely seek
participation and a broader role in it.

Some tentative generalizations, however, begin to take shape.
Phrases like "Black Awareness," "unity," "Black Pride," and "respect" are heard ever more frequently, especially among young people. There is an overwhelming conviction, expressed with equal
vigor by college students and street youngsters, that blacks in the
ghetto have no more real independence in 1969 than they had before
the violence of August, 1965. Whatever the depth of their feelings
about whites in general, they are visibly and volubly discontent
with a dependency upon the patronizing (or politically expedient)
"do-goodism" of white people. They demand greater control over
the institutions in their community, and a more meaningful voice
in the decisions that govern the present and shape their future. Undoubtedly they exaggerate the degree to which *white* people in this
country effectively decide their *own* individual destinies. The notion
of the all-powerful and self-directing white is a child of the myth
of "white superiority," but from the viewpoint of the ghetto resident the "power gap" between Watts and Beverly Hills looms large.
No one can gainsay that the structure of employment, education,
and law enforcement is fundamentally more responsive to the interests of whites than of blacks.

Political and "community" leaders are targets of deep mistrust
and suspicion. Among white politicians, only John and Robert Kennedy have aroused genuine enthusiasm (perhaps with the exception
of militant young intellectuals) in the ghetto. Negro politicians,
as a rule, are not trusted much more than are the white. The pervasive feeling is that the "leaders" and the "spokesmen" have drift-
ed away from Watts, and that they serve their own interests before
those of the community. Among the publicized "leaders" on the
national scene, one alone—the late Malcolm X—appears to be pro-
foundly admired and respected by young people of almost all personal philosophies. His autobiography and his recorded messages
are basic texts among the youth. They cite his observations with
confidence and pride, conscious of the fact that Malcolm was himself a product of the slum ghetto. His experiences and problems,
they stress, are akin to their own.

The role of Martin Luther King is not quite so clear. Most of
the youngsters admire him as a person, and his martyrdom has
further strengthened his image in the community. Their reaction
to the philosophy of nonviolence, however, is another matter. Some
are prepared to accept it as a *tactic* to be used on occasion, but few

will adopt it as a philosophy. King, of course, was different from Malcolm in background and personality, and the significance of this is not lost on the youngsters. King was a minister, at a time when the youthful respect for "preachers" was plunging. (To be sure, Malcolm was also a religious figure, but obviously not in the tradition of the Christian church.) Perhaps more importantly, he did not emerge from the slum ghetto: he was the son of a well-established Southern minister, the beneficiary of an impressive education, and someone who always seemed to be well off from the standpoint of a poor black in Watts.

Perhaps because they wish it to be so, many of the youngsters claim to perceive a growing similarity between the ideological positions of King and Malcolm. They observe that King was moving away from integration and toward separatism, implying that he must have been disillusioned by the white racist resistance, or the white liberal weakness, he had encountered in the North. Few of the young people demonstrate much active interest in "integration"; their goals, they say, are equality and independence. Integration, if it is to come, is a later step, to be taken only when it need no longer be accomplished on the white man's terms. I leave to the reader the personal judgment as to whether this is a correct assessment of King's ideological direction, or merely a projection of the youngsters' own feelings and desires.[1]

I suspect, on the basis of fragmentary evidence, that the older people are stronger in their admiration for King—more respectful of religion, integration, and nonviolence as a philosophy—and less inclined to idolize Malcolm X. One notes pictures of King (and of John Kennedy) in many of their homes. They are probably less aggressive and impatient in their views, somewhat more attached to the "other-worldliness" of traditional religion. The depth of their commitment to religion, and perhaps some of the reason for it, is evident in the reminiscences of Mrs. Hitchcock. (*See* Chapter I.)

All of this reflects, I think, an aggravated case of "generation gap." In some ways, the revolt of the young people against the standards of their elders is even more bitter and abrasive than their rejection of "white supremacy." Here, as elsewhere, the natural and universal distance between teen-agers and their parents is widened by the effects of racism.

---

[1] It is interesting that the youngsters never mention the apparent movement of Malcolm X in the direction of *less* "separatism," hinted at in the last pages of his autobiography.

The young people and the few older persons whose views are represented below are neither paid professionals nor spokesmen for organizations. They have no ax to grind, no cause to plead. All of them have lived in or near the Watts community for long periods and have spent at least some time in the local schools. Like Armstead and Townsend, most of them belong to families which migrated to Los Angeles from the South. Their educational backgrounds are varied, most having graduated from Jordan, but some having dropped out. A few have gone on to college, but still return to their homes in the Watts area whenever they can.

Among the out-of-school kids, work experience is irregular, and most are or have been involved in special programs administered by the Watts Labor Community Action Committee, Westminster Neighborhood Association, and other organizations or agencies. Gregarious, personable, and intelligent, the youngsters have been active in groups such as the Sons of Watts and a Teen Post (a federally funded center for recreational and cultural activities), but few would be regarded by school officials as part of an elite. To the contrary, their unconventionality and independence have led them into occasional brushes with teachers, administrators, or the law. They probably represent the "mainstream" of youthful thinking in Watts, insofar as that can be identified.

We shall start with three contrasting impressions of the Watts community, as it existed during the first year or two after the riot. Each, I believe, is reasonably typical of the group represented: a bright dropout with a "record"; two college-bound youngsters; and an older woman. Then we shall examine several individual views of "leadership" within the black population of this country and this community, again as it prevailed after August, 1965. Finally, we shall hear in this chapter from several residents, young and old, on the value and necessity of community control and the new roles they would assign to both the blacks and the whites.

Some Contrasting Impressions of the Community
(1966 - 67)

Bill: I can't speak for everyone, I am an individual. I guess I feel the way they do, you know. The community where I live is all right, I suppose, except for a few minor things, like police. I guess [for] the poor people in my community, it's bad, it's bad, down and out a little bit.

I came here when I was quite young. When I first got here,

I thought, "Wow, this is the grooviest," but looks like later I found out different, the hard way of life. Nobody told me nothing about Watts; I didn't know when I first got here, but I am learning. I still don't know all about it; I am making a little progress now.

Well, if I had known something like the riot was going to happen, I would never have came. I almost lost my life during that incident, "uprising of the people." Yeah, I participated . . . [this was] my chance to "get over." Things just seemed to come up that way. I got picked up several times, and I got roughed up by the police. I still came out on the good side; things I have that I didn't have before, you know.

[The idea is to] get over, just like Whitey. I want to have it made; I want to live up in the hills, just like everybody is talking about. I don't want to live in the slums all my life. . . . Whitey's streets aren't with a whole lot of cracks in them, not trash cans all over the place.

Really, I don't care myself [about the term "Whitey"], that is what everybody else calls them. I try to be with the in crowd. The people that are with the crowd, they seem to be getting over one by one. I just say if I follow the crowd, maybe I will get over because I don't seem to have no other way that I can get over. . . . Whitey's got a fine car; he got a fine home; he got fine clothes; he got everything. I don't hate Whitey. As long as Whitey respects me, I respect him.

[In a taped conversation, Armstead and Townsend reflect on conditions in Watts in the late summer of 1966, one year after the riot and two years after the preparation of their special report excerpted from in Chapter I.]

Armstead: I think it is interesting that now everyone is taking pride in the fact that we had the biggest and most renowned riot in history. At that time, people weren't sure of how to feel about it, whether to feel embarrassed, whether to be ashamed that we are living in an area where something like this happened. But now everyone is proud. . . .

I wouldn't say that the economic level has risen [as a result of activity following the riot], nor are the people satisfied with the present condition, but the inconveniences of having to go way outside the community to a store, I think that these kinds of things are some of the factors that influence people not to riot again. Not only that, I think that some of the people don't have their tensions relaxed until they've had this chance to express themselves; peo-

ple are looking back now and asking, "Why did we do this?" They
are really trying harder to express themselves. But then again, there
is this element that we have to do it again and again to make sure
they heard us. Most people have had enough of riots. Going back
to this pride, I think that the American tradition is to be first in
everything, and the same thing is going on here; it's happening
all over the country now, just repeating what happened last summer. All we need is to be first, we keep on pushing in different directions. . . .

A lot of jobs have been developed around the main idea of getting youngsters off the street, and doing something constructive,
giving them something to do with their idle time. They have started minds to working, thinking about what happened and why it
happened, and thinking about the situation now, like "What can
I do?" It is working, it is getting kids off the streets, and giving
them something to do, and I think, in this respect, the Federal government has achieved one aim of the poverty program.

Townsend: Some thoughts of not wanting to identify [with Watts]
stem from what you might call the post-World War II era: that
Watts is really the Watts that you might have read about in the
magazines, or the paper, about the killings and murders, the gangs,
and what have you, and this is the type of atmosphere, the stigma,
that still lingers in Watts. The people that live in Watts wouldn't
like the things their friends say or would say if they knew they lived
in Watts or used to live in Watts. Many of the people have had as an
ultimate aspiration to move out of Watts. This attitude has changed,
and I wouldn't say as a result of the riots, but as a result of . . .
the way people feel about themselves and Watts. . . . Jordan High
School has many kids I know who would not have gone to college,
had they been going to any other school in the city. Due to the fact
that many of the kids went to Jordan High School and not Washington High School or maybe Manual Arts [schools in other parts
of the ghetto], they got scholarships and money and these are things
that these kids can't overlook; they need the money; many kids
got jobs simply because they lived in Watts, and this has an effect
on your life. . . . Some of the people realized this, so the attitude of
the residents in Watts is changing towards Watts. . . .

When I said "the residents in Watts," I was a little too inclu-
sive in stating that, because the attitude varies through age, economic groups . . . severely in some cases. I'd say basically that the
people that are in the very lower economic bases, along with young-

er age groups, say under twenty-one especially: it seems that their attitudes towards Watts have changed greatly. They have taken a great deal of pride from what has occurred recently. . . . At our school, when you divide what could be called achievement levels, there are even different attitudes on these achievement levels at our school, and there are different attitudes between the kids who go to school and those who don't go to school. There are even splits in the opinions of the kids who don't go to school . . . but they boil down to basically whether or not you have taken up the flag and joined the bandwagon in total pride of being black, or maybe of being a Californian, or an American; something similar along these lines divides the issue in Watts right now.

Meanwhile, a little more basic, community attention has been taken away from some of the things that caused the riots. Right now, as I see it, there is a tremendous power struggle going on throughout the Negro superstructure . . . between what we might call the moderate factions and the extreme factions and even the factions that go unnamed. . . . There are a number of programs, large-scale programs like antipoverty itself, that took the attention away from civil rights in Watts. These diverted interests have resulted in . . . a non-idleness of ideas in Watts now. Right now, for the most part, more people are thinking about what is happening in Watts than were ever thinking about it before.

[Mrs. Brown, an older woman in Watts and another long-time resident of the community, notes down her impressions of the attitudes and problems there in 1966.]

Mrs. Brown: Most people view the community as a "drag," and that all the publicity given Watts is "for the birds." There are vast differences among groups. Old-timers usually can tell you things as they really are. The migrants are show-offs. The employed is determined and shows hope; they refuse to be intimidated and will not let anyone get them down.

There are no natural leaders. There is, however, hope if the young men now elected to public office think of their communities instead of their wallets first. The general opinion about politicians is that they are crooked, very bad, and liars.

Ministers are even lower than the politicians. They steal from the poor to pad their pockets and what they sell is emotional garbage. Most are self-ordained "fakers."

Merchants in Negro communities usually ask twice the price you would pay in nicer stores.

Teachers are doing a job, but are usually given too large a group or class to be truly good teachers. Social workers again are given too many cases and far too much paper work; hence they are failures.

Policemen in general are decent; a few bad ones are around, but I would hate to be without their protection.

Agencies like _____ [a major local organization] stink. Most of their personnel are migrants to Watts from eastern states. Except for the few neighborhood aides, most of their funds remain in the pockets of their staff. Let's fact it—for the riots to have occurred at all screams failure of agencies.

Some view the riot as revolt. Others say it was a bunch of rowdy punks that had nothing, that will never have anything, that blacken the eye of the City of the Angels. Many are trying now to make Watts a better place; even those that rioted are trying to present a better image.

Negroes in areas like Watts can never completely control their communities: first, they are too divided, and second, they are too short on "bread."

Generally there is no antagonism toward whites. Give Negroes employment, decent homes, things most people take for granted and Negroes are denied, and black and white can live together. I would say [black and white] teachers are regarded the same in the community, merchants also, but I hesitate about police officers. But a rabble would not stop even for Negro officers.

"Leadership"
(1967 - 69)

The dynamics of "leadership" in a low-income ghetto is considerably more complex than the usual journalistic version might suggest. Many of the Negro leaders and spokesmen identified in the press are unrecognized in Watts; a few, like Martin Luther King, Stokely Carmichael, and local militants such as Ron Karenga and Tommy Jacquette, are known to the young people, but the reactions vary sharply. Of course, the late Malcolm X has wide recognition among the hip youngsters, and his reputation appears to be more favorable than that of, say, either King or Carmichael. Roy Wilkins of NAACP, Floyd McKissick of CORE, and Whitney Young of the National Urban League are virtually unknown. The youngsters have heard about NAACP, but tend to regard it as primarily an older people's organization. Negro politicians like Adam Clayton Powell, despite the publicity and frequent controversy attached to their names, elicit little or no interest. Most of the youngsters and many of the older residents are cynical about the motivation of those elsewhere labeled as their "leaders." Though the volume of their information often is small, they are surprisingly incisive in many of their observations.

Chuck and *Wally*:   I don't see where Stokely Carmichael is really progressing, I don't see what he has gained.

It seems he change his whole theory about everything. When he first came out, people listened to him, and then after a while, he gets to pushing himself, he is for this, he is for that, he never got any backing. So now he's lost his hold on Watts. First of all, if you are going to start out something, why not keep it that way, just don't start anything and then end up on something else.

When he first started off . . . the Negro people, they figured that he was a true Negro, he had a reputation for [trying to] back up the Negro and open an opportunity, a chance for the Negro, and then he let down . . . and by his making that trip to Cuba, I don't know what he has accomplished. I mean, they couldn't help him. . . . I believe he was getting pay from another organization beside, or another society beside, the Negro. . . . To me, he started out as a great man; I was really interested in him, now all I can say is, he is a black phony.

Chuck: Malcolm X, I studied his philosophy and his writings. . . . All right, he had the majority of the Negro people behind him; they would listen to what he has to say, but then, when he got to this point where people was really behind him, he was killed. So I feel like this: a Negro . . . will set out to do a job, he has this power being over him, he can only go so high. After Malcolm X was killed, a lot of people still believe in his philosophy, you find quite a few people like to read his books. Seems like he is another type that struggled through life. He went through what I'm going through now.

The power structure only lets you get so high. . . . Once you get too powerful, you have a lot of backing, and you have a lot of force, you don't know what might happen to you; you could be walking down the stairs, walking in the front door, it might blow up, you don't know what's going to happen.

[His idea] was to get everybody together, just don't fight among each other. He was against the Caucasian man for his own personal reasons. Yet and still he believed in a balanced power structure; you know, you got a Caucasian president, why can't you have a Negro president.

Wally: I believe that . . . at the time [he was assassinated] he was expressing strong feelings about Negroes, and thoughts and ideas, and . . . right there he was getting across to the Negro; all of a sudden some man come up from nowhere and assassinated him. I feel . . . that outsiders was involved in it, too.

He was a true leader toward the black society. Whatever he said, you know, it got across to the Negro. He wasn't the type to like to incite any type of trouble, such as Carmichael. Seems like every time he [Carmichael] address a person or people, the first thing comes out of his mouth is "violence, violence," and the whole crowd is younger persons, are kids, or teen-agers, and everybody watch him, and he say what they want, there is a big riot.

Chuck: Yeah, you can't just go out and say, "violence, we can't have this, we're going to violence," especially if the peoples is following you, now all of a sudden, "pow," you are going to change like that; a lot of the young people around and get to hollering "violence," things start happening.

George: The students . . . in schools like Jordan . . . know what's going on behind having black dignity and about when is the next mass meeting at the Muslims' auditorium, such and such, like that; they know what's happening, but they don't take it under too much consideration, you know. I think the most thing the students want to do at that age is to get that diploma; then they can worry about what's happening on the outside. I guess you know most A12's and B12's, all together they are having a problem in school, and they can't give too much of their time to thinking about Muslims, and maybe they don't take it under too much thought. Once they drop out, I couldn't say too much for them. But, for those that I do know, they have joined the CCC [Community Conservation Corps, run by the Watts Labor Community Action Committee] and the Sons of Watts. And they more or less hang around liquor stores, you know; seeking jobs, too.

Chuck and *Wally*: Martin Luther King just goes around hollering "Brothers, we shall overcome," that is his talk. They're going to kill him, and he goin' to holler, "We shall overcome." About the only thing he has proved is that a Negro can go anywhere, *walking*. But all this blah, blah, "We shall overcome," everybody knows sooner or later everybody is going to overcome. A man is going to attack you from behind, and you're going to stand up and "turn your other cheek" and holler "We shall overcome." Man, what's he talkin' about?

Because when the white man hit him, he don't strike back, he just take it and walk on; another man hit the side of his head, "Oh, I'll turn around, I got two cheeks." That's nonviolence, you know. "Do anything, as long as you don't kill me." Ever since he won that peace prize, he just fade away.[2]

Louis Lomax [an author and host of a local TV discussion program] just like to talk; he has a split talk, he talks in two different languages.

Muhammad Ali [Cassius Clay] proved himself in the community. . . . You know I agree with him but to one extent. He knew that there is no possible way you could beat the power structure, so therefore he eliminated himself by just walking into the trap; he is going to pay $10,000.

It was his religion. He signed a contract with the organization: "I shall not do this; I shall not do that." And once he breaks that treaty, that paper, the organization . . . plots against him, they try to kill him, or get rid of him. If you break a contract, there is no hope for you.

And he got quite a few people backing him. . . . It is against his religion to participate in any combat, like carry a gun; he will go, but he refuses to kill a person that he has never seen before.

The Catholic religion is the highest religion, the first religion. All right. Now this dude, Pope John, if they think they will have him go in the service, you think he would go?

Paul (1969):   Malcolm went through so many different things and hit every black person from middle class to no class at all. I think he could have solved the problem, and the majority of the black people related to this solution.

Everyone looks up to Huey P. Newton as a god: If he sees something wrong, he is gonna fight it immediately. And they respect Eldridge Cleaver too, because he's gone through the experiences that the majority of black people have gone through. The thing is, times are changing; Carmichael took a lot of people with him. Martin Luther King was coming to the reality himself, maybe that's why he got shot. I don't talk about Carmichael that much anymore, because he split and left his people for his individual concerns. Like his relationship with a woman. I think the movement just went to a higher level. I wouldn't leave the people.

I know there is a possibility of a race war, but I am more concerned about the economics of it. If there were a race war, I don't

---

[2] These comments about Dr. King were made several months before his assassination.

know whether the black man could win. I know a lot of people would die. I'm fighting for humanity. As far as revolution is concerned, if it's an economical revolution for all the poor people in the world, it would be very successful; if it's a racial war, all I can see is a lot of people dying.

Several adult women of Watts discuss the politics and psychology of leadership in the black community. Juxtaposed to their comments are the observations of a young adult man who was present at the discussion.

Mrs. Andrews: Let me tell you. That black Mr. Charley; of course, we realize that when white Mr. Charley goes in, he goes in for an ulterior motive, too, but you see, when black Mr. Charley goes in there, he sells out his folks for a few pennies, just like Judas. It's okay to go in there for a personal gain, but then help somebody at the same time that you are doing that.

That's why if we ever going to get ahead of the white man, you got to get education, with your mother wit, and you put the two of them together. But you cannot put people up there that don't know what they are doing. They always got these so-called leaders, just like Eartha Kitt. She goes up to Washington, she isn't got no business saying nothing in my behalf; she don't know nothing about the way I feel, so don't talk for me.

Mrs. Coleman: Just get a bulldozer and run over Martin Luther King, that's all you need to say about him.

Jerry: You know how much Martin Luther King makes in a year? Let me tell you, he makes more than $50,000 a year. He sits on two different boards, he is making $5,000 for each meeting. Those meetings only last fifteen minutes a year.[3]

I hate Martin Luther King just like I hate the white man. King done told us one thing, King told me when I get slapped on one cheek, turn the other, and I don't believe in that. When a man hit me, I believe in hitting him back. Martin Luther King stopped us from having freedom in 1963, with the best President the United States ever had. . . .

Rap Brown is a sellout, just like Stokely Carmichael. (*Mrs. Benton*: Just like the rest, all of them.) Stokely Carmichael was taught

---

[3] These assertions are erroneous, but they are presented intact as illustrations of a frequent cynicism about the motivations of "leaders."

everything he know by a man that was known by every black person on the face of this earth, Malcolm X. Instead of doing what Malcolm had devoted his life to doing, Stokely Carmichael and Rap Brown are doing just the opposite. Malcolm X never would have left America to go to the Bahamas because he committed a crime that was wrong. Stokely Carmichael and Rap Brown did.[4] Stokely Carmichael and Rap Brown never in their life went without some armed weapon. Every time you saw Malcolm X, he never had a weapon on him. This is why he's dead today.

In late 1968, *after* the assassination, Jerry expresses a more moderate, and I think more typical, assessment of Dr. King.

Jerry: If you look at Martin Luther King and Malcolm X, you find they are talkin' about the same thing, but from a different personality. You take Malcolm X, Martin Luther King, Tommy Jacquette, and the rest of these Protestant, Baptist, and Catholic preachers. They are all fighting for what Malcolm X said he was fighting for. It's Black Nationalism!

See, people fight in different ways. If you're involved in two, whereas if you lose in one, you might win in the other. Martin Luther King and Malcolm X were close, very close to each other. When Malcolm moved, you noticed, King did too.

In 1963, three weeks to the day after Malcolm had given his speech in Detroit (that's on the album), King took a group of people, no preachers, and they marched on Washington. The only one thing that was accomplished, that they said they was going to do, was take 20,000 Negroes and lay on International Airport runway, and don't let an airplane land. The rest of it was a picnic on the White House front lawn.

The night before that march, there was a meeting in some hotel, between the Big Six [Negro leaders] and John Kennedy and some others. John told them, "You gotta stop this march," and they said, "Boss, we didn't start it, we can't stop it." You know, that first day of the march, you didn't see no white people or anything. The next day—Spanish-Americans, whites, everybody, thousands of 'em.

You know, back in 1954 [Malcolm X on the record, "Message to the Grass Roots"] they had a Bandung conference, and it tickled the shit out of me. That motherfucker was made up with everybody in the black race: black, brown, red, and yellow. Every-

---

[4] The reference here is evidently intended to be to Adam Clayton Powell.

thing but a white man. The dictionary says a nigger is a member of any very dark-skin race, and so there is only one race that is not a nigger: the white race. If I take a school and bring those militant groups and Christian groups in with each other, and convince them to cope with each other and come to a conclusion of how we are going to fight this matter of getting independence, then we can get all our people together.

[Two of the most prominent "nationalist" leaders in Los Angeles are Ron Karenga, head of a group called US, and Tommy Jacquette, head of another youthful organization called SLANT (Self Leadership for All Nationalities Today). By background they are markedly different, though their philosophies seem equally militant. Karenga is a college graduate, the holder of a Master's degree in African languages from UCLA, a potential doctoral candidate, and a facile polemicist. Jacquette is also sharp and articulate, but his language is the language of the ghetto streets in which he was raised. Unlike Karenga, Jacquette "belongs" in the low-income community and is both physically and temperamentally close to the youngsters of the Watts area.]

Wally: The majority [in the Watts area] would favor Tommy Jacquette. There is a lot of people doesn't understand Ron Karenga, and what he is trying to do. Seems like he is out for himself. Now, when Rap Brown or Carmichael is in town, Ron Karenga is in back of him, a bodyguard, and once when Rap Brown split, there was an opportunity for Ron Karenga to step in and speak, say what he could bring across to the Negro. It's like a competition. He figure that Carmichael didn't accomplish anything, and he is a phony, so here is my chance. "I am going to sneak in while the door is open, speak and see how many brainwashed Negro persons I can get to, and what I can get," and he got less than the majority people in Watts. . . . For Tommy Jacquette, I have more respect than I will give to Ron Karenga.

Chuck: We don't see much of Karenga or Jacquette. [Karenga] talks as though he is a philosopher, like he know everything. Actually he just touches things lightly that should be taken within consideration. You can't change just overnight, you know.

[In late 1968, two college students — Robert Mason and Richard Townsend — discussed King's role in the black movement and their conception of his transition to a more militant stance. Both Mason and Townsend were raised in the Watts area and are still based in the community.]

Robert Mason: You see, the movement never got started until King, because King had an influence and an ideology, two things that the movement never had before. Therefore, King became a leader, and all these cats—Malcolm, Stokely, Rap—are nothing but cats that were involved with King, and King is their reference point. King is the real origin of organized dissent in this country.

Sure, integration became unpopular, and King lost a lot of his influence. But he was trying to keep up, and he was very hip. The origin of his movement was to play upon the humanitarian conscience of the entire society, of the entire world. And the thing is, King had more patience, period! Stokely went down one time and got hit on the head and thrown in jail and he quit, that wasn't his bag. But SNCC worked very closely with SCLC and still does, though they kind of left King a little bit. Even though King had this beautiful thing, I think he really knew that separation would come about, that the separatist movement was a *necessary* movement. But these cats took over the vanguard from him and I don't think he was ready for the way that Stokely swept the minds of black college students and people in the ghetto who felt this great sense of urgency. You see, King was always a well-off man; he was never broke, so he couldn't exactly share the sense of urgency that people in the ghetto feel. But I think eventually he would have merged with the separatists.

We are fighting a war, and people like King and Stokely are the generals. Now, when you're fighting a war, you don't rely on one tactic; you attack from the front, you come in from all sides, and it has to be a *total* concept. We are going to have to free the cat on the street, as well as the cat up here in Baldwin Hills. We're going to need doctors, and lawyers, so how can we alienate these people and still consider ourselves a movement for liberation? So the diversity really represents a united front even though people think it's fragmented—it is one big push for one thing. It's just with different tactics: one guy is in Intelligence, someone else is in Propaganda, someone else in Infantry, and so on. It's a total concept; there's always jealousy and bickering among the different services, but they all combine to form an army to fight a war.

Richard Townsend: You know, when Martin Luther King was in Cicero, he knew what was happening, he knew what the reaction would be each time he went there, he knew what he was showing

to the black people. He's going to show black people that, in the
North, that was the hardest place to change. Nothing had changed.
He knew that, if he was to follow integration, he would never have
gone there and confronted those people the way he did. Black people read in the paper, "Martin Luther King, integrationist, goes into
Cicero in the North, and the white people throw bricks and bottles,"
and the whole bit. I think he knew what it would generate in the
black community. He knew it would generate a sense that would
have you identified more with the separatists. And he took black
people through a stage: before that point, black people began to
think the only way to make it was to have a white person as a friend.
He took 'em through that. They begin to understand how the system
works, and then he went on to expose the system even further. There
is no doubt about it, like in his last remarks, he was attempting
to show blacks that integration didn't work. And he was aware that
it didn't work.

"All Power to the People"
(1966 - 69)

One concrete result of post-riot activity in Watts has been
a movement to build organizations and institutions which are led
by, and entirely responsible to, the residents of the community itself. Even the youngsters of the "parking lot gang," regarded by
many as incurable delinquents, organized themselves into the Sons
of Watts. On all sides, almost without exception, the demand was
heard for community power and responsibility. The role of the white
liberal in this process is increasingly obscure, and the more articulate militants make it clear that the black community should be
allowed to "do its own thing," free from the gratuitous advice and
guidance of outside meddlers. Whether the "system" is adaptable
enough to permit this remains to be seen, and one's judgment on
this possibility ultimately determines how revolutionary one is in
thought and action. The revolutionaries, naturally, regard the dominant system as one massive, monolithic, and essentially racist bureaucracy, while the less radical see it as a more diverse collection
of institutions which are responsive in varying degrees to political,
social, and economic pressure. First we shall examine the views
of four college students, all of them back in Watts for the Christmas holidays of 1968. Then we shall hear from out-of-school teen-
agers and young adults—and a few older people—on the same general issues, their comments recorded over a two-year period. Oc-

casionally juxtaposed is a comment from one or more of the college-bound youngsters.

Elaine: I think the decision-makers know that the poverty programs are not doing any good. The token changes aren't real, and they know they aren't real. Like, in the poverty program when SNCC got some poverty money and started some Liberation Schools, and OEO was against that, but that was doing something to re-educate black people in the sense of Black Awareness. You have a Head Start program, which may do some basic good, but it still keeps black people under the thing that, in order to do even as well as whites, they have to have twice as much training, which keeps them in that inferior role. And, to me, those are the only things that they want. They want to reinforce this black "inferiority" idea, and that's what the poverty program is always saying and doing for us, and I think that's what the programs are meant to do. I don't think they are meant to help anybody.

I think Moynihan (and other white liberals) had a basic misunderstanding of what was necessary. I think only black people understand what black people mean. You know, white people control the things that are going into the ghetto. They can't gear them to the minds of black people, just because they are not black. And they refuse to admit that, either to themselves or to other people that are in positions to do something about it. They want to have this liberal role of contribution, and even if it is token and you tell them it's token, they reject that. And if you tell them what they can do is work in white communities to change white attitudes and white values, they say, "No, we have to work in the ghetto."

I think the idea now is to get a Black Awareness or Black Consciousness across, through public education. That, to me, is the only way. I'm talking about Black Mentality, a state of mind, not just the pigmentation of one's skin. Of course, I don't mean to say that white people can get Black Awareness.

[In stimulating this awareness] I think community control of the schools is essential, not just in the sense that black people say what black students are taught, but I mean the people that are teaching them, the administrators, and so on, their role models should be blacks. The superintendents, the school boards, they should be controlled by black people. You shouldn't need an extra poverty program for the money. Whatever money is given should go through the public schools.

That's what I think it should be, but I don't really think anything *within* the system is going to do anything for black people. So, in a sense, this is hypocritical for me to say, because I don't believe black people are ever going to get community control of the schools as long as white people are going to be in position to decide whether they get it or not.

And it's impossible for a white person or a white system to give anything toward black independence, that's self-destroying. I think that if you get an awareness of what the system is and what it has done to black people, you can't become anything else but a revolutionary in your thinking, and white people will not create revolutionaries. The conservatives, like the Rockefellers, the Reagans, the Johnsons, and the Kennedys, those are the ones that have basic control in this country.

There is a black value system, and it's basically different from the white. [In African societies] the family was very important, but it wasn't a capitalistic-type situation where you work to get ahead or for material success, and I think that materialism is part of capitalism, which is definitely part of the white value system. Somebody said that the supreme thing in the white value system is property, where the supreme thing in a black value system would be people.

I don't see how we can deny the fact of a community or a ghetto mentality as it exists now. There is a common bond among black people, the fact of alienation is the same throughout the community. And the Muslims are really the only ones that have a practical, united, black movement. Like, if America was to be destroyed today, if everything we're complaining about in this society was to be destroyed, the only group that could still function is the Muslims.

Richard Townsend: I think what we should realize is that all these poverty programs and all these educational programs resulted in one thing: showing black people where the system can't be moved and where it can be moved. Sometimes the system moves. The State Legislature just passed a resolution saying that Black Studies should be taught from elementary schools through college, and in the wording it is pretty much like the kind of Black Studies program that black students wanted at San Francisco State. At Santa Cruz, Professor Blake is pretty hip and he taught [Black History or Sociology, as in the case of Nat Turner's rebellion] like I think it is. I think those kinds of courses are developing.

In some ways, I think the "system" does produce revolutionaries. They can get you into Berkeley and try to teach you the ways of the society, but it just so happens they're producing revolutionaries at the same time. You look at these colleges in the South; they try to buy them off with Ford Foundation money and all that, and it's not working. They are still creating revolutionaries; they don't have the power to stop it. They can't set up an educational system now that's aware and enlightened, and teach the truth, and prevent people from becoming radical thinkers.

People in the ghetto can react two ways to these little model "econo-fab" houses they are building in the neighborhood. People are going to say: "Well, I'm going to do everything I can to get in that house and be like every other American family," or the houses can make people very angry. And like Eldridge Cleaver says, you have people cooped up in these ghettos with steaks and nice houses on their minds, you can have a reaction, especially if you can't supply them.

Robert Mason: In any of these programs, especially these federally funded programs, you have to have money appropriated. But the point is that, with every program, there's always the dependency thing. You see, black people have always been dependent and if it's left up to the system, they will always be dependent. The black community has to stand by itself; it needs economic and social and educational independence.

There is a problem of leadership of the black people: do we have a *program?* You can't complain that white people are coming in and taking over and running the programs, when you don't have anything to submit.

At this particular point in history, there is a necessity for black people to have separation, and the Federal government will never support separation.

My thought is that any black community has to go through three different stages. Number one is the destructive stage, in the case of Watts the '65 revolution. The second stage would be the unity stage, with the idea of self-reliance and socio-economic independence of the black community. Number three would be integration or, at least, peaceful coexistence. But at this particular point in time, black people realize that there is no such thing as integration. Integration has to be done on the man's terms. It means accepting the society and accepting white values and white laws. But this isn't *us*.

Right now, what we have is a rejection of the existing structure of exclusion from the system, and a rebellion against being

defined by someone else; so now, in the pursuit of unity, we are trying to define ourselves. We have been fighting against ourselves.

But I don't see how we could really model ourselves after Africa
when we are in an entirely different situation and Africa's problems
haven't been solved by their means anyway. I mean you have to
work with what you have. You can't go from here to there without
going through all these points between. People say, "We want to
go back to African culture, we dig African culture." But we have
no relationship with African culture. There is a common bond among
all the oppressed peoples in the world, and that should be our point
of reference.

I don't think black culture has reached a point where you can
define a black person by this culture. You see, a culture of someone living on 103rd is different from a person living in New York.
How do you relate to black people in New York? You even find different mentalities in Watts, or you get a different vibration from
a person in Watts than you would, say, from a person from the Glad-
iators or Slauson.[5]

In developing a culture, you want your culture to be perfect.
You want your culture to express your purpose, your goal. We could
sit back and look at the world, and examine all philosophies and
all cultures, and pick out what we think is best. We are in the position of *building* a culture.

You see, our [so-called] "culture" is really a *sub*culture, it's
purely reactionary [a reaction to rejection and oppression]. We ate
chitlins and hog maws, and found that the pig is bad for us, not
healthy for the human body. So we cut that loose. We are in a position where we can change, we are developing culture.

I spent a long time up at Seattle University, and the mentality of the Negro people there is nowhere near like it is in Watts because they have never experienced the type of oppression that we
have; I mean they don't worry too much about police, they get along
pretty well with whites. They don't have the sense of urgency, don't
feel the strong sense of culture, and the strong ties of blackness.
The Black Panther Party there has about twelve members, and
no community support.

There *is* a common bond among black people, but the bond
isn't as tight as you might think. An interesting story is the story
about this cat who started a circus and he had this big sign, "The
Greatest Show on Earth," the most unusual show, the most unique

---

[5] Other areas of the Los Angeles ghetto where youth gangs are common.

show, and thousands of people came to see it. All they had was ten brothers pulling a rope, and everybody said, "Is that the greatest show on earth? What's so unique about that?" He said, "Have you ever seen ten Negroes doing anything *together?*"

We have to sacrifice individualism for the sake of unity. This is what black people are going through now. You take orders—that's what I think is so beautiful about Islam. Even though I don't dig it, as a [religious] movement, discipline is beautiful. When Elijah speaks, it is done.

Each one of us is our own little organization, with our own goals and our own everything. We are united just for one purpose, to attain liberation. If we were given the land, the entire country, or the three or four states that we wanted, and all black people put in there, what would happen? Anarchy, power struggle. The best type of government in a situation like this is a dictatorship.

I favor something I like to call "economic communalism." Have the ghetto economically independent, with [black] people centralized *within* the community, yet have the so-called community organizations and institutions *de*centralized *to* the community, not run from downtown. Jordan [High] shouldn't be operated the same as Hollywood High.[6]

Paul Williams: What we have to do is to build self-pride and identity, start building up the community. The whole thing is to build up this independent ideal: the people in the community building it for themselves, whatever it turns out to be, whether it is revolutionary, if it doesn't work within the system, or if it does.

The black man is confronting the problem: is he going to work in a group, or is he going to continue with individual goals, like this desire to get up high in the society? This is the whole problem of broadening individuals and turning back to tribalism, to where we can be more effective. One way to do it is to use what I call "constructive hate."

One thing whites must realize is that the whole philosophy of this country has been divide and conquer, divide within countries, civil wars, in foreign policy, divide within the community. And give the attitude to black people that they can't work together, can't live together, that the organizations are going to kill off each other, so they can't really establish the idea of working together. What the black movement is asking for now is actually a restructuring of the system, restructuring of the institutions in the black commun-

---

[6] Mason explains "economic communalism" in more detail in Chapter IV.

ity, to have black people work together and for them to have the
image and the concern and the desire to work with each other, and
the respect to work with and for each other.

You see, black people are going to need encouragement and
the self-identification where they can relate to the past and to historical factors. Motivation—they need this extra boost at the present. I don't think the black man is going to develop to the point
of being a racist. Racism means that one culture will dominate another. Once black people reach the point where they feel superior or
equal or whatever it is, I don't think it will go to their heads.

And once the separation is obtained, at the same time there
are gonna be people, not ministers or people like that but people
like themselves, demanding integration. For us to ask for a Black
Studies Center at Harbor [College] is just demanding *integration;*
asking for more black clerks, secretaries, cafeteria workers, black
administrators, is just demanding integration. Some people might
say they [the blacks] are getting more than their share. Myself,
I haven't found the point of what is a "share" of freedom, what is
a "share" of participating in the functioning of the family of institutions.

I think that white people must learn to give up their morals
[value systems] and beliefs and change the structure of this country and establish more of an insight for relating to people. The only
thing that will save man is his social being, his relationship with
other men—that's the only thing. Once people learn to respect each
other on a level that they can communicate on, *then* they are going
to have integration, but I don't see it in my lifetime. Maybe outside my lifetime there'll be progress toward whole and complete
integration.

You can talk about "assimilating," but the norms and morals
of this society are not what many people want to assimilate into.
The only realistic way I can see to assimilate is to restructure the
norms themselves, to develop norms somewhere that will fit everybody. So that both white people and black people can survive. If
you have twelve people living in a house together, and the morals
[norms] are only structured for eight of them, the other four will
either destroy the house, because they can't live under those circumstances, or be put outside the house. If you live in a society
and the society is geared for a certain kind of person and you can't
be that kind of person, you can't live in the society. The main thing
is to change the *society* so that all of them can live in the house together. There'll always be a minority and a majority, and that's

fine because without disagreements you won't have corrections and modifications and developments, to make progress and solve the problems. But if the minority reaches the point where it can't function, there must be something wrong with the system. The society is not being effective.

I think the black movement rejects the [white, capitalistic] idea of materialism. Materialism, to me, is a philosophy that matter is primary and consciousness of self is secondary, that consciousness derives from matter and material gain. The first thing we have to realize is that consciousness of self is *first* and that things that are material are *second*. And that you have to start relating to the individual, before you start relating to material things. You have to change the whole structure.

My main concern is working with people. The determining thing now is that black people work with each other. Now, the majority of middle-class people doesn't relate to people in a different class structure. The majority of middle-class black people—the so-called NAACP—when DuBois was in charge of it, the idea was to get more doctors, get more lawyers, these other different things. And the thing is, what he was doing mainly was relating to people who went to college and went to school, and these people—the professional people, the so-called educated people—should come back to the community and establish themselves as working *for* the community and not outside factions or just working for themselves. They should try to motivate black people who don't have an education. This is the main function: middle-class persons relating to the person who got trapped in "suppression." Just remember that every time he [a middle-class person] gets a higher job, there are five or six people who are not working. Economically the whole country is not functioning, economically it is not sustained. When everyone is working, then the whole country is more stable.

The Uncle Toms that are in office now will have to be changed, to where there's more representation, more people who want to have things for black people, instead of puppets to the white man.

A lot of people say there's communism going into the black movement. I don't think so. A lot of people who are concerned with working in the community may adopt some part of communism or socialism but by the same process they take something from every system, from socialism or capitalism, coming up with an economical system that might have everybody working. I see three different movements going on at the same time: the movement of reform and change, the "due process"; the communistic movement of total revolution to change the whole economical structure; and the movement of people concerned with working in their communities. White people really trip me out when they say there's communism in the black movement. To be honest, I don't know. Maybe there's communism in the movement, but the thing is that the black movement is surviving on its determination to work for the people in the community and I don't care how much communism is injected or inserted into the movement, it's never going to co-opt it. Of course, there's the communal thing of everyone working together to survive, but at the same time black people have their own individual concerns, their own desires also, and I don't think that's going to change: black men, independent, but with more participation together in solving the problems. Basically, the force that will make this country more stable is the black people.

Paul Williams (April 1969):   I'm just laying back, just saying and thinking a lot of things, any way my thoughts run. I think about a lot of things. The first thing I think about is how fortunate to have been in a family who do have some kind of desire or determination to do something; so I'm working actually on something that I really don't know what I'm working on, but I'm just doing it. Basically I'm just a person that talks and likes to relate things to people. When I start relating things to people, I have to relate things to myself; when I relate to myself I find out there are a lot of fallacies and a lot of things that are wrong with me, which I'm trying to figure out. Who can I blame it on? Can I blame it on myself? Can I blame it on the white man? Can I blame it on the country and the way they run things?

It all boils down, something is wrong with me, maybe what's wrong with a lot of people. But the problem, as it exists now, is black people in this country, and I'm black, so I'm part of the problem. You live with the problem, you die with the problem, you think with the problem, you do everything with the problem.
I think I have a unique responsibility. I don't know if it's to my people, for my people, whatever, but I kind of think more than just about my family—I think about everybody in the neighborhood. I think about what they are thinkin' about, think about what they are doing, you know. I think about my friends and how they are going to relate to me in the future—they might not relate to me, because you know how you separate as you get older and you just go on your merry way. But when I look at the problems of people, you know, I say, "Wow, that's my problem too, and I should do something about it." A lot of people say, well, you should be basically concerned with yourself and not with other people. But I kind

of think of being concerned about a lot of people—might be the cause of my death, cause of me being irresponsible all the rest of my life, cause me never to achieve anything in the future. Well, this is really what I'm concerned about, what I'm interested in—people and their problems.

And black people who live in Watts, they don't seem to have a unique problem, but they have a problem that is very common among black people. They are living with their families, their mothers—economically unstable, suppressed, psychologically defeated. You know, as I tripped through high school I had to impress people, I had to do things that were somewhat significant so I can get *attention*. Maybe this is what I didn't get at home. But as a black person I wonder: what am I really supposed to get at home? What did my parents get when they were at home? And like, wow, I got attention, but I didn't get the right kind of attention, and, you know, you are supposed to learn how to read, write, and this is why I'm talkin' on this microphone now, because I can't write and I have a problem reading, going to junior college. But I think I have something that I can offer to people, and I feel that I should express it.

This common situation in Watts, this common problem of black people being unhappy, being suppressed, being winos, being dope addicts, being broke, don't have any moral convictions and the whole thing—who is really causing the problems? People blame it on the white man, and some people blame it on the country and their policies; history shows that their policies have been quite racial [racist], but when it all boils down, there's *poor* white people and there's *poor* black people, and the poor people seem to have this problem. I'm never going to get away from my people, I'm always going to live with my kin, my environment, my peer group as they call it. If I don't relate to them, I'm not really relating to anybody.

But since I am in this problem, I've been thinking about it a lot, and I been trying to figure out what in the hell's been goin' on—this shit is ridiculous, you know, all black people's minds all fucked up, and my mind is all fucked up, and what are we going to do about it? How do you really work together to achieve something? The whole country is based on making a lot of money. I feel that the country should be based on the spirit of *producing,* of everybody producing so everyone could live comfortable. I'm talking about black people living comfortable, I'm talking about poor white people who are not living comfortable, I mean everyone living comfortable.

Now, in this society some people call themselves living comfortable, but they are not living comfortable, because their conscienc-
es either are bothering them or something is bothering somebody,
and this man is going to always have a problem. Now in black communities, basically, it's an economical problem, but to really solve
the economical problem, you have to solve the problem of the black
people's minds so they can learn to manage their money in such
a way to where the economy of the community would grow. I think
people can work together. It serves everybody's benefits—well,
some people are greedy and some people not greedy, and I think
people should have the freedom of their desires and their goals also,
along with working with each other. You know, they're ambitious
and they want to work a little harder, to make a little bit more. They
should have the opportunity, but also they shouldn't deprive others who, say, are not working as hard, to live comfortable also.

Now this problem, this country has had a problem with black
people for 103 years, and now the problem's coming to the point
where people are ready to invest their lives, I'm ready to invest my
life to make black people comfortable, and I'm gonna try when, where
and how I can, and I'll try to do it in the most logical way I can,
and the black movement and the black history tells me that we've
been fighting for something that this country is supposed to be
constituted under: equal rights and everything. But there seems
to be a *racial* difference, then there is a *class* difference, and [with]
the combination of both of these, you can't hardly make anyone
comfortable, someone is either still inferior or superior.

I think people should learn to live with each other under their
cultures and their beliefs. Now, as things are going, the black man
is beginning, just beginning, to believe in himself, believe in his
ideas, his whole thinking, create his own symbolism, define his own
meanings to everything that he stands for. When you do this, you
know, you have some kind of identification of yourself, and to really
know yourself is something else, and when you relate yourself to
something else or you really have something that you can identify
with, say Africa, also you can identify with yourself *here*. Then,
to me, it's groove to really have these things, and it's not the reading and writing that I've been determined to go to school for, but
it's just in knowing that there is a past and there's something really
pertinent to *me* as an individual. So what I've done is kind of encouraged myself to really do some deep thinking about how to help
black people and how to help myself, and the only way we are going
to do this is that we get a meeting of the minds and understand-

ing of each other. Now we'll just work on something better for my mother and your mother and everybody's mother to live comfortable, financial-wise.

The movement has grown to the point where it's drawn all parts of black people into it, including me. I believe in the social man and the black movement, black power, has drawn me in as an individual who is concerned on helping people, black people specifically. Now I know, to solve the problem, you have to solve the problem of black people first. Then you can solve the problem of the other people. I think the white people know, to some extent, that they created the problem, and now they are trying to alleviate it, but they have to learn also: they have to change *their* culture, *their* beliefs and everything to develop a real logical thing of learning to live with each other.

The movement has brought me to a point to where I'm president of a Black Student Union, and I think this is the most beautiful thing that there is. But is this going to exist in the high schools? Why doesn't it exist in the community? I keep thinking: something is holding it back, holding back people working together in the community.

We're trying to change educational institutions, to where the educational structure is relevant to black students, and also to white students; it's going to be hard as hell to do. But there is a lot of things that is really pertinent to black people and the only way it is going to be pertinent to them is to motivate their interests. These Black Studies departments or majors or centers have motivated black students' interests in college. The thing is, when you are dealing with the administration of a college, the administration wants to agree with the solving of the problems, but they feel that they have to do it their way and there is still something missing, and it gives a person a real uncomfortable feeling when you have to continually go over and over again and find that this group of men don't want to work with you. I think the only way you can solve a problem is to work with someone who actually *is* the problem. Maybe you can solve their problem, [but] if that individual is only concerned for himself and not concerned for the overall problem, that still does not solve the problem because the problem is in the *masses* of black people, not just directly in individuals. Now, I'm at the level in the black movement of strengthening my insight on the exterior world, the world around me, and I find that some people in the movement are not basically concerned with the black problem which is immediate and they should deal with it first. But I find [also] with people being hungry all over the world, I find myself broadening out.

The stimulation of self-pride and the discredit of another individual is somewhat going against my convictions, but I find justification in doing it, you know. Discrediting of a white person is justifiable because they *need* discredit. They need this down feeling, this feeling of being below because they've put themselves so high on a pedestal to where they just fell off because it was off balance. I think once black people build this pedestal it won't get so high to where they'll fall off. I think they'll strengthen the whole concept of people working together, and through the reality of black people working with black people, and black people being proud of themselves, [they'll] change their whole conception of hustling and killing and beating up each other. They're going to start something that's really going to be a much stronger thing.

I keep telling myself that the black man is going to save this country. I keep hearing the statement: man is extinct, man is destined to destroy himself. To me, as an idealistic, optimistic individual who believes in communicating with people, I feel there is some need, some way, to solve the problem. The immediate problem is black people in this country, and the next problem is the problem of all the poor people all over the world, then there is the problem of the white man and his so-called control over everything and [his] desires for land and everything. I keep feeling that man has to be optimistic in solving the problems. He has to be determined to do things, to put things together, to make this place a lot better for people to live in. I really feel that people can communicate. Being in the movement I find [sometimes] I'm going off leaving my brothers behind, that don't have the self-pride but still [cause] the destruction of black people. Well, I must go back, don't leave the ones who are straggling behind—bring them up to the movement, always motivate someone, try to stimulate them to have the same direction, the trust and honesty of working with each other.

But I find the conflict going on to a further thing: of economical value and not being [simply] on the thing of motivating black people, but just trying to convert *all* people. It's not a racial thing, it's more of an economical thing, and I want the people to see the economical problem and the psychologically defeated poor man— his mind is warped and destroyed and he consistently lives in a poor atmosphere and people keep saying, "Well, you know, people want to live like this because this is the way they are," but hell, I live around 'em all the time, I sleep with them, I eat with them, I really feel that they think this way but I don't feel they want to be this way. I feel that all of them have desires and goals and there is always something holding them back, and [for me] the thing is to fight the problem, whatever's holding them back. Even the international thing.

I have a conception that as I fight for Black Power I fight for "people's power." And this includes white people, which they call the devil and everything else. If it ever comes to the point of, say, killing ninety or one hundred white men, *to solve the problem,* I'll do that. But the thing is, what is really going to solve the problem? You can talk about "divide and conquer the white man," but what is the real purpose of "divide and conquer?" You know, conquer for supremacy, conquer for equalness, conquer for what? I find myself asking what the hell am I conquering for? And it all goes back to [economics].

You know, how do you kill a man? What is killing a man? Just physically—shooting, stabbing, poisoning? A man can be dead if he's psychologically defeated. It's like having a horse that can't run and you have to shoot him, and he is much better off dead than alive.

The means to our goals is the revolution, but we have to think about the aftermath of the revolution too. You know, there'll be no more climbing up the stairway of status into a high class, the whole conception of this country [now]. Poor people and black people are in an alliance with each other. Black people and white people are coming to this realization. White people also are realizing they are poor and psychologically defeated. Man has in the past [created] a technical world, but he has fallen back, he has regressed, the technical world is too far beyond him. The masses of people who cannot relate to these machines have to relate to each other. I'm black and he's white; he's low and he's cool and we are all here together and not talking to a machine but talking to each other. And this is the real thing, that people are beginning to have some dialogue, people are beginning to communicate, people are beginning to reason, people are beginning to find the truth of the real world and of themselves. But first they must discover themselves.

I think people nowadays are coming to another age of reasoning, where we will find truth, and we are coming to another age of reality where we can communicate and experience, relate, participate in all activity that exists in this country and have a common goal. But after the revolution, what do you do? Eliminate the aristocrat classes and have people come together and we eliminate the economic structure which is so at fault, very superficial. High class, low class, middle class upper and lower, and all these classes: this is just role-playing. [In] the situation after the revolution there is time for people to reason and understand, but we are going to have to do more than just play roles, but try to inject reality into every so-called occupation we have in the future. This is why I feel that it is very important for black people to come to this reality and white people come to this reality. After the revolution they must reason.

You can't kill a man's ambitions. A man must be ambitious to exist, have desires and goals, but selfishness has to be eliminated when one man is overeating and another man's undereating. He's going to have to give up all the extra that he has, for the equilibrium of people surviving and living comfortable. Man can mass-produce to where he can really survive on this earth, [but] the evolution of man is leading to where he will destroy himself just like another animal. Social man, who's been evolved out of philosophy, sociology, psychology, and all the social sciences—the study of man himself has developed social man. If he can resolve to reason after another so-called revolution, he can respect another man's ability [tendency] not to have that drive, to not be ambitious, and then in the next society that's gonna exist, that man is gonna have to inject this particular drive or ambition into every other man so everyone can be ambitious enough to where they are gonna live, or their children are going to live, comfortable under their own circumstances.

When I use the word "comfortable," I define it as not being really luxurious, not really middle-class, but I just think it is a basic thing of surviving. "Comfortable" can mean a lot of things. The goal is to mass-produce for everybody, not for just a certain segment of the people. Now, a lot of people go to these factories and they produce millions and millions and millions of dollars of these types of things and they don't get their equal share. [In the new society] you are producing for everyone within the society, and each one of these people go into these factories, they have in their minds that they are not just producing for someone else's profit, but they are producing for their own profit so they can live comfortably in the future. When you think someone is making a profit *exploiting* you, you are not really comfortable psychologically. Now, even the ones who are living comfortable are consistently being aggravated by those who are not comfortable, those who are psychologically defeated, and those who are trying to motivate themselves to be more ambitious. I think this would make him uncomfortable also, because he has to worry about his money, about the status that he has. But if he is to exist, he is going to have to give up a certain amount of his profit for people to survive. Now if he still is ambitious, and he still has this desire to be ahead of everybody, he is going to be ahead [in terms of] producing for everybody, not just producing for himself, or making a profit for himself. And I'm not saying, tear down the economical class; I'm saying, restructure it in such a way to where everyone is benefiting from what is being produced.

Now we are mass-producing damn near everything in this country. We are producing a lot of luxuries, a lot of conveniences to a man's home to where everyone in this country should have a convenience. If you don't have a convenience, someone is making a profit of stockpiling this stuff in somebody's corner, in somebody's warehouse, or somebody's destroying it to make sure that someone else doesn't get it. Now I have a strange feeling about this country that they *are* producing enough for everybody, but they are not giving it to everybody because the whole economical structure is built on a war and military complex which [makes] the country blossom in the sense a lot of people are working during wartime, and not at wartime people are not working, and the whole thing has just evolved around keeping people down to where *other* people can be over-comfortable, you see what I mean?

Now when I'm looking to the relationship of a high-class person and a low-class person, it's only going to be basically on the man's ambitions, and not of the color of his skin or him being deprived of anything. Equal education, not only equal opportunity but equalness of freedom in his mind to really develop as much as he wants. My desire is to be a teacher. Now if I would have the proper education, I probably would have a higher desire. Now someone who has had the education and who is not motivated to be something higher in society can also find a professional job to where he can live comfortable also and won't have to strain. The person doesn't go through the process of dying while he is alive, which is a very independent thing from death. He [and his children] have the advantages of being stable when they do enter into the world of competition.

Now I don't want to relate [push] competition to the extreme point because I feel that competition is necessary. I believe in competition, but I don't want a competition to stifle any man's mind or any man's feelings on developing. And this is the whole thing: that we have been caught up in a world that has psychologically defeated people, suppressed people, exploited people, have done so many things to people to where if their minds are not straight, they are being killed. So what I mean by being "comfortable" is that a man can actually have the freedom to think and express himself and to produce. Only just now it seems that they will never be comfortable, but if the technical world reinforces the social man, I think there might be some progress in the world because technology and automation has dominated man's mind to where he only thinks about inventing something for his own selfish desires and not for the masses of the people. And this is very important, it is actually a contradiction to reality in itself and to have a contradiction in reality is really bad, you know, because we can't continue to live without relating to each other.

Once he becomes equal, he's free of the changes that have been holding him down, he's gonna compete with each other. I mean, keep within a form of competing not to be greedy, or selfish, or destroy other men, but to compete to increase production, saving man himself and not man saving the machine. The thing is that man is going to become ambitious to the point, first, he establishes, "Well, I'm equal, now I can compete on the level of really being free." And they are gonna all be coming together, a meeting of the minds, to analyze the present for the future, to produce better for their children, for the future generations. And competition is gonna be more a factor in motivating the people to produce a lot more for themselves, not individually for themselves but for the masses of everybody—mass-produce for the people. Competition is going to bring this about.

Paul Williams (continues):   Black Power is social, political, and economical. Socially, black people must live together, socialize together, in the framework of continued everyday understanding of different class groups within the black community. You have your lower classes and then you have your bourgeois so-called elite, the black elite which is supposed to be middle class. The bourgeois black man thinks he is gonna be higher in the class than what he is gonna be. The majority of bourgeois values lie within the context of lower-middle class, and therefore they want to live higher and the standards [are] higher and want to socialize a little higher, and socializing anything higher than middle class outside the black community is actually and definitely socializing with the white man. But day by day black people have begun to fall into the trap of honesty and sincereness and found out, "Wow, I'm not really that high in the status group of this country," and once black people realize that, then they can mingle with the ones who do not have this value structure, and develop a situation where black people are more understanding with each other and can communicate with each other and learn to live with each other no matter what happens.

Now, political power is something that is gonna be based on a lot of tactics and ways that the black man shows the white man he is politically educated enough to handle the situation. But if the black man is not politically educated, he can be totally suppressed, exploited. Black people are forced to become politically aware, to have more black representatives as mayors, as congressmen, as senators. But once black people see that even their own kind in this class group has been corrupted by money, by material wealth, by the concern of man only for himself, and if the black man is out basically *for his people,* it's gonna prove for a fact that politics in this country is corrupt and he's gonna get himself assassinated just like the rest of 'em.

King was beginning to see the significance of militant groups working with all black people no matter what their philosophy is. He was beginning to see the insight of this, and in my opinion the man assassinated King because he was getting politically involved, educated, he was beginning to motivate the people to do a lot of different things. That was the last nonviolent demonstration that he was gonna have; I know his next statement would have said: All black people work together and use each other's means to their goals and that means, if it is necessary to have violence, let violence be. If it is not necessary to have violence, don't let violence be.

You can either empty this whole racial mess into the trash can by reform, or in a revolutionary construction of politics you don't deal with conventional politics at all, you deal with any means necessary to definitely handle the situation of this country. That means either a partial, compromise change in the country and this structure of local, state, or federal government, or a total, complete change of this country, which is definitely needed. And without complete change, the survival of this country is definitely down the drain, 'cause the economical class is superficial, unrealistic, dehumanizing mankind himself, and politics in this country is proven to be totally corrupt. As they have run it for the last forty to fifty to sixty years, it has been basically military or a war economy. So the poor come to see this country in a very unique way. It is very significant that they get politically educated, along with the modern science and insight that man has, the extra, technical insight that the white man has, to really beat him at his own game, show in his own country that he can either be rectified or destroyed as necessary for humanity itself to survive. And this is what the whole thing of Black Power is behind, is *humanity*.

So, if this country really wants to survive, this country looks inside itself. This country can survive, but it seems like they don't want to survive. 'Cause their problem is here and it's not in space, and it's not over in Asia, Africa, Europe; it's here in their own home. The problem is existing within the quagmires of black people and white people, [where] black people been corrupted by the white man and then the white man's mind is corrupted because of what he believes in.

What I'm trying to say is that economics is the thing, economics is gonna cause the social uplifting, economics is gonna cause the political education of the black people, economics is gonna cause the uplifting of the smallest proletariat in the black community, even the wino who doesn't want to work. Economics is gonna stabilize the community, cause the black community to control its own within itself. Economics is gonna be the power base of approaching each of the institutions in this country. For the black man, economics has been small and petty. Confrontations, power plays, between black militant groups over money. But who benefits? When black people get to this point, of not reasoning, you can say, who is benefiting, who is making him not reason and, well, there is the white man, there is the establishment that is continually starting these confrontations among black people, "divide and conquer," and make sure that black people never work together, and he [the white man] will consistently put organizations or things within the black community to make sure that the black man never works together again. This method of "divide and conquer" may come from two sides, but it's not going to be a thing of the black man dividing and conquering the white man, but it's gonna be the poor people and the white people who have the insight to see that the problem is not basically a racial thing, but it's basically an economical thing. White people themselves are going to see the truth and reality and they are going to see the honesty that the black people have in this movement and they are going to totally relate to it.

This country has failed to supply the black man with the economical means that he needs to motivate or stimulate his mind and his environment to survive. White people are going to divide themselves, they are going to conquer themselves, because they are going to see the honesty and the realness within black people, to make proper changes in this country. And until that time, there is going to be a lot of people dying because the establishment is going to suppress, continually suppress, any movement that is going to benefit the people, not only the black people but *all* the poor people.

The black man is suffering because there are so many devices and ways to suppress his mind, his will, his physical ability, and everything. He is under total exploitation, his mind has been robbed, [but] he is ridding his mind of all these things, this past world of corruption and misunderstanding. Now the white man is misguided because he gets higher in the status class and he [this] discourages the relationship with anybody. The morals of higher living have corrupted his mind.

The middle-class white man is the one who can establish the relationship between rich and poor, black and white. He is in the middle, he has to understand. And in some particular cases he does have the insight to see the corruption of this country through the form of not communicating. The middle-class white man is going to have to see the realness in himself and relate to that. The poor white man is coming to the fastest reality that any man ever came to. He is gonna have to see that he is never gonna get rich. So, if he is working for someone else who *is* gonna get rich, and he can't get rich, he's gonna have to develop an insight to fight the establishment, or to fight the white race, or the white race's moral standards, which are totally wrong.

The relationship between the black man and the white man is getting worse and getting better at the same time; as they begin to get closer to hate, they begin to get closer to reality at the same time. The black woman and the white man are getting further and further away [from each other], because they can see the reality that the white man's moral structure is totally poisoned and for her to be living within the white moral structure, she is gonna find that she is gonna be superficial, she is gonna be unreal, she is gonna be further away from her man, her mate, and [if] she sees her mate turning to these white women she is gonna get violent, and solve that problem herself. She is gonna be more woman, more honest, more sincere to her own man, her black old man. And this is gonna cause the success of the black race being stable. The black man involved in the movement needs a strong black woman to consistently push him foward, having him do things that are reasonable and honest.

Economics is the black man's problem, and the white man must supply more than he can ever imagine to stabilize the black man in this country. And once the black people see that Black Power is not only realistic but for the benefit of black people, they cannot fight it any longer, they are gonna be forced to live with it, white people are gonna be forced to live with it. Black Power is gonna develop into *people* power, a whole conception of real power for the people to live comfortable in this country. Economics, through political science and social science, is gonna cause the uplifting of the black man and the black man cannot and will not fail. And when he's saying "power to the people," he's not saying only black people, but white people too. Black people will realize, and all people will realize, that they have the power to correct or develop or modernize this country in the most constructive and successful way there is.

[Some of the out-of-school youngsters discuss the formation of the Sons of Watts, a spontaneous organization of the "hard core" which emerged during the summer of 1966. On the anniversary of the riot, the Watts community staged a festival, with parades, exhibits, and several jazz concerts on the athletic field of Jordan High School. The massive crowds, integrated though predominantly Negro, were patrolled by the Community Alert Patrol, a group of local residents who had originally banded together to check on police practices and record incidents of brutality or harassment. The crowd handling, a complicated and delicate task under the best of circumstances, was performed with remarkable efficiency and the almost complete absence of incidents.]

Jerry: I'm going to tell you, man, this organization called Sons of Watts . . . this is the best thing that's happened in Watts in the last five years, I should say . . . You got the worst criminals in Los Angeles. We were all drunk one day over wine. Wine, Red Devils, and any other narcotic you can name. We were all intoxicated right after the festival. Someone said if we can keep that many people together, white, Spanish, and black, without any mishap, we can do it at all times. One person said it and didn't know what he was saying, so three other people got together, called it the "Sons of Watts." Young men who were raised there, got half killed, come back, went to jail, come back. In other words, they were raised there in a town no one even thought exists, just started calling themselves "Sons of Watts". . . . They worked in unity; they worked together.

Sam: The reason why the Sons of Watts really want to gain is because I myself, as a teen-ager in the area, I am going over the path that they have went over, you know, like throwing all these different things, stealing cars, having fun. See, they've been through all this, and they know what is going on, they know what that man is going to give you up there . . . the jail, the police; like this man here I talked to, he can tell what the jury's going to give you if you go out there and take a man's car, or take his battery out, he can tell you what the jury's going to give you, you understand? It's going to be just like he said, and it's best for them to tell you and to stop me now while I am young. They tell me, "Boy, you go to school, gets you an education . . . do what you can, get you an education like the white boy got." Excuse me, I am not prejudiced. Like this man says, "Just you get that education that he got, then you can wear newer shirts or white shirts with a gold pin, you don't have to dress like any other old colored person." . . . This is what I figured that the Sons of Watts group meant to be, like they are today . . . because they don't want us to go on through what they did, and they done been through hell . . . if you go back, I am not an old dude and I am not a young dude, from what I done heard and from what people done told me about different things, and different kinds of brutality that police gave you in '58, '49, all back down in the later days, that is not too groove goin' to jail, I know it is not too groove.

Sam and *George*: Anyone that wants to [can] join. All you need to do is to have enough courage to go down there, when they have a meeting. . . . What I am saying, man, is like the Sons of Watts' idea is a good idea, and they have done a lot, I mean, like who would ever think of setting trash cans at every corner, man, and going around suggesting to these peoples not to litter the streets. . . . You go to South Gate, Huntington Park [adjacent areas] or somewhere, you'll see a trash can on every corner. That is the way it is in Watts too, now, "Sons of Watts," every corner.

Those are not trash cans really. Those are just barrels that they went and took their time, and oil drums, and sprayed, and wrote "Sons of Watts" on their own time, and put 'em on different blocks, at different corners, yes, on every corner in Watts. See, this is something that our government, all these peoples in Washington talking about improving Watts, there are small things they could do that can even make us happier than we are now, but the Sons of Watts, I mean, how come they couldn't think of this five or six years ago, to put a trash can in Watts . . . how come that as long as I've

been living in Watts, man, the best Christmas decoration I ever
seen in my life in Watts is this last year, 1966.

You know who put those decorations up? Parking lot boys and
the Sons of Watts. That is right, they care, man.

[In mid-1966, the Student Nonviolent Coordinating Committee (SNCC) of Los Angeles, in company with other organizations
generally identified as "nationalistic" in sympathy, proposed that
the predominantly Negro south central area be incorporated as
a separate city. Most of the area is now a part of the city of Los Angeles, though some of it lies in unincorporated county territory.
The stated purpose of this move was to provide local self-government for the mass of Negroes in the county, through the election
of their own mayor, city council, boards and commissions, and so
forth. A much-debated issue in 1966, it received less attention in
1967. Nevertheless, it remains a microcosm of the issues and arguments which beset the Negro community not only in Los Angeles
but in other urban ghettos of the country. Armstead and Townsend
offer their own reactions to the proposal; others from the community give their comments separately.]

Townsend: Since the [first] Watts festival I have heard a great
deal [about incorporating the area]. It's what you might call a split
vote . . . especially if you were to contrast the thoughts of maybe
the nationalist with the thoughts of the moderate. You'll find primarily the nationalist will say, "incorporating Watts will have its
advantages," which can easily be seen by the moderate. The people will have a sense of pride, will have to support themselves, it
will be their own, and of course you always protect your own. . . .
The moderate might criticize . . . the fact that you are alienating
a community; what you are actually . . . creating technically and
officially is a ghetto and he looks at it on a long-range basis. You
have to balance whether or not forming a ghetto now will force Watts
to become completely alienated from Los Angeles, and will it allow
Watts a chance to grow up so that it may be able to disseminate
its culture . . . into the greater Los Angeles area in later years. It
is really on the edge of a balance, and for the most part, you find
that most moderates would prefer staying in Los Angeles. . . .

If Watts were any other place, it probably would be a very good
idea [but] in Watts you find a massive political struggle . . . which
might result in a number of things such as neglect of the obligations
of being a city. . . . And you would find yourself isolated even more.

. . . Educationally, I could see this as an advantage, a tremendous advantage in that schools could make exceptions that they cannot make now, concerning curriculum. . . . Personally, I think that, as radical as it may sound . . . if we were to secede from anything, I favor seceding from the Los Angeles City School District, without necessarily having to incorporate. Because I think now things like fire departments, trash cans, and so on are relatively important [time-consuming] and we wouldn't have time to concentrate on these things. On the level of education, this is where I feel that we could do a lot more. We would be more flexible, we would appeal only to our needs, we wouldn't appeal to the needs of University High School, which the Board of Education has to do right now. The books they buy, they buy books for University High and Jordan uses them; so why not have Jordan buy their own books? Books with more pictures in them, which might be the case. This is just an example. I think that this is something I would offer as a definite solution, seceding from the Board of Education.

Armstead: I don't really think it can manage as an incorporated separate city. I don't see the advantages. The main advantage supposedly is to . . . let you identify with something, but I think that the situation is that Watts as a community now has enough to do that will give the sense of pride of doing without having to incorporate into a separate city. Secondly, I can see a disadvantage which might have a real effect on the community, if let us suppose Watts was incorporated. . . . The way it is now, financially it is almost impossible, but if it was financially started somehow, and it failed, that would have a definite effect, and it is very possible that it might fail. . . . We must consider the effect this might have on the people. If your initial purpose is to perpetuate pride and then you fail to find this, you know what might happen then.

[Other youngsters react to the proposal for incorporation of the south central area into a separate city.]

Chuck: Well, actually it is not the people in the community that are saying all this. It is the outsiders, people that come from outside that are saying Watts ought to be this, Watts ought to be that. Actually, it should be left to the people who dwell there.

Another point about Watts trying to become a city. Watts can't be considered as becoming a city. It takes money to run a city, and this is something that Watts cannot have. There is not really enough money right in Watts, in order to make Watts a city, a separate city from Los Angeles, and it takes money to run a city, and therefore being a part of Los Angeles and Los Angeles County, it does have the government's money to function.

George: I feel that the people in Watts, they want to be a part of Los Angeles. And this idea about separating Watts, the so-called ghetto area, from Los Angeles—just like letting it be a city—that idea isn't too swell, as far as people living in Watts are concerned. We sort of have a goal there, which Bill said earlier, and that goal is to get over. By this, he means to really have the feeling of having something of your own, like when you are older than you are now, you have grandchildren, you can say something like "Well, I went out into the streets, I worked, and I made my money right, I did not steal anything," like this; this is a nice, warm feeling you see. This is how I feel that most of the young people . . . of Watts would feel when they get to the age of fifty or sixty, maybe.

An adult man, somewhat older, separately expresses his opinion of the movement to set up an all-black city.

Tracy: We have Black Power groups that are for isolationism: "We want our own community, we want a complete self-government, we want to isolate ourselves within the nation, but we want all the rights and liberties of the other men." I say this is not possible. We have to become an integrated part of the woof and warp of the American fabric of life.

Right after the riot, they contemplated making Watts independent because of the economic repressions and other things. But so many people are here we could not support a separate school system, we could not maintain public utilities, we would have had to support ourselves out of our own taxes. The unemployment rate out here would have killed us; we would have bogged down in the mud and so we would never have been able to lift ourselves out of it.

[Though most of the residents seem opposed to incorporation of the area on technical grounds that are obviously sound, this does not mean that they necessarily want to break up the ghetto and integrate with the white majority. What they appear to seek is equality, and a freedom of choice to integrate or not to integrate on terms and conditions acceptable to them. Individual feelings and choices, of course, differ widely. In the following section, "Jerry," as a representative of the militant hard-core group, gives a few of his impressions about the question of integration vs. separation. An older man, experienced and knowledgeable in "civil rights" activities, then offers his view. Finally, Richard Townsend, then seventeen years old and just out of high school, describes his reaction when people tried to classify him according to their stereotypes and thereby denied him the option of choosing his own individual "bag."]

Jerry: You know, as far as I am concerned, I don't think integration even enters the people's mind in Watts. If you want to integrate, they're ready; if you don't and you say, "Damn them," "Damn you!" They have one objective, that's to be equal. They are not thinking about integration, not at present.

I think they feel the same way I feel. They don't want no more than what you got; they don't want you to have no more than what they got. If you got $1,000 and you have a good job to make that $1,000, that is all they want. But it's their job to make it, because you give them a job, they are going to make it.

If the whites are going to give the blacks anything, they should give them . . . the mule and forty acres. All right, we can say if the federal government want to pay every Negro family in the United States, from 1864 to today, a mule and forty acres, they'll give that Negro family over $200,000. . . . Then . . . Ron Karenga and no one else will have anything else to say. If we are all free and equal, sure, prove it, give them what you promised them. . . . This is all they could be asking for: a nation within a nation. We are going to combine them. Give another family a mule and forty acres, we keep putting that land together, we are just going to spread into a wide-open field and build what we want on it. . . . Everything that McNamara and President Johnson is going to do in Vietnam is what we would do with a mule and forty acres.

Mr. Martin: The goal is equality. The method, the method of getting us equal, you can get it two ways: you can completely separate and go off on your own, or you can integrate into the American society. . . . We don't have one black person in policy-making position in any of the big industries in this country. You don't have one black person in the policy-making positions of the financial institutions or the government. Take General Motors, for instance, in order for us to be equal, we'd have to buy shares in General Motors; that is equality. Once you come into General Motors with a power bloc,

a stock block, say this man owns 100,000 shares, they may set him
on the executive board. Now, that's equality, because he comes there
with 100,000 shares, see what I'm saying? But if the man in General Motors turns around and appoints you onto the executive board,
well, you'd be a Tom. Then you would be an appointee, and you
say "yes," when he says "yes"; he nod his head, "no," you nod your
head, "no". . . .

You see, in order for us to be equal in this country, we have
to have the same things, that means we have to be in Washington,
D.C. Why not have a Negro Vice-President? If you want to make
sure Johnson don't get shot at, have a Negro Vice-President; they'd
make sure he don't get shot. And if somebody did shoot him, they'd
have him stuffed, and they'd sit him up behind the desk. As a guarantee of not shooting the President, let's make a Negro Vice-President. There is no way in hell they would kill the President then.

[In the summer of 1966 and again in 1967, articles about Watts
appeared in a number of prominent magazines. The theme of most
of these pieces was that nationalism and anti-white feeling were
rampant in the area, and the views of "nationalist" spokesmen such
as Ron Karenga and Tommy Jacquette were given prominence.
Townsend gives his own reactions to the articles, and in the course
of the analysis he reflects the dilemma confronting him.]

Townsend: The articles really show that they were written by
a person who either had a limited acquaintance with the community or felt that generally the more extreme aspects or the extreme
points of view of the community were far more important than those
of the majority of the people of the community. For instance, they
entitle one article "Watts, Still Seething." Now, I think, from living in Watts and knowing the people, that Watts is not seething
at the present time, nor was it seething in July [1966]. . . . It says
also while the riot cry was "Burn, Baby, Burn" in 1965, the ghetto
today is still close to flash point. Watts is not close to flash point
right now. You look at the rest of the country, and then you look
at Watts; Watts is very quiet . . . I think the article was quite sen-
sationalized. It brought up a few good facts, especially things concerning the hospital and public facilities available to the people of
Watts. But other than that, the account it gave of how life is today
in Watts is very untrue and distorted. . . .

One [article] contains a picture of a group of kids who, as the
caption depicts it, are playing on the railroad tracks. In fact, the

kids are coming from school, and they are taking a short cut across the railroad tracks as they leave Markham Junior High School. This is found throughout the magazine. There is another place where they picture a boy holding three fingers. They state in the caption that the three fingers stand for "Burn," when in fact in Watts—this is known all over Watts—three fingers only stand for Watts itself; it does not stand for "Burn" at all. . . . To contrast that, in the north-west part of the southeast central area, which is commonly known among teen-agers as Slauson, the sign there is two fingers held in the air. Here is another point in which they really stretch the truth and give a very poor impression of the people in Watts themselves . . . it never points out the fact that there are a number of kids in Watts that have actively involved themselves, who have really found some hope for themselves in many of the programs that have been started in Watts. And as a result of the riots themselves, they have really found some hope in the near future. This article only discusses a small per cent of the people in the Watts area. . . .

White people somehow seem to think that the true Negro, the only Negroes who are right, is the one that is downtrodden and the one that is on the street corner. . . . O.K., you take a member of the Student Committee now—I'm talking about sixty-six people— you take that leader and fit him there and then you take a guy that is the head of a gang, that represents maybe thirty hard-core cases, and sit them side by side: the one that *Life* magazine is really going to regard, the one the *Post* regards, the one that all white people regard, and the one that television regards is, at this point, the gang leader, as the one who "really talks for the Negro" today. . . . A good example is the news program, when they asked Stokely Car-michael . . . why he represented a lot of the Negro sentiment, and he said that the polls say he represents nineteen per cent, but "there are a lot of other guys that are up above me and they ain't here." So that indicates something right there. The point was that he rep-resented only a very small amount, due to the very nature of the way they felt and the way they acted. . . .

Projecting this down on a lower level, almost on a personal level, you take Jordan High School where sixty per cent of the kids really are not hard-core cases; they are kids who could get along in this world if they had the opportunity to get along. You compare them to the others' percentages . . . and whatever they want to come up with, "we want a real Jordan High School student, we don't want an honor student, we don't want this." They go and look at the kid and they say to the kid: "Why don't you have conked hair and why don't you talk with slang, you are not really a Watts kid, you are something different." This is the thing that has really hit me in disgust the most: the fact that they really deep down in their hearts have a stereotype of what people in Watts are really like. When you see a person from Watts who has on a neat shirt and maybe a tie, then he is not from Watts. This is really shocking, because even at the camp in New York [a summer citizenship camp attended by Armstead and Townsend in 1966] many of the kids . . . wouldn't accept the fact that Bill and I could have possibly come from Watts. This really got me; I mean the only way I could prove it, I left my class ring . . . but then I said that Bill was the Student Body President, and they expect the Student Body President to be the top gang leader. This is the attitude that has really stuck in my throat, because . . . the average kid in Watts is not the hoodlum-type gang leader, and O.K., you can't ignore the fact that there are a lot of kids that are in gangs, and they are the kids that need the most help. . . .

There is a thing in *Mad* magazine where they have this kid that is in the gutter and they are saying, "Keep our gutters and slums because each kid has to rise out of the gutters and slums," and most people seem to have the thought that to be honest and pure and sincere, while being "middle class," is almost impossible. I've been a victim of this myself, and that's why I've become so heartset against it whenever I talk to somebody who I think feels this way. I have to remind them that I live in the project and that at night I have bread and rice for dinner . . . and they don't believe you. . . . I have to keep reminding them of this, or else they say "Oh yeah, he goes to this school or that school" and he has forgotten. It's just the attitude, and when you get a car, it's all over practically, because if Negroes have a car, it's kind of like you have been successful, and to other Negroes it seems like you are trying to leave Negroism. It's really so crazy, but it is basically stereotyping what a real honest poor person is like in Watts, and I think that most people are no more honest than I am, although I have had the educational opportunity which allows me to be dishonest in very discreet ways.

Yeah, I have to admit that a lot of my sentiments have been torn, but basically . . . maybe I have been brainwashed . . . because I can see my worth . . . and the way I'll do what I want to do has changed considerably and has made me tone down many of my thoughts. I am still the same, although I talk about it in a different way and I look at it different and I dress a little different now than I did then, and I act a little different, and I don't get all upset and

worried. I guess I've been brainwashed, still the point is that I'm
going to do something and I think that is the most important, speaking out of personal value; I feel I'm going to do something, even
if it is just mess up something, and even if it is criticizing someone
who just falls apart, I still have got to do something; so that is something I still hold even if I am "middle class," which I am.

[Two themes recur in the opinions of the youngsters, whether
in or out of school: Whites must relinquish their domination of the
ghetto and their insistence that blacks become carbon copies of
themselves; and blacks must achieve greater unity among themselves and greater respect for one another. The reactions to individual whites will vary, but the demand is consistent. Sometimes,
however, their bitterness is directed against the older generation
of Negroes, and most particularly, the "successful" ones who have
moved into the more affluent sections of the city.]

Sam: This is what I have known to be true, that a white person
can*not* come in Watts and tell me what I *should* do, and what I
shouldn't do. He should go home, go back in his mansion, in his
own land, and tell his people that we are not animals, we are not
dogs, what they say we are, and he should train his people to respect
me as a human being when I go to Huntington Park or Inglewood
or any other white vicinity—not to look at me like I am a dog, or
talk about me, or not wait on me just because I am colored, or to
say they don't have this kind of material and push the material back
in the sack. And when my mama, his mother, and everybody else's
mother walks down the street, the man can't whistle; you know,
the white man, he would be whistling and like that.[7]
  A time ago, we had these Caucasian people come out and show
us different designs, modern designs, which I was ignorant to the
fact because I had not went to school that long to understand what
these designs really meant. They told me one thing, and the blueprint was showing another thing, and the only way I found out the
blueprint was . . . actually told in a different story, was [when] we
held a meeting . . . when they had all those blueprints telling how
they are going to move all these homes out and build a hospital and
all this business in Watts. I ain't seen nothin' yet. I ain't seen nobody
come back; they got some peoples down there at that Economic

---

[7] Sam, just eighteen when he made these comments, was raised in Mississippi, and his observations seem to reflect his experiences there.

Opportunity Board, whatever you want to call it, talkin' about all
that money, and this and that; the peoples talks about 'em so bad
out there in Watts, [and] I ain't heard nothing else from them or
ain't seen nothing else from them.

Jerry: The best thing a white person's coming to Watts [could
do] to help is to be himself. You want to come in and act as *yourself* and not like somebody that's got $50 million. If you've got $50
million, keep it to your own damn self.

All you're concerned about is what the problems are. . . . Be
yourself, ask around. Then you want to do something about it? Take
your money and do something. Don't tell us what you are going
to do with it—with your $50 million—because I don't want to hear,
because I done heard so much. I done heard so much that the white
man has promised my people.

Trash!

Promises, promises.

George: What scares me is that a Caucasian comes into Watts
talking about he got $50 million; I mean, we don't want to hear that
because all that is going to do is to make us want it. Make us try
to think of ways to get it, the ways we arc going to try to get it,
like stealing, like knocking somebody off, or going into their pockets, purse snatching, everything.

[Still, there are variations in the attitudes of young people
toward whites, and toward the question of separation.]

Chuck: You know something? If it does happen, say, the blacks
do get a country of their own, so all the blacks just move off in their
country; yet and still, the Caucasian race will still be here, and there
is going to be just that much more conflict, because it could be . . .
a civil war.

Sam: There was a time, right on 103rd, that peoples actually came
in the Teen Post with guns, threatening Miss Welsh [the young
white woman who then directed the Post]. Told her, you get out
of here and leave my people alone, this or that, but she wouldn't
leave. See, this is what made me really like this woman so much,
and up until this day, I feel like there is not nothing in this world
I wouldn't do for her. I'm going to tell you, without the Teen Post
and Miss Welsh, I wouldn't have knew what I know today about
a lot of things; I wouldn't have knew that you can go to this dis-

trict, sit on this conference, sit in on these different things, because this is just the fundamentals of things that should have been happening ten years ago. Sitting in conference is no big thing for a white boy living in Burbank, or Eagle Rock, or Pasadena. His school goes through this every day; conferences with peoples livin' in Washington, Canada, distant foreign peoples coming from different countries and things, coming over here talking. First time I saw a foreigner, I laughed at him. That is how ignorant I was. . . . I didn't understand, you know. I didn't know what was up, and I was seventeen years old, man. To us, going to these conferences was a great thing.

This thing of "he is better than I am," and "I want this, I want that" is ruining us, destroying our mind, man. A white man, he can bring a boy from Nigeria, or Tulu, Africa, or anywhere, I don't care where it is, and put him in a mansion, you understand what I mean? And he could be famous just by being informed.

George: Well, this is the way I feel. Like, when a Caucasian comes in Watts, man, from things that I have heard, the impression that the Negroes in Watts get, fables and things that he is a blue-eyed devil, he comes here to take your dough. I mean, he has an education, he has a little bit over you, he can con you because you don't know any better. From the impression I have gotten from a lot of white people that I have met down there, they are only trying to help; some of them are, I am not saying all; some of them are prejudiced. From some of the ones I have met, they try to help. Things that I haven't even thought about having, I have gotten. What we should do is just . . . abandon this thing out of our mind, man, just get rid of it, because people are equal, everyone is a human being; we should look at a person as being a human being, not because they are black or white or red or anything, man, that doesn't make any sense; that is a sign of ignorance right there. "I am [representing] Black Power, I don't like Whitey even when Whitey is right."

[Some of the comments about "Uncle Toms" are heated. The young people often express resentment and frustration about the fact that older persons will not heed their advice or are not sufficiently militant. The statement below is extreme, but gives us some idea of how wide the gap can become.]

A Young Adult: When you overthrow a system, I'll be damned if I would put anything in front of me, because I am apt to kill my mother if she gets in my way. I'm not going to sit up and let a sixty-five-year-old woman keep a twenty-six-year-old young man from having what I know that belong to me. If she done lived her life, let me live mine. This is what I say—I feel everybody over the age of forty-five needs to be shot down.

Do you know why China is the roughest, toughest country on the face of the earth today? Because they kill off their Uncle Toms. . . . There was a nine-year-old girl [in China] had the point of a gun pointed at her father's head, and pulled the trigger. . . . And they lined up a whole generation of Toms, all of the old, old over forty-five, and they just kill them all. Ten years later, no more Toms in China now.

[The cry for "unity" sometimes takes the form of a bitter indictment against those who have deserted the slum ghetto but continue to speak for the "community" and reap political or personal benefits from the performance of that role. The following judgments about individual politicians reflect a widespread cynicism among the more militant youngsters.]

Jerry: We are going to have a revolution. What is a revolution? Killing everything that gets in your way. What are they doing in Vietnam? Killing everything that gets in their way. . . . They are making the Vietnamese think the way we're thinking. Like the Africans, they're making the Africans think like we're thinking.

A revolution in the United States has to come overnight. You are going to sleep one night, you'll wake up and look out your window, you might have a shotgun flying right through the window into your face. No one will ever know when that revolution is going to occur. . . . The dark nations ruled at the beginning of time, and they will rule at the end.

As far as I'm concerned, Ron Karenga and Tommy Jacquette and none of the rest of them is going to start that revolution. One man cannot start a revolution, and no group of three can start it. A revolution and a riot are two different things. Now they might be able to start a riot. Three people have done it. . . .

The only revolution the Negroes ever had was on March 5, 1770, in Boston, the Boston Massacre.[8] That was a Negro revolution, not a black revolution. Negro revolutions are statewide; a black revolution is worldwide.

Right, all nonwhite nations will come together and overthrow the system which they feel is their enemies. Like in the Bandung

---

[8] Crispus Attucks, a Negro, was among the first Americans killed.

conference, [when] all dark nations came together and they wouldn't
let the white man in. Once they found out they could not let him
in and get their business taken care of, then they knew they were
all going to fall right in line. It's the same thing with these Negro
and these black people; they are going to have to do the same. King,
A. Philip Randolph, Roy Wilkins, Adam Clayton Powell, Ron Karenga, Tommy Jacquette, all of them, they have got to get in the
same room together and leave the religion out of it, and come together as black people, before they get rid of the man's system.

I quit going to church when I was eight years old. I read the
Bible one time, and it said: Thou shalt not kill, Thou shalt not commit adultery, Thou shalt not commit false witness, all that stuff
in the Ten Commandments. This is what God was supposed to have
said. And in the law book it says the same thing. And at the same
time, if I committed adultery, if I committed a murder on somebody,
they gonna kill me. So here is the law stating this should not happen and God has stated it, and at the same time, them lousy white
motherfuckers are taking our lives by the gas chamber or the electric chair. That's what learned me what the society is really doing
to people.

I am not against religion. I respect religion for what it stands
for. But the black race is not like that Spanish race or that white
race. You know how it sounds when a Caucasian lady goes in and
have a baby? What does she do? She just "mmmmmm." And the
Spanish girl goes in—"ay-yi-yi-yi." And here come this nigger—what
do she holler? "Oh Jesus, help me Jesus!" That's the first damn thing.
Now I believe in God, or some force of Supreme Being. There is something up there, or down there, but the only thing that is stopping
the black race from getting independence is the religion.

Sure, if I was _____ [a Negro who holds high elective office],
I'd be doing the same things he is doing. I'll sit right on my ass until
them niggers woke up and asked me to do something. If I didn't
take the time to write _____ a letter and tell him I wanted something done, I wouldn't expect him to do nothing. And that is just
what he is doing. He isn't doing a damn thing. When the niggers
learn what a vote is, then they'll know how to use it.

The main thing is to teach them niggers respect for each other.
Respect is something beyond life. Build me one school, anywhere,
in Watts maybe, and teach them niggers respect. Don't give me
a white teacher, don't give me a white administrator, don't give
me nobody in [my] school that's white.

Now, I can get to those students. But, boy, it will be hell tryin' to get to their mommy and daddy. Tell them motherfuckers that James Brown is at the Forum or Ray Charles is at the Cocoanut Grove, and them motherfuckers will dress up and go there in a minute, but they can't do nothing to help their people.

I'll tell you why the whites are smarter than the Negroes. Like, back in history when the Turks had the whites surrounded, and one of them black niggers turned their back and let one of them white men out of there. Now that one white man stopped and he thought: How can I get the rest of them white people out of there so we can rule the world? So he finds a way. But if a nigger was in that circle and he snuck out, what's the first thing that nigger gonna do? Well, he's gonna say it's not his problem at all. They got to get out on their own. He got out. He's free, but them niggers have got to find their own hole: "I ain't going back to tell them where to find it."

Now, take someone like_____[another elected official]. Where's he living at? Somewhere on the west side. But where did he come up at? The ghetto. Why did he leave? He advanced. Which any man would do, but make sure you bring somebody with you. Every time you go up a step, you bring somebody else up a step. _____ doesn't give a damn about us now. He got what he wants. That's what is always in our way. One nigger going one way, one nigger going the other. We've both got to go at the same time and the same way.

IV

Employment and Economics

Everyone agrees that more and better jobs are desperately needed in the Watts area. Lack of employment was a critical problem long before the summer of 1965, but most policy makers remained insensitive to it. Many of the traditional jobs had begun to vanish as a result of automation, shifts in industrial location, recession in building construction, and other factors, while the inflow of unskilled and relatively uneducated migrants from the South continued unabated. Yet the community had conspicuously failed to provide new and improved job opportunities to replace those lost.[1]

Since the riot, programs directed mainly at young people have multiplied in the area. Neighborhood Youth Corps (NYC) jobs are available to students and out-of-school youngsters at $1.40 (until recently, $1.27) an hour; the Watts Labor Community Action Committee, under a contract with the Department of Labor, employs youths aged fourteen to twenty-one (and some adults) in various community improvement activities, administers cultural and recreational programs for younger children, and sponsors skills training for returned veterans and others at its new facility leased from the city; Westminster Neighborhood Association employs or trains residents in a number of programs; multiservice centers, run by the State of California, combine placement and rehabilitation services under one roof; several training centers, both publicly and privately funded, operate in the south central ghetto; the OEO-funded Neighborhood Adult Participation Project (NAPP) hires local people as community aides at $4,000 a year; and a private business group,

---

[1] Documentation of these points can be found in *Hard-Core Unemployment and Poverty in Los Angeles*, 1965. See footnote on p. 22.

led by businessman and former Undersecretary of Commerce H. C. McClellan, claims to have made about 18,000 gross job placements from the south central area, a figure which (if accepted) would suggest that the entire unemployment problem has virtually been wiped out.

The degree of progress observed by residents, notably the so-called "hard-core," is considerably less than the volume of publicity would indicate, though programs such as WLCAC's Community Conservation Corps have had substantial visibility. Many of the governmental programs are limited to young people, offer little or no promotional opportunity, and establish such low earnings that some local residents are disinclined to abandon alternative, and sometimes illegal, sources of income. While *overt* racial discrimination may no longer be pervasive, subtle and indirect discrimination, often based on cultural biases or whims, has taken its place. Police records, inadequate or inferior education, lack of work experience, and purely personal mannerisms or appearance disapproved of by employers are handicaps borne by many.

No one really knows how many are unemployed or underemployed in the area, though very precise figures are often cited. Serious problems would remain even if all employables were to be employed: the female heads of households cannot leave their young children untended, many have health problems or are too old, and the pay for some jobs is insufficient to raise family income above the poverty level. Obviously, the provision of jobs with both long- and short-term promotional ladders, the essence of the "New Careers" principle, would enhance economic and social stability, but it remains to be seen whether new public and private programs will fill the plentiful gaps that still exist.

Even the more innovative programs must, at some point, defer to the established institutions. Employment in the schools (especially in teaching capacities), in civil service, in private industry, and in apprenticeship programs remains controlled by a complex set of rules and stipulations which change slowly, if at all. Because they lead nowhere and are frequently associated with efforts to keep things "cool" for the summer or for some other period, the special jobs created for the ghetto seem to reek of second-class status. Many of the residents, especially among the youngsters, are inclined to view them as purely token measures designed to buy off the population and serve as a camouflage for unwillingness to do anything really meaningful and fundamental about the problems.

Most of the "manpower" programs use special federal or state

funds to provide temporary (and usually low-paid) jobs for the unskilled, or skills training in certain identified occupations where
shortages of qualified labor have been certified. A few generate
potentially long-term employment for those who do not qualify
under prevailing hiring standards and for whom vocational training, as conventionally applied, is insufficient or inappropriate.
These few represent institutional change, in the sense that normal
hiring, promotional, training, and educational procedures are over-
hauled to meet the particular needs of the formerly disqualified.
The more typical approach permits the employer to retain whatever qualification he has established and, generally, imposes the
obligation of change upon the job seeker himself. Of course, the
opportunities to secure specialized training in several fields are now
more accessible and more plentiful, but many administrative barriers and cultural and psychological inhibitions against their use
remain undisturbed. The larger society demands relatively little
change of itself, but a virtual regeneration by those who have been
excluded for so long.

The established norms of government, industry, and education conflict with the suspicions, the impatience, the pride, and even
the creativity of many of the young people. Racial discrimination
aside, the mere complexity, cumbersomeness, insensitivity, and
lack of imagination characteristic of bureaucracies will "turn off"
a great many of the youngsters (and not a few of the adults). On
the streets, there is always a ready "training program" in how to
acquire a few bucks to meet immediate needs. The youngsters are
quick to apply themselves, and their very cleverness and smart-
ness ultimately become liabilities. Sooner or later they will have
a record, which further impedes their entry into a career and com-
mits them almost irrevocably to the path on which they have embarked.

One of the major reasons for their cynicism and frustration
is the unimaginative and almost Kafkaesque routine maintained
by society itself. Obviously there are cases where jobs simply do
not exist, a circumstance which a service or referral agency cannot
control and for which it may not be responsible. What remains un-
forgivable is a rigid adherence to procedures which make it doubly difficult for unskilled or unsophisticated persons to exploit those
limited opportunities that might be available. A few concrete examples, drawn from observation and experience, will illustrate the
point.

In 1967, a conscientious youngster from Watts, desperately

in need of work and unqualified for the better-paid jobs in industry or civil service, applied for low-paid employment through one of the antipoverty programs. Before Tommy began his work as a custodian in a housing project, he had been compelled to make ten separate visits to buildings scattered throughout the central Los Angeles area, fill out three different forms—in addition to being fingerprinted—and take a routine physical examination despite the fact that he had been given (and had flunked) a Selective Service physical about three weeks before. The whole process, indeed, had been initiated by his referral from the draft board to a local Youth Opportunity Center, as a "Selective Service rehabilitant." An intelligent and dedicated program administrator later eliminated or simplified several of these steps, but was unable to persuade Selective Service to make available extra copies of its medical examination records. The steps that remained, even after the simplification, were formidable. Some are inevitable, and others are of possible interest or value to a youngster from Watts. The point is that the mere complexity of the process will anger or frustrate a great many young people who may already be inclined toward cynicism.

In 1968, a bright youngster, with a record of several offenses, was referred by his Probation Officer to a job opening as groundskeeper with a local Recreation and Parks department. He performed so well in his examination for the job that he was hired on an "emergency" basis, which meant that any additional checking of his background would take place *after* his employment. Though his performance on the job was quite satisfactory, he was subsequently dismissed because he had not listed all of his past offenses on the application form and because he was still on probation. He had worked under supervision, and no proof had ever been submitted that his record, or his status as a probationer, necessarily related to how well he could do the job. While one section of government—the Probation Department—was asking employers to hire probationers and men with records, another section was adamant in its refusal to employ these same applicants. It was not clear how "government" could, logically, ask private employers to do that which it was in large part unwilling to do itself. The reluctance to employ ex-offenders in legitimate jobs leads, ironically but inevitably, to their reversion to the streets and a further career in crime.

Tommy's brother, whom I have called Chuck, had had his own experiences with the bureaucracy. Then a twenty-year-old high school graduate, he is a personable youngster who has had one encounter with the law and is on probation. His applications at the Employment Service have resulted in the completion of numerous forms—and little else. Each time he visits the local office, he is referred to a training program, "as soon as there is an opening." Like many other youngsters with his background, he is not easily attracted to mechanical training, especially if it requires an indefinite period of waiting. He had concentrated in pre-business courses in high school, and, rightly or wrongly, is inclined to focus his job search on possible opportunities in that field. It is not always possible to measure the conscientiousness or persistence of his follow-up to a job referral, but here is an example of one experience.

Chuck had been referred to a job opening in a private hospital located in Redondo Beach, about fifteen miles and several bus transfers from Watts. It turned out to be a janitorial job, paying $1.50 an hour, but the interviewer was disturbed by the distance Chuck would be required to travel and, even more, by his one arrest. He was involved in a car theft, but the charge was reduced to a misdemeanor and he had served no time. Nonetheless, the interviewer was agitated: "Naturally, we have a lot of valuables lying around in a hospital." Chuck was told that his application would be considered, but nothing resulted.

One of Chuck's buddies, whom I have called Bill, has had a different experience, but one which typifies another facet of the labor-market problem within the ghetto. Bill had accompanied a relative to the personnel offices of an insurance company, and, on an impulse, had submitted a job application of his own. Most of the ghetto's residents find their jobs through informal channels, often guided by tips from friends or relatives.[2]

Bill is an unusually bright eighteen-year-old, a good reader and writer, quick-witted and verbal. Like many of his peers, he did not make an appropriate "adjustment" to school, and was transferred frequently for disciplinary reasons. Eventually he dropped out, and has been intermittently employed since leaving school. He was arrested on at least two occasions, and was on probation at the time of his job application. On the application form he had faked the information on his school background, claiming not only high-school graduation but some college attendance. It is also possible that he concealed the facts regarding his delinquency record.

[2] A survey by the Institute of Industrial Relations in 1964 showed that the vast majority of persons in the area found their jobs without assistance from the Employment Service or any other formal organizations. *Ibid.*, pp. 155 - 56.

On the basis of his application and his score on standard tests, he was given a job.

According to all evidence, he performed well at his job and was given added responsibility. Supervisors liked his work and recommended him for promotion. In evaluating the recommendation, the company's personnel department investigated his school record and discovered the misinformation. He was then fired from the job, and he returned to the streets. The discharge was not related to poor work performance or to dishonesty on the job, but merely to the falsifications on the initial application. It is highly uncertain whether he would have obtained a job at all if he had submitted a completely truthful application, but obviously he was able to fulfill the work responsibilities. The net result of the experience was another stain on his record.

Whether or not such experiences reflect special treatment, or simply the application of rules which apply to everyone, is beside the point. The ghetto youngsters have a low tolerance for the kind of frustration which is associated with administrative routine, and a corresponding resistance to rules imposed by their elders. Their comments reflect a consistent suspicion about the motives of the older generation, and especially the adults who run antipoverty programs or administer contracts and grants. The "better jobs," presumably, are reserved for those with the proper political pull. This is not always true, and the young people are sometimes excessively cynical about motivations and intolerant of regulations which are sensible. Nevertheless, their insight is essentially correct; the promotional ladder is indeed blocked for most of them under the prevailing rules of the game. The rules may change, and some have already given way. In too many cases, however, the change comes too late: the self-confidence and self-respect of the youngsters have already eroded.

Starting with Richard Townsend's views in 1966, the following section looks at the impact of manpower and anti-poverty programs in Watts since the riot. Each of the youngsters has been directly involved with a major program in the area, and their comments generally parallel those made by the adults, one of whom was the local director of a key project.

Townsend (Summer, 1966): Just speaking about the jobs and the new programs that involve community people, probably to capture their interests or their time or keep their hands busy doing constructive things, there has been some criticism concerning this

approach to solving these types of social problems in Watts. . . .
There was the basic issue, brought out in the Moynihan report, that
talked about the split in the Negro family; many people feel that
if there was a unified family there would be more direction, more
intensive responsibility, you will find in many cases. I heard this
from a person who had done a lot of work in the community; that
now the kids are off working, maybe in an NYC [Neighborhood
Youth Corps] job during the day, or they are over at some summer
camp; the mother is working with NAPP [Neighborhood Adult Participation Project] recruiting voters; while the father still doesn't
have a job. So here you find, now everyone is out of the house, and
they are even further apart now and they don't even have a chance to
discuss things, because they don't even meet now. In the intent
and the aim, it is helping, let's say, the mothers, but still the fathers
are out of work right now. They still need places, and they will be
here for thirty more years, and they must have jobs right now. So
I think it is failing in one major place: it provides NYC jobs paying
$1.27 [now $1.40] an hour for kids, and Conservation Corps jobs
for kids, but still the adults don't have jobs. I say most definitely this is the critical point, providing jobs for those who must feed
families, people who have to support a family, not just people who
have to buy notebooks, milk, and cookies for lunch time.

Chuck, Fred, Jerry, and *Herbert (1968)*: There are *no* poverty
programs that are worth a damn! For one thing, some of the people that you have leading the community are trying to make it over
for themselves in all one lump sum. Next thing is that you have
too many older people. All right, then, the younger people are the
type of people that know the problems and the ones that face these
problems every day, and that should be running the program.
    We need something like an educational or cultural center where
. . . the teen-agers and young adults can have what they think is
best for them.
    All our poverty programs that are in the ghetto areas today,
the man put them there because he feels this would calm us down
and the people he puts in charge of it are people out of the ghetto
areas not knowing the problem in the ghetto areas. Now . . . the
person under him don't have a damn thing to do. Any poverty program you go into today, you will see that that person is not doing
a damn thing. That job is not even enough to say that it's [requires]
a junior high school education. They call them "manpower" programs, but . . . they never taught you skills, and even if it taught

you skills, it couldn't put you on a job because it wasn't in contact with a job. For one thing, the Negroes who run [programs like Job Power] didn't have any contact with any major enterprises.

I don't care what poverty program you go into today ... if you are a grass-root person, you are not gonna make over $333 a month. $333 a month does one thing, and that is, it keeps you in poverty. Unless you're living by yourself, that's no money.

The majority [in the community] isn't working. And now they're in something where a man is gonna give him $333 to sit on his ass. Who wouldn't take it? It's better than going out stealing and robbing every damn night. If I can sit on my ass and make $333 a month, I'm gonna sit on my ass. The NAPP program is to give people a first stage in a new career. A career is supposed to go up, not be dropped. When I got through working with NAPP I was dropped. Because of the sixteen months.[3] If the agency in which you are working does not hire you, then you're through with NAPP.

Sure, they [NAPP] contacted me with the Sheriff's Department, but the Sheriff's Department don't want me. I didn't even go down there.

Instead of having ten or twelve programs in our area, all of us [should] have one program in this area large enough for the capacity of the crowd. They can just take one program where all the money could go to and then they can get the right facilities for somebody to learn something and go out and get a job.

Jerry: But I don't want no nigger in there that has got anything to do with no church. I cannot afford to have any preachers nowhere down the line. If we put poverty [programs] under them, then they're gonna have more money than what they got. The whole world is run by gangsters, which we all know.

Let's talk about A. Philip Randolph, Roy Wilkins, Martin Luther King, Celes King [local NAACP leader], Adam Clayton Powell, and Louis Lomax. These are the guys who get the money. If they showed up tomorrow and asked for a million dollars for a program, they would get it. If you showed up and asked for a million dollars for a program, you wouldn't get it.

All Four: The game is the same but the name changes. The same people who are running NAPP are running CEP. The same people who are running CEP and NAPP are running the job training. The

---

[3] NAPP aides are automatically terminated at the end of a specified period.

same people who are running those are running the skill centers.
The same people who are running the rest of the poverty program
are running OIC. I do feel that OIC is the best training project that
they have in the poverty program.[4]

The problem is communication. Some people know what the programs are there for and what they got to offer and they benefit from
them. Other people don't know what they're there for and they go
there by mistake.

I very seldom hear Urban League knocking on people's doors,
actually sitting down and talking to them and explaining to them
what this program is and what it's there for. But in OIC they got
eight young men in that office who actually get off their ass and
knocks on people's door.

Actually a poverty program to me means you start out at this
and then you raise up. It all depends on your ability and how much
you try for yourself. I'm giving you something now but if you're
gonna try and better yourself, then I'm gonna help you better yourself. Then you can go out, and [they] give you more counseling and
then go out to the job you're trained for; if he can't hit it, well—you
come back in the program and try again.

CEP and the Youth Opportunity program on Figueroa, in the
summer they send you to different places and pay you $600 like to
pick cantaloupes. If you want to be a fool to accept $600 to go out in
the hot sun picking cantaloupes, you go ahead. Well, I did this once
and I stayed two weeks. Two lousy weeks and I couldn't take it
no more.

You can't show me a nigger who won't work. If you pay a man
enough money, he'll work.

Right. It depends on what kind of work. Negroes are choosy.

They're not only choosy. I look at Negroes this way. They don't
behave any differently from anybody else if you put the conditions
the same. You set up the conditions, you run a person one color
through this box and another this box—if the conditions are the
same they behave the same. But the thing is, if the boxes are different. . . .

I can see putting a supervisor over a person and being strict
on them as far as the job or the training is concerned. To make sure
they produce during training, you gotta have a kind of guy who

[4] Again plagued by internal dissension, the funds for the Opportunities
Industrialization Center (OIC) were temporarily cut off by the Los Angeles
antipoverty agency in May, 1968, and finally suspended in 1969.

goes in and says, "Man, you are not doing well on this training. What are your problems?" For example, maybe the guy's got two brothers who just went to jail and he doesn't quite know what to do about it except to drop out of school and try to help them work out their problems.

George: There is only one place in Watts where you can go and get a job, and they are filled now. This is Watts Manufacturing, that's groove. They manufacture bombs and things, on El Segundo and Central. They got a loan.[5]

Chuck: You know what I think, I think if they go in and, like, put about twelve Caucasians right here, and maybe twelve Negroes, and maybe twelve Mexicans over here, the ones that have the ability to do a job, number them up. You know, if they pass this law, there has to be these many people in here this color, or else. I think the problem with employment would be damn near solved.

Herbert: [In a poverty program I am in] I do my job, then do a little bit more, all the time . . . trying to work myself on up, but they don't want to give anybody a break. I would take over the work from the man above me, and, you know, if you get a man from a lower-paying job . . . and he is doing the job that the higher-paid man is doing, well, he is supposed to get the same amount of money. They want you to act like you have a regular job, on the street, yet and still they don't want to pay you like that, they say, "Well, you try to get a nigger to work for a nigger, the nigger won't even act right." Well, in the first place, the nigger that is in the boss' job, if he doesn't act right, you can't expect nobody else to act right. . . . I've been there about a year, and haven't made any progress either up or down. When I first came there, I gave my age and they tell me, "I am sorry, you have to work at NYC first, and then . . . you can start to move up and advance." Really, I am where I was when I first get there.

In the offices, they might give the young ladies a chance sometimes, but most of the young men, they pick their favorites, you know: "I am a friend of such and such a family," or "This is my old girl friend," something like that.

The young adults had a lot of talent; we organized, but the big man didn't dig it. They want to talk about the improvement, stuff like that, [but] they [the adults] really don't know the prob-

---

[5] Watts Manufacturing Company is an affiliate of Aerojet-General.

lem, people can help themselves if you give them a chance to help themselves. . . . [The kids] expect some help, not a whole lot of group counseling, this and that. . . .

I want to go back to school and . . . be an X ray technician, and that will give me some kind of advantage, where I can cut the streets loose, and I'll make a decent income. And as times go, I can keep on bettering myself . . . and I can grow with it. . . .

Yeah, I want to go back to school and everything; I mean, the only thing I can really enjoy, a lot of social life, that's what I like. But seems like ever since I've been working there and everything, I haven't come in contact with anybody, just been a loner, you know.

I don't want to be no rich man, or nothing; all I want is to live comfortably, where I don't have to be bothered by the police and everything, where I don't have to be worried by nothing, but just left alone.

Chuck: See, Westminster started off with a [home] maintenance, a caterer, an answering service, and a delivery service. And this delivery service could be used by any community within the Los Angeles district, in which if you had a package to be delivered, you call Westminster, and . . . they deliver the package; the fee never did exceed $3. All right, this will build itself, they would clear $1,000 or more a week. All right, it'd be the same with the answering service.

The [maintenance] crew would go out, clean up apartments, everything. The work was so good, we went to different businesses, went on plane rides, one man took the crew to Shelly's [a jazz spot in Hollywood]. . . . It's just the idea that . . . the group really wanted to work, they just kept motivating themselves, they cleared $1,000 a week. . . . Then somebody raised a squawk about the books; somebody is getting the money; the whole program is cut loose.[6]

George: And what makes one want to work, you know, it wasn't like a regular office. You can go there, you can work, and then maybe on a Friday and Saturday, have some kind of social activity, in which you can follow through . . . and enjoy yourself.

[Job hunting is never a pleasant experience, but it can be doubly frustrating when the job seeker is black, ghettoized, and dependent on public agencies like the Employment Service or leads from rel-

---

[6] This program, called Operation Job Power, was terminated when questions were raised about allegedly missing funds and kickbacks, though the formal charges were subsequently dismissed.

atives and friends. The adult male employed in a full-time, non-menial job, who might guide him into employment, may not be available. The Employment Service will not be of much help unless the job seeker is quickly adaptable to the hiring norms of middle-class businessmen, not a likely possibility for those raised in a low-income ghetto. Several residents, young and old, describe their experiences in job hunting.]

Mrs. Harrison (In 1967, a NAPP aide under the antipoverty program and later an employee of a training program): People discriminate very subtly now. Now it's your height, your weight, your educational background, how many years of experience that you had, and all this. I remember once, a few years back, I went to the Telephone Company, and a few years back the Telephone Company was very, very prejudiced, and I think they are better now. But at that time, they had only a very, very few Negroes working for the Telephone Company, ladies . . . working on the switchboard in the back . . . and all of those were the light skin, long hair, and straightly figured. And I went in there, and at this time I weighed about 165 pounds, and I passed the written test, and I got to the oral, and the lady and I had somewhat a personality clash. We had this because I could just feel . . . that I was going to be discriminated against. So we talked, and finally she came out with how much did I weigh, and I told her; so she gave me this bit about they couldn't hire me because I weighed too much. I could only be a maximum of ten per cent overweight, not more than that. I saw a white woman in that office that weighed four hundred pounds. I asked her about it, and she proceeded to tell me that the lady had been with the company for a long time, and gained this weight during that time she worked for the company. And I just blew my stack, and I got so mad until I cursed her out, and then I cursed the fat woman out, too.

Let me tell you another excuse the Telephone Company gave me; this was on another occasion at another office. At this time, I had two children, and she asked me what kind of child care did I have, I had to be available to work on call, in other words, day shift today, the swing shift tomorrow night, maybe graveyard shift the next night, and I had to have child care facilities set up myself, and they didn't consider the father as an appropriate baby sitter, they didn't consider the father. Now, I can stay home during the day, and my husband can keep the children at night, but this is not sufficient for them.

This one company I know won't hire women as secretaries who

are wearing wigs. Then there is this girl in our group that is constantly being rejected, and she is disqualified because she wears a natural; here is Whitey that says, "If you want to work for me, at much less than what you should make anyway, then put the straightening comb in your hair. If you want to be an individual and wear a natural, then I can't hire you."

George and *Chuck (In 1967)*:   We go over to the Employment Center, but it's no action behind them. I went there when they first started, and I tried to get a job; I filled out a job application, but no one called me, so I just gave up on it. At the present, I am looking for a job, because I will be out of school in five weeks, and I don't want to just be walking the streets, doing nothing, with an empty pocket.

They give you a routine about what type of work could you do, you will have to go through a physical and all that, just for a training program.

I didn't even bother to call after that. I thought it was a waste of time; I could be out in the streets looking for another job, you know, while I am sitting back waiting for them to come, and they didn't get in contact with me.

They have some little plan at Jordan, I guess NYC, and they will find you jobs, and the majority of the people that have the jobs are the ones that are known by the administration and the faculty, those more or less that would be sort of in good with them, you know, goodie, goodie partners with them. You don't know anyone at the administration or the faculty, you don't stand a chance of getting a job. That's the way they work.

I have been out in Hawthorne, I've been out in South Gate and Inglewood, looking for jobs, because there aren't any jobs offered in Watts. . . . A lot of times, the newspaper ads are misguided; they'll list the jobs, about three days, you know, and you finally decided to go in, the job was taken two or three days before.

A friend of mine went over to the Medical Building on 103rd, he went in, he applied for a job, and they were all filled, so he left his application there. I think about two or three weeks after he filled out this application, they called him; and at the present, he is working in place of another person, making $1.50 an hour, and the work he is doing consists of mopping floors, this and that, backbreaking work for $1.50 an hour; and he told me that he asked the man that he was working for, why couldn't he get paid as much as everyone else since he wouldn't be working there permanently, it is just a temporary job; everyone else is making $2 and something, I think $2.47 an hour . . . and he told him something like, "I only pay schoolboys $1.50 an hour, because that's all the work they can put out," so he quit. I think he started Tuesday, and he was supposed to work until Monday, so since his money wasn't right at the job where he was working, he quit. I don't blame him; I would have quit, too.

George: I've been down to every employment office there is. A time ago, they had this job-a-thon thing [a job placement TV special, promoted by commentator Louis Lomax]. I went down there a week after it started, and didn't get a damn thing. When I was going to school, they were trying to prepare the A12's for going on to work, so they were trying to get them jobs before they left school. So they sent every A12 that wanted to down to the Medical Building on 103rd and Compton [where the Employment Service is located]. Everybody filled out those forms, you know. They had us to go down there, thinking we are going to get jobs, and nobody was called. I waited two months myself, they didn't call me. "We'll be checking with you," you know; "you seem to be a very nice young man; you have a nice personality, well-groomed," this and that. I waited two months, wasn't even called. If you want a job, you got to get out and look for it yourself; that means walking.

You can go over, say, to the Urban League. It's a gas, they told me that Continental Airlines was hiring. I drove way out there, and the dude came in and shook my hand and took me way back in his office, made me feel as if I was going to get a job or something. He comes telling me, "We'll call you after the Christmas holidays." This was right before the holidays, and he still hasn't called. . . . You know, I think there must be a quota [for Negroes]; there are just so many that a business will take.

You know what [should happen]. You should go within your own community and get a job and make money, not too far from the pad, just walk, and enjoy your work. I mean like, we need more jobs developing in Watts. Young people, we shouldn't have to go out of our community in order to seek a job. They should have a job for us in our own community, and solve our problems right here. That's why we can't get no jobs, because like if we want a job, we probably have to go to the Employment Office and then get a job way out in Seal Beach or Orange County or something like that. Like you don't have a car; transportation is a gas, and [there's] not too many people in Watts that's actually trying to make something out of themselves that got transportation, and the buses aren't even accurate.

Actually, you don't know how it feels, wake up in the morning, and jump out of bed, say to yourself, "Well, I am going to look for a job." Maybe you might have $1.20 or something to catch a bus, and you go through this every day; and it's a gas, man, it will make you blow your mind. . . .

And you see everybody making it. People that do have a job, you see them riding in nice cars, doing what they want to do, making it through life young, and you want to do the same thing, but you can't. This is what makes people get together and say, "Look, man, we're going to start running around cutting these honkies' heads off again, in order [for them] to see we not jiving," you know, this big old crime wave, it was easy for us.

Who wants to trip way out in El Segundo every day just to hold a job, keep a little money in his pocket; man, that don't make no kind of sense, especially if you don't have nothing to start with.

I think if they put the skill centers in Watts, and made it more like a school, go to your skill center for about two hours, and then from there go to an assigned job which you are training for, I think that would be cool.

Right now, you go to school for a certain amount a month, and then, if possible, you might luck up on a job they might have. It is not concrete that they will give you a job as soon as your training is over with.

[Many youngsters are cynical about training programs, viewing them primarily as sources of immediate "bread." There are some worthwhile programs, but communication with the community is weak; some potential applicants are discouraged because of past failures, police records, or both; the selection and referral process is sometimes excessively complicated, and may even screen out the so-called "hard core"; internal dissension has been a problem, at some point, in almost every major program; the linkage between training and a good job, with upward mobility, is often not strong enough, or visible enough; and some trainees suffer personal or emotional difficulties which hinder their adjustment to training or job routine. The same drawbacks apply to many of the "community action" programs.]

Chuck: Everybody can't get in the training programs. People are moving in Watts every day; the population is getting heavier and heavier. People want to do this and that, and the training program can't take everybody.

I could go for a training program myself, but I want to continue my business college-prep major. I think I know enough about office work to succeed in a training program within office work; but, you know, they go through too many changes; like you fill out an application, you have to wait and wait and wait. By that time you get tired of waiting. You can't wait forever, you know, just for an application to be answered.

George: The kids go to the Westminster [Neighborhood Association] training program just to pick up the $20 allowances every week. You know, the classes are not interesting; they don't make the classes interesting at all. I mean, I think that if you are going to be taught, they should do something to make you want to participate in the class activities; and people, they just won't sit up there, and not doing anything if the class is popping; and if the class is boring, the students won't be that much interested in school because the money is involved.

A kid might become a dealer in drugs because he needs money. I mean, everybody is going to try to keep a little money in their pockets. Without a job, what can you do? This is the opportunity for him to make the buck—easy, quick. Just like shooting dice.

Sam and *Bill*: Now they got a new training program over on 103rd. It pays something like, maybe, $40 or $50 a week, and everybody goes to school there. The dudes that used to be over at the Westminster program are at the new place now.

A lot of the programs are just to keep the boys busy, cleaning up vacant lots and things like that. They will cut loose with some money to get the juvenile delinquents off the street, so they won't be harassing people, you understand? They don't mind giving up a little bit of money so that . . . people who go to jail . . . can come back to Watts . . . and get a CCC (Community Conservation Corps) or Watts Labor Community Action job.

[In 1966 and 1967, several of the youngsters involved in Westminster Neighborhood Association activities were prominently identified with so-called "nationalist" organizations, or were vociferously anti-white in their expressed attitudes.]

Sam: All those people over at Westminster . . . have been talking Black Nationalism, Black Brothers, Mr. Charley. They're talk-

ing about the white man, and start working for him again, you know.
. . . I have seen several young men, my friends, now they are riding around in brand-new cars. They don't even know me anymore.
They work for Westminster. . . . When they were getting up to $20
a week for going to school, there was a big talk [about Westmin-
ster]. Then other programs came in, and they could make $60 a week,
so there is nothing much Westminster has to offer to the community anymore, no more than talking about the white man. And I hear
that all the time. I can walk out on the street, and somebody hollering about Whitey, Whitey, Whitey.

A lot of people . . . act like a pack of wolves or something. . . .
You know, as one fool jumps into the river, all the rest of the fools
jump too, and drowned themselves. . . . You've got jobs and things
to keep the kids out of trouble . . . but this is not going to do it, keep
them out of trouble, because some of them stay two hours there,
three hours, and then they're back to their same old bag again. They
are talking about Whitey again. All it takes is one bottle of wine,
three fools to get together, or two fools, or one fool and a bottle of
wine, and that's it. Because once he get to talking about Whitey,
everybody else is going to talk about Whitey.

A lot has been done to help the community, but . . . they [the
community] haven't took this up yet, because they didn't know
about it. Like me, until two or three weeks ago, I didn't know anything about TOP [Transportation Opportunity Program, a training program in truck driving, auto maintenance, and driver education, sponsored by the Teamsters Union], and a friend of mine
got me together and took me over. I didn't know anything about
it, and I live right there in Watts, and it is right on 108th there,
right off Central. . . . It has really been a great help to me, because
. . . at present I cannot read too well, and . . . here is a man over
there, a very nice man; he takes his time out. I'm supposed to be
going to school there to learn how to drive. He takes an hour of his
time out to teach me how to read and write, me and several other
people. This is the kind of thing, not just going to school and learn-
in' how to put that bolt into that hole and turnin' it and screwin'
it. You take a dumb man, the greatest dummy in the world can do
that. So many people . . . don't know how to read.

It always falls back to the Southern white man, because he
don't start the Negro kids in school until they's seven or eight years
old, see. I started [in Mississippi] when I was seven or eight. . . .
In California, the kids are even going to pre-school, and get an idea
of what ABC means, and one, two, three, four, five.

Now I heard about the Watts Skill Center [another vocational training institution, staffed by the City schools and funded by the federal government under the Manpower Development and Training Act of 1962], but they make it so difficult for a person to get into it; I mean, like they say, you have to have some kind of standard there. They have got to make some kind of standard for these programs, but they make it so hard for a person that doesn't have an education really to get in a program to function, to get themselves to moving, until it's almost impossible for him to get in. He has to cheat his way into it; or someone has to push him through there that has position. This is what happens.

For a fact, some of the people there at _____ [a local organization] have been there from the first strike of gold until now; and they are still there, and . . . our fellow brothers get in this position, and, well, they are interested in a poverty grant. They're thinking about, well, I am going over there, and talk to this man, and see what I can do for myself. "I'm not thinking about the community; I'm thinking about myself." This is the spirit; everyone is looking after themselves.

Like _____ [an administrator of a local antipoverty program]. He had a nice thing going for himself. . . . He likes to talk his point of view; he don't like for a younger person to come to him and lay it down on him, like, "This is it, man. I feel this here way about you." He is up there talking to me. . . . Now, I think maybe he has come to himself. He knows . . . that the young people they need help; they are beaten, worn, and he sees now that this is very true. You can't put the kids off in a trick bag, tell them a bunch of lies. He is worried about girls' dresses being too tight and too high and too short and too long, and the color of their hair, and all this. This is for the church, or for the home, not for him to decide what they should wear, and what they shouldn't wear.

Sam (reacting to participation in a training program in 1968): Throughout the days that I was going, I had left Watts. I had left the majority of Negroes and fell off their bag. I mean I'm not around my own people and I know how to adapt myself, I think, which I have overcome. . . . I found out that you can no longer go around hollering "this white motherfucker," "this white son of a gun," this and that, because the simple reason is . . . this world is no longer in this stage. . . .

Myself, I've been called a "house nigger," because I have associated with whites. . . . When I got to California, talking about the

Whitey was a big thing because back home there wasn't nobody that talked to Whitey. I don't think I really got the chance and opportunity and ability to have enough guts, enough know-how and courage and motivation about myself to see all these things happening in the world if I didn't come to California. . . . There's a great conflict in how to run [this] organization and how everyone wants to be the boss. There's always going to be something wrong with the means one way or another. If we reversed the whole course and put the black man over Whitey and we had all the riches in the world and he was our slave and he did all the dirty work, it would be the same thing all over again. . . .

I wants to see a program . . . where we all relate together as humans, not as Mister so and so, the head of the whole program; not as so and so who has been to Washington five or six times, and he knows the President of the United States; not as the great white father, the owner of all the corporations and he wants to give us help and support and all this here. I want to see the time when I can go back to class and I can feel free; [now] I can feel this hatred, what I would call fear of someone saying, "You Uncle Tom, man, look here, what are you going to be doing working up there in that office. What you be telling them people, man. What you be doing?" You see, this is a fine example . . . that my brother had a bad understanding of what I'm doing. As long as the white society stay up here behind the desks, out in the field you know the dark has unity and togetherness; just seeing them every day and not saying more than "Hi" and "I'll see you later," that doesn't mean anything because it doesn't take anything from you and it doesn't give you anything. It just makes you say, "Well, there goes that old white man again." He might say the same thing, "There go that poor black boy again." I've seen the time when it's been so cold that the white man has had to turn his head because he couldn't take it. And I seen the time when it's been so cold that the brother had to turn his head because he couldn't take it. So I'd like to see the type of program where we all integrate together and be as a whole, because if you don't try to make any effort as white, I'm not going to try to make any effort as black.

And the Mexican definitely isn't going to make any effort, because he don't want to be associated with you mainly because you are black and he don't want to be called black. He wants to be white in some means of the way. I'm really in three worlds: a black world, a white world, a Mexican-American world. And in each one of these worlds I go through different changes and . . . they don't want to

adapt themselves to certain ways and be responsible to certain obligations that they must attend to. By this I'm saying they don't
want to give no black man a chance to prove that he has any type
of culture, any type of motivation about himself at all. All the time
there's nothing planned; there's nothing ever planned for him to
really see himself as he is. Really look at himself. Really think and
say, "What about tomorrow; I'm getting tired of living the days
as they come."

Why not give the black man like me responsibility? I believe
that the black workers and the white workers and the Mexican workers could run this program without any sort of boss man, anybody
to tell them what to do, how to do it and what not to do. Most of
the time, they just don't like to have one correct them because when
you correct someone, someone thinks you're making fun of them,
you're trying to take advantage of them, you're [the trainee] doing
things you shouldn't be doing.

Ted: I applied for training, but they said the area I lived in was
too high an income area. I live between Central and Avalon [just
west of Watts, narrowly defined]. They didn't say *my* economical
status, or my parents' economical status; no, they said the income
in the *area*. I was married at the time; I had a wife and two kids.
O.K., my wife's living with her parents and I'm living with mine
because of the fact that we don't have enough money to move into
a home of our own.

[Some of the residents are conscious of the fact that most of
the jobs created are abortive. Only occasionally do they lead into
a career, or into supervisory, professional, and administrative positions.]

Paul: They are not training people for, say, above middle-class,
professional jobs. . . . They will give you a skill in which you will
be making just so much, and they haven't given [you] the economic opportunity of gettin' higher. I'm saying, just move it up a little bit; like, you can make so much money and be comfortable with
your Cad, with your hi-fi and your pad.

A lot of things they do are just token. I feel it's just a farce, like
this pad on 103rd, this "econo-fab" pad is a farce. All that bullshit
they're pulling. The man is just disguising a bunch of things. This
isn't establishing security.

I'm not talking about giving anything; I'm talking about giv-

ing people the educational ability and ambition. They should change
the whole educational system, more basic education.

Miss Stanley (the former director of an antipoverty unit in Watts):
You see, the thing with job development is that . . . they are not
doing job development. They are placing people in agencies . . .
and then the agencies tell the people, "Well, now, you've been here
a year or two years," whatever the new maximum is, "and now you
are eligible to go out and get jobs some place." Well, granted that
people will have some more skills, maybe a lady with practice has
become more skilled in typing. But the fact of the matter is, in
job development it means that you are developing jobs that never
were there before, and that isn't being done. So what do you have
now? People who are even more frustrated because they are not
on welfare anymore, and in some cases they have been the antagonist to the Welfare Department to help others, so they really don't
want to go back there, and yet they are having just as much difficulty now finding a job as they were before. Also, people in the
community say, "Well, it's my turn to go off the _____ payroll.
Can you help me to find a job?" And they are as desperate now to
find a job as they were when they first came to the office when I
was there, and they were looking for a job, and we were able to hire
them. But now where do they go?

[A great many residents volunteer a belief that more locally
owned businesses in the area would give them the security and the
independence they need. They may not recognize the economic difficulties inherent in establishing such businesses in a low-income
community, but their views must be given weight. Whatever the
economics of the problem, the perception is important; the ghetto
will retain its colonial status until it achieves some degree of economic strength and autonomy.]

Jerry: You know poverty money is coming down in the ghetto
area, coming to the people over the age of forty-five or fifty years
of age. Now these are people that any young adult would consider a house nigger, or an Uncle Tom, or however you want to put
it. Now you let these young adults put that money where it is supposed to go, I think it will go a lot farther. . . . Like, there are lots
on 103rd Street, where businesses used to be, build more businesses with that money; you are automatically putting people to work;
you are giving them experience at the same time. Why not do this?

What are you going to spend $232 million a year [in California] for, to let them sit on their ass?

Chuck: It's always a person that is considered the middle-class man here that gets the position. They should let the people that are in the area handle the situation themselves. You know, we can get enough money right on 103rd, and . . . we could be bringing money within the community. There should be things going on around the community, because . . . the young kids don't have no recreation; they have no place to go, seems like. Things is so far for them to get there, and they can't get there, so they just get out and do anything they feel they want to. If they can find something to have them entertained all this time, they won't be thinking about [setting] all those fires.

George and *Chuck*: Now, the Muslims, they have businesses and stores; they're trying to do something. They want [the community] to be together. All of them in one big batch, that's all they want. Just like they say, "give me a piece of the United States." It's just like the record says, "forty acres and a mule." We deserve what we're supposed to have. It's cool.

Things are happening every day. It's going to take some time, and . . . are we willing to just sit back and live in "the white man's society," and try to wait . . . for something great to happen, [or] you can just go out and join some sort of organization, and try to make it as fast and as soon as you can.

Mr. Kelly (An older man): Why not get loans and establish a shoe shop in Watts? There's profit in any neighborhood anywhere where people have shoes, particularly in a poor neighborhood. I'd do better here in Watts than I would out here on La Cienega [in the Beverly Hills area], because, for one reason, you'll have your shoes repaired more often and the man that don't have to have his shoes repaired, he can throw 'em away and buy a new pair.

Robert Mason discusses his concept of "socio-economic communalism," after a philosophical and historical introduction which traces the origins of the black man's plight in America.

Throughout our existence in this country, black people have not experienced even a notion of the constitutional right of self-determination. It is for this reason we have suffered and still do suffer the helpless, powerless, inferior role of second-class citizenship in the United States.

During the time of our physical slavery, self-determination for blacks was totally eliminated by the Southern power structure. The notion was met with guns, whips, ropes, and dogs if a black man attempted to realize his right to determine his own destiny. The destiny of black people was determined by auctioneers and plantation owners. Bought, sold, traded, bred like beasts, black people were powerless to circumstance. Self-determination was denied black people because freedom cannot be given—only denied. Black people were denied the basic concepts of human existence: self-identity, self-concept, and love for one another. Africans from the same tribe were separated as thoroughly as possible, to prohibit the exchange of objects like trinkets, drums, and clothing, which natives could identify with and by which communication could be established between the slaves.

This destroyed the early slave's only chance to identify with someone or something. Even though he had bondage, race, and emotions in common with his companions, he could not communicate. These facts, coupled with the fear of the strange, new environment, held the early slave powerless.

As communication developed, freedom and self-determination were the two prevailing ideas. As blacks grew in number, they became more defiant. As self-identity developed, so did the notion of self-determination and the number of runaway slaves. The vehicle for communication was a broken form of English picked up from their white masters. Blacks had no other positive figure with which to identify *except* their white master. For he was the man to be envied—he had everything. He lived up in the big house, his woman didn't work, he didn't work, he had a soft warm bed, the best of food and comforts, while the slave had to toil without reward, half-starved and half-alive. "Yes, suh, Missa Charley sho' got it easy." So whites became the point of definition, the source of identity. Most slaves defined themselves with the white man and allowed themselves to be defined by him. But a few slaves, unsure of who they were, knew exactly what they weren't— white men. These few demanded the right to define themselves and began encouraging and leading rebellions, increasing the numbers of defiant blacks: men like Denmark Vesey, who organized a rebellion in 1822 and led 9,000 slaves into Charleston, or the "brothers" who fell with John Brown at Harper's Ferry in 1859, or even Gabriel Prosser who organized thousands of blacks in Virginia in the early 1800's. These men were the vanguard of the black man's struggle for self-preservation. Writers like Frederick Douglass escaped from the South and wrote to inform the country of the plight of the black man in America. Growing sympathy for the black cause, coupled with economic disputes, separated the North and South and aggravation eventually split and plunged them into civil war.

With the subsequent Northern victory and Reconstruction period came the first of many false hopes of emancipation. The mass migration northward began our period of economic and psychological slavery. Self-determination for black people has been combated by politics, socio-economic repercussions, poverty, and the pen, as well as police, National Guardsmen, and later the FBI and CIA. But instead of being totally eliminated, self-determination was restricted. As the abolitionists attracted slaves and, now, ex-slaves northward, the power structure was horrified at the mass invasion of freedom-seeking blacks. The large, industrialized cities were naturally the targets for migrants.

Upon arrival in the North, the "free" blacks were forced into rundown sections, employed in low-paying, all-day, second-class, menial jobs, and harassed by white policemen. Utopia turned into a sham, another more painful, more sophisticated form of racism. Hate hung over the air like a blanket, the kind of hate seen in eyes and smiles; the type that fills your nostrils and makes you want to vomit or spit. The black man found himself powerless again; even though living in highly concentrated city centers, his role was still being dictated to him. He had left the South, but his reputation for being subhuman, lazy, stupid, and inferior had preceded him North. Held in bondage of poverty and discrimination, the black man turned to the white man's promised means of escape: education. Black children, whenever possible, attended city schools. In 1854, Lincoln University, the first black college, opened in Oxford, Pennsylvania. An educated black class was formed, but on a white scale. Inculcated with the white man's education, the new black intellectuals began attacking the conditions of their wretched brothers. The first attempts to aid the cause were through legislation and sympathy.

The NAACP was formed in 1909 in New York after a series of race riots. Langston Hughes dramatized the woe of blacks; white and black middle-class liberals under the NAACP banner worked to get federal legislation passed to relieve the existing conditions. But this, as I said, was a middle-class movement; the masses turned to the church. The promise of God made it worth suffering hell on earth to gain heaven hereafter.

In the ghettos the church became the main social and political organization. The church had an ideology. The minister was a powerful and respected man. For these reasons, coupled with the church's adaptation to the struggle for equality, the Reverend Dr. Martin Luther King became, in 1955, the vanguard of the civil rights movement. In his civil rights movement, King employed the basic principles of freedom and Christianity to aid his cause. The church is a universal institution, therefore a power base. King adapted the teachings of Christ to his theory of black liberation. Christians couldn't very well renounce the Gospel and many integrated into the movement. The movement's first target was the desegregation of public accommodations. The purpose was to legislate equality and then to integrate public facilities, sometimes forcibly. Armed repression of civil rights workers became grounds for condemnation of the historical Southern white policy of separation, but in the process it further enraged already enraged Northern blacks. Northern blacks joined organizations like SNCC and CORE. These organizations led the freedom rides, sit-ins, lie-ins and other demonstrations for public accommodations in the South.

As more heads were cracked and bodies bruised and jailed, general conditions did not improve, self-determination was still a myth. Younger students began to turn their eyes to the revolutions in Africa, China, and nearby Cuba. They began reading Mao, Marx, Guevara, Castro, Kenyatta, and Kwame Nkrumah, as well as Malcolm X, Frantz Fanon, and Eldridge Cleaver. Integration meant that blacks could only be accepted on white terms, "superior" terms. The notion of self-determination revived. Self-identification, self-pride, self-definition became the watchwords. Leaders like King and Wilkins lost the vanguard of the movement to Carmichael, Forman, LeRoi Jones and El Hadj Malik Shabazz (Malcolm X).

In a very real sense, black people see themselves as living a neo-colonial existence in the country. We constitute a country within a country. Our sections of the city are designated to us by economic discrimination and we are chained there by poverty, poor education, and discrimination. Our resources, both physical and human, are exploited by foreign officials who hold foreign investments. These foreign officials care nothing for the natives or their homes; they care only for their imperialistic greed; they don't want to integrate. They control our social, economic, and judicial systems. They even control our communication system. The blood and sweat of our brow is exploited for the profit of the mother country. Foreign troops (policemen and National Guardsmen) control our country, adequately armed to suppress any sign of restless natives.

Newspapers, radio, television, etc. are controlled by the mother country. She exploits us, dehumanizes us and castrates us for her own best interest, and then she expects us to respect and love her, to salute her flag, fight and die for her and feel grateful for all she has done for us. While she teaches that "violence doesn't solve anything," in Vietnam she represents the fact that "power legitimates." While she is horrified at "crime in the streets" in the North, she charges through the ghettos and the South with guns and badges, killing and maiming. While she shouts "liberty and justice for all," she denies me the right to be a man—the schizophrenic bitch! Our official leaders, white man's stooges, still try to hide behind the petty bourgeois clichés and tokens, but the masses are realizing the need for a socio-economic revolution. As LeRoi Jones says, "The struggle is not simply for equality or 'better jobs' or 'better schools,' and the rest of those halfhearted liberal clichés; it is to completely free the black man from the domination of the white man," and to achieve the independence of black people. Cuba was attacked by the United States because she refused to let herself be exploited solely for industrial interests of this country. Patrice Lumumba was killed because he resisted the same neo-colonial designs we live under. "Communism" was their tag, and the U.S. justification; our tag is "Black Nationalism."

We want independence from the political, economic, social, spiritual, and psychological domination of the power structure. Whites tend to see themselves as the omnipotent ruler and protector of humanity. The economic exploitation and the psychological indoctrination of all other people go under the heading of "white man's burden." "Negroes in this country do have problems," they say, but whites don't have any. They either blame others for prevailing conditions, feel guilty and work to help the black man, or apathetically feel indifferent.

We black people realize the need to assert ourselves, to define and identify ourselves rather than to be defined and identified by whites. Whites feel rejected, indignant, and hostile toward the new black self-image. Most seem to feel our problems can be solved using the existing structure, unaware that the structure is the basis of our problems. We demand the right to decide what is best for us. To white people, "Black Power" means we want to take over the country and kill white people. To blacks, it means assertion and mastery in every aspect of human endeavor to form a consolidated front to achieve total liberation. This implies that we must create our own institutions to develop our culture, our ideology, and our citizens to determine our own destiny.

These institutions depend upon the freedom to seek and expose the truth. White history paints a negative picture of blacks. How can a people work with a negative self-identity? We must rewrite history to capture the positive aspects of black history. Both whites and Afro-Americans must be able to face the truth and deal with reality. There must be permanent black institutions, not the token programs from the government. These institutions must create masses of self-sufficient citizens, as well as allow intellectuals to capture, develop, and communicate the black experience in America.

My solution is socio-economic communalism. First of all I need a product: a product that can be produced on a multi-million-dollar scale. It has to be a new (or relatively new) product so I can corner or even monopolize the market. I shall select the community of Watts in which to build this factory (because it is the place of my origin), but it could be any black community. I find a site on which to build the factory, on the corner of 103rd and Alameda. Alameda is the state's truck route and it is a low-rent zone. A general plan of operation and estimate of production costs is drawn up.

The cost will be very high, because to be successful this factory must employ thousands of skilled workers from the community. This labor force could be trained in government-financed training centers attached to the factory. The factory could be subsidized by a combination of Federal and private donations. The unique factor in this venture is that it is non-profit and therefore tax-deductible. The factory will be communal. It will be run by a salaried administrative staff responsible to the people.

One might say that I intend to use government funds for a socialistic cause. Or some may say that I am begging. To the former, I answer that the U.S. government is presently engaged in socialistic programs like medicare, social security, and welfare to combat the evils resulting from capitalism. To the latter, I figured the interest on forty acres and a mule for one hundred years, times the number of black people who have labored without a payday. I did not even consider the immeasurable wealth created by four hundred years of exploitation of black people. No, I would say the government is getting off very cheaply.

The "profits" from this communal factory will be diverted to the solution of other community problems, such as a community-owned and operated shopping center. Everything from aspirin to xylophones could be sold at discount prices. Both of these ventures would be self-sustaining after a time and "profits" would be directed at solving community problems.

Other alternative investments for surplus funds would be low-cost housing tracts, constructed and sold at cost. Low-interest loans and reduced insurance rates could also be considered by the factory in conjunction with the Federal government.

Public schools and pre-school centers could be subsidized to upgrade the educational system and make it more relevant to the community. Research and experimental projects could be conducted by students into community problems and solutions. A communication center (T.V., radio, newspaper, magazines, etc.) could be established to project a realistic, positive image of black people to the community.

You should understand that economic communalism would not be the entire solution to the existing dilemmas of the black community. Instead, it would serve as a secure economic basis to subsidize, encourage, and enhance the establishment of other black institutions so necessary for our people. With economic communalism comes the psychological stimulus to inspire black people to achieve unity and self-determination. Self-help would give us the experience in business administration and responsibility necessary to survive in this computer age. Our *own* businesses, our *own* labels, our *own* people would be enough to lift our socially demoralized, economically deprived, psychologically whitewashed, spiritually feeble masses to the summit of human achievement. Economic communalism could be the way to the fulfillment of Malcolm X's dreams, Martin Luther King's prayers, Nat Turner's visions, and Huey P. Newton's sacrifices.

V

The Police

Few issues arouse as much emotion in Watts as the problem of law enforcement. When the late William Parker was Chief of Police in Los Angeles, his arrogance and insensitivity in relation to minority groups—Mexican-Americans as well as Negroes—only aggravated an already complex relationship. Parker ran a generally honest and efficient police force, but his gratuitous comments on the alleged criminal proclivities of certain minorities (of "cultural" rather than "biological" origin, he later explained) earned him the deep hatred of most black people. His death in 1966, and his replacement by an apparently moderate chief, brightened the prospect for a better rapport between the police and the black community, but the resulting improvement seems to be limited mainly to that broad and amorphous category known as "community relations." So far, the young people report little observable change in the day-by-day actions of the policeman on the local beat.[1]

The problem of law enforcement is even further complicated by the process of enforced ghettoization and the concomitant restriction of legitimate economic opportunities available to the residents. Denied equal access to the educational and occupational privileges taken for granted by the majority, and introduced to the "street economy" at an early age, many are impelled to seek an income (or possibly some other gratification of personal needs) in illegal or illicit ways. Unemployment and underemployment are more

---

[1] After the assassination of Martin Luther King, the Chief of Police and community groups ranging from moderate to militant, established a communication which was without precedent. Whether this foretells a permanent change in relations, however, remains in question. Ironically, the Chief, Tom Reddin, resigned in April, 1969, to become a TV newscaster.

severe in the south central ghetto than in any other part of the country, and existing manpower, unemployment compensation, and welfare measures meet only a part of the problem. In such circumstances, "hustling" comes naturally, and a youngster soon accepts the fact that, in large degree, the law is an enemy, full of double standards and arbitrariness.

It would be wildly incorrect, of course, to suggest that every Negro in the ghetto is hostile to policemen. Indeed, many of the residents feel that there should be *more* police services within the community. An oft-heard complaint is that the police are slow in responding to calls, or that they are not tough enough on wife-beaters or young punks. The youngsters themselves object only to what they perceive as discrimination in enforcement or harassment, not to law enforcement itself. Obviously, a great many are convinced that policemen are more inclined to detain and harass them and are less respectful of their dignity as human beings than is the case in Anglo communities and the Anglo suburbs.

Much of the friction between the community and the police emerges from the "stop and frisk" practices of the local cops. Technically a policeman must have "probable cause" (a plausible reason for suspicion of illegality) for detaining and searching anyone, unless he has a warrant, but there is a pervasive conviction in Watts that the typical cop requires much less "probable cause" there than in Beverly Hills or Long Beach or Pacific Palisades. While recent court rulings supposedly expand the rights of the individual in relation to police power, the practical situation has changed very little. The discretion of the policeman remains broad, and unless there is strong evidence to the contrary or witnesses are present whose testimony impresses the court, the "dude" accused of an unlawful act will find that it is simply a case of "his word against the cop's." Judges and juries are rarely inclined to give more credence to his assertions than to those of the police. Provided that he was reasonably careful in reciting the required statement of an accused's rights, and avoided the use of excessive force *in public,* the policeman still has little difficulty in making his charges stick.

If the individual had access to private counsel, and if the available appeals procedures were used to the fullest, it is quite likely that the conviction rate would be markedly lower than it is. In practice, most arrestees must rely upon the public defender, who rarely appeals a conviction, and the legality of the arrest procedures usually remains unchallenged. Many of the youngsters expect to be searched for drugs or narcotics whenever they are stopped by the police, and again it seems probable that police power is applied more broadly in Watts than in the Anglo communities.

For instance, the *Handbook on the Law of Search and Seizure,* published by the United States Department of Justice in 1968, clearly states that an arrest for traffic violations cannot be used as a pretext to search for evidence of another crime. It instructs the policeman that, "If you use a traffic violation arrest as a pretext to search for products of an unrelated crime the search will be invalid" (p. 44). But the statements of the youngsters, and the personal observations of the editor, suggest that this restriction is regularly violated.

The *Handbook* further warns policemen against searching a home without a warrant, except under certain, strictly defined conditions. Under no circumstances, the *Handbook* declares, should officers enter a private residence in order to conduct a general search (in effect, a "fishing expedition"), and a legal search without a warrant can occur only in emergencies, or during "hot pursuit," or when the officers observe that contraband may be destroyed, or when incidental to a valid arrest (p. 27). The scores of experiences cited by the residents of Watts demonstrate that some policemen invade their homes on pretexts that fail to meet any of these criteria.

"Probable cause," from a layman's standpoint, appears to be a flexible and subjective concept. Certainly, a youngster from Watts gets the impression that a policeman is empowered to detain and examine him for any reason that seems appropriate to "Irvine" at the moment. In many instances the cop will give no explanation at all, and, if pressed, he is often likely to say that the "dude" resembles the description of a suspect wanted for a crime. No one, least of all the youngster himself, can know for sure whether this explanation is honest.

In one case which I observed at close range, the youngster involved (John) had been arrested on a "possession of marijuana" charge. He had been apprehended on 103rd Street while walking along the sidewalk in midday; a police car cruising down the street had pulled to the curb just in front of him, and its two occupants got out and went toward him. On the surface, his activity did not seem to be suspicious when the police car came into view, and during the preliminary hearing the arresting officer had been asked to explain why he had glanced at John and why he had stopped the car. He knew, he said, that John had a long felony record, and he observed that John acted suspiciously when he became aware of the police car.

In fact, John's previous conviction on a felony charge had occurred some years before, certainly before the arresting officer had been assigned to the area. However, John had recently been *accused* of assaulting a policeman, but his trial had resulted in a hung jury. The officer's statement about a "long felony record" was incorrect, and it seems reasonable to infer that he was motivated by an awareness of the unproved charge and by his resentment against John for apparently having beaten the rap. Of course, his additional statement about the "suspicious behavior" could neither be confirmed nor refuted by witnesses or by other evidence. The judge readily accepted the statements as sufficient indication of "probable cause."

The youngsters clearly distinguish among law enforcement agencies, and among individual policemen, on the basis of the degree to which the enforcers detain or harass them when they are not engaged in unlawful behavior involving injury to persons or property. They will admit, without hesitation, though perhaps without pleasure, that the cops have a right and duty to apprehend anyone who is committing a burglary or theft, or firing a rifle, or driving dangerously under the influence of liquor or narcotics. They even feel that the police are sometimes derelict, in failing to protect the lives and property of black people. At the same time they deeply resent any official concern with their private morals, particularly when convinced that different rules are applied to whites.

In the following section several of the youngsters describe their own experiences with the police. Except for Marvin, each of them has been arrested at least once. Most of these experiences took place between early 1967 and late 1968, after the riot and the death of Chief Parker.

Marvin: While Parker was Chief, a Negro in Watts would be walking down the street, coming home from a party—it might be quite late, let us say, about two or three o'clock—and they would pull you over to the side and actually hold you up with stupid questions, call you "boy." They wouldn't come up to you and say "son" or something like that.

Like an incident when . . . I was coming home from the beach quite late one night, and I was in a hurry because I had something to do early the next morning. I spotted the officer's car. I was going south; it was passing me. I didn't pay any attention; I was just walking. Within thirty minutes, that car pulled up on the other side of the curb. One of the officers jumped out of the car, and he said, "Halt, boy," just like this, so I freeze where I was; I didn't try to make any getaway moves or anything like this, fear of being shot or wounded or something like this. So I stopped, and he harassed me, threw my arm in back of my back, and it hurt. He got me in the car. He asked all kinds of stupid questions, like have I stolen a car before, and I said, "No," and he actually asked me where did I hide it, questions like this. He had a report on me that a lady said I was peeping in her window, and I was in a dreadful hurry, I did not want to be retarded in any way. . . . But since Chief Parker has died, the police has slacked up a little bit. . . . They are not as much discourteous as they used to be.

Eric: There has been a slight change, but . . . when they approach you, they still approach you in an insulting manner. It seems like they feel you are beneath them. In some cases, they tell you why they stopped you, but take this incident that happened to me. I was coming along, and all of a sudden, out of the dark, they came. Forced me into discussion. "Where are you going, boy? It is too late to be on the street, boy." I felt just like getting out of there. . . . As a Negro, you feel low. It makes you feel cold inside, you are different from them. Like trash. The only thing that you are different in is the color. . . . It happens so frequently, you just learn to go along with it.

    I don't think that Reddin [the Chief of Police after Parker] really made a difference. . . . It's the same thing, but with a different approach. Just like three, four, five years ago, when you need the police, like emergency call, it was a hour or two hours before he got there. And when he got there, he acted as though it was a rush deal: what's happened, what took place, how long ago. They say "Sir" or "Madam," but it's not sincere; just a cover.

David: The game is the same, but the name changes. Reddin is doing it one way, and Parker was doing another. But it all means the same. When you are running a country, nobody else can win. Because you are the one that is running it. You always leave ten or twelve loopholes for yourself.

    I think the police been on my case since I entered junior college. I just know from what one white officer told me one time, "Don't let them know that you go to school." But the reputation that I had at that time, and then somehow they fucked around and found out. That's when I was dead—'cause I was a militant motherfucker.

Eric: You know, you went through this stage of militancy, you expressed it more when you were younger. That was my daily situation.

You know what, man, you never know what they stop you for. If they stopped you for a traffic violation, you'll never know it. They just stopped you on GP [general principles].

A time ago I was stopped by one of those black-and-white [police] cars and there was a Negro policeman and a white Caucasian in it. It was in front of the pool hall. The policemen jump out of the car, Negro policeman comes to me—runs toward me. No, he didn't go in my pockets—I backed away from him, but by this time my back was against the wall. Same time I am saying, "What have I done?" The white Caucasian, he is standing off at the side; the Negro is talking, he gets smart. He is telling me all about the training he is going through. So he wants to get my hand behind my back and take me out. Right away, I can't say I'm getting an understanding with him. I'm still going to ask him, "What have I done?"

Then I turn to the white one and I get to talking with him. Then I try to get an understanding with him. So finally I get an understanding with the white policeman. They said I looked like Herbert and you know damn well I don't look anything like Herbert.[2] The white policeman goes back to the car and tells me to go back into the pool hall. The brother's just standing off on the side.

Ray: Now, in the black community, if you are sensitive, if you show too much fear, you will automatically be considered guilty. I've been stopped right out in front of my house and the policeman told me that I didn't live there. They were two young guys and they was going to take us to jail just for suspicion of burglary. I was in [a friend's] car—he was getting ready to go to school—we was just sitting outside. So these two policemen they passed by, you know, and they saw us and they turned around and they came back, behind us. They started talking about the high burglary rate and this and that, and they searched us all the way down and everything. Young cops are the worst; they are a gas, man! See, these were recruits.

Now, I know, my little brothers they were busted about three blocks from home and I know they were clean when they left the pad; whether they ran into something on the way or not, this is beyond my knowledge, but I do know they were taken to jail.

What I am trying to say is this: once you get a record and become recognized [by the police], don't do any suspicious action.

---

[2] Eric is slender and built like a lithe basketball player; Herbert is about thirty pounds heavier, built like the football player he is.

David, Joe, Marvin, and *Eric*:   There ain't but two or three policemen in Watts that we all know: Jesse James, Billy the Kid, Uncle
Tom, that white one name Wyatt Earp [local nicknames for cops].

LAPD cops get a reputation from Watts, like this one, well,
he put fourteen Negroes in jail in one week. He cracked down on
four gambling joints in two days. He cracked down, he gets this
reputation. One white cop will give you a fair chance every time;
he gets a lot of respect, and he earns that respect. You know, you
don't catch him coming in, beating people on the head, kicking them
all in the behind; the others will poke you, "What's your name?
Where're you going?" He'll say, "Everything all right?" You might
have been doing nothing, you might be in a liquor store, need three
more pennies, he's going to find it and give it to you. Tell me, what
other cop would do that? If every other law officer would work like
he was, I'll tell you that community would be one hundred per cent
better. . . . He knows the area like the back of his hand.

David: Now _____ is a good white man; he's all right. You want
to know the first words I ever said to him? I called him a lousy motherfucker. And do you know, man, we have been friends ever since
then. That man has found twelve warrants on me and wouldn't take
me to jail. I have seen that man stop boys with narcotics in their
pocket, put it in his hand, tell somebody to blow it out, look at his
hand, say, "I ain't got no evidence," get in his car, and drive off.

. . . I wouldn't want them all to be like that. Let me tell you
why. I wouldn't want 'em to be like that because at times I think
if it wasn't for the police, we would all be dead. You would be after
me, and I would be after you. . . . You would have a revolution,
you would have a black-and-white revolution. The revolution they
are fighting over there in Vietnam, that ain't no revolution compared to what we'd have here if it weren't for the police.

David: It takes a long time for police to respond to calls in Watts.
From forty-five minutes to an hour. One time I's about to die. It
took the ambulance an hour and twenty minutes to get there. . . .
Now the Fire Department, they respond so abruptly. . . . See, they
got to go.

Mr. Martin: Might be the man's liquor store on fire. . . . There
might be something of their own down there.

David: When one of them niggers gets to cuttin' up that other nigger . . . he is not going to come down and get me, if I cut you up. . . .
That's just one less nigger, one nigger gone. That's just one he

doesn't have to be worried with. . . . Maybe two. He don't care, he going to give them time to kill each other. That's why it takes so long to get there.

Now, just like about a couple of months ago, a little cat named Richard Wiley, police jumped on him. Now, you know them blackjacks aren't supposed to break, but they beat that boy so bad, hit him so hard, that blackjack broke on his ear. And then turned around and shot him in the arm.

Now, when I was over there beatin' that man over the head with that pipe, somebody called the police, and it took them about an hour and a half to get there. Everyone knows that it wasn't anyone but I kill that man, or that man kill me. . . . They knows there's no white people out there. . . . There is only two people, there is only two races that they can't save them in trouble. That's Negroes and Mexican-Americans. They don't care nothing about them.

Eric: I wouldn't mind becoming a jailer, or something like that, especially in the Sheriff's Department. LAPD, mostly what they have to offer are patrol officers, and I wouldn't be a patrol officer, anywhere. Well, anyone is your enemy, because the suit you wear is the enemy to the public. People . . . are not aware that the man in the suit might be helping them. As long as he has the uniform on, he is "no good."

Joe: But, you know, there are police officers of LAPD [that] has time and time again "brutality" towards Colored people; they harass the peoples in the community. And in different communities, I don't care if it is Westwood, Hollywood, Bellflower, I don't care where you are, the police are different. . . . I can get arrested anywhere and you [a Caucasian] cannot, because this is embarassing to you, because you will bring out the point how embarassing it is to you. If I bring out the point I am embarrassed, I am embarassed because I have a black skin from my mother.

LAPD is worse than the Sheriff's office. LAPD feel within their mind that we have already established a bad enough reputation, harassing us, taking us through these unnecessary changes when we are not within our community, as though they are doing themselves and their community a favor by getting us out and keeping us out. For one, we know from the start they don't want us there, and they will more or less be establishing a reputation for themselves; this is bringing them up in the world, bringing their standards up a little higher; I am pretty sure they want that increase in pay.

The Sheriff's Department has its own bad points also . . . but definitely, the Sheriff's Department will not stop you at four o'clock in the morning when you're driving down Central Avenue or Compton Avenue area, and I've seen the Sheriff's Department, he will not say anything, he is going about his business; he is looking for the robber, he is looking for the peoples who is breaking in homes, he is looking for the peoples that is really doing something, but police in L.A., they are more concerned with the, more or less, younger generation, teen-agers, carrying drugs about with them; there would be this man over here robbing this store, and this man over here breaking into a few houses there, they should be patrolling that instead of stopping every other black person on the street.

When they stop you, you go through all the changes. If you don't have narcotics on you, or cigarette tobacco in your pocket, you might go home, and then again you might go downtown for suspicion. . . . That's all it would be is suspicion, suspicion, all day long, all night long; you can go to the felony tank, and you'll find more people in jail in the 77th Precinct than anywhere in the city of Los Angeles, on suspicion, suspicion.

The first thing they say to you when they stop you is, "Where're you going?" And after, "Where have you been?" They will ask you, "What's your name? Have you ever been arrested before?" If you have, then it is a long haul, and if you look like you're criminal—don't wear tennis shoes, because if you wear tennis shoes, you might go to jail, you might go to jail for suspicion. Now if you are highly dressed, just like you're coming from a party, or something, they might pass you, but if you are in plain ordinary everyday clothes, like normally the Negro people, tennis shoes and T shirt, they will stop you, they will search you, they'll take out this little white card, they write down the area you are in, what vicinity, precisely what time it is, call down [to the station] to see if anything been happening on the street. If it has, if it has, you get in the car and you go down to 77th for suspicion, you understand? They can hold you two, three days, and it's not your fault, if you're in this particular area at this particular time when something else is going on. Then they tell you that you shouldn't have been there in the first place.

They never tell you why. They take you downtown, they get you down and find out it wasn't you, then they may tell you. They might. They search you in all ways. You spread your legs. If you put your hands on top of a hot car and you burn yourself, you take your hands off, you might get hit. They make you go through your coat, take all your pockets out and put it all on a white sheet of paper, dust your pockets off, see if you got any narcotics on you. And they might tell you to be quiet. And don't be eating anything. Spit it out. You're actually chewing, they get the impression that you're eating narcotics. They will say—and don't have the match cover tore off the back of your match book—"Where's the rest of the joint at, or where's the rest of the dope at?" This is the type of routine they are doing. It's about the same as it was a year or two ago.

The police don't want to be wrong; they hate to be wrong. That will make them look bad, if they stop you and they can't find any other reason. That's probably why they gave Jerry his citation, is because they hate to look bad. They got to be right, they have to be, regardless what things are, they are going to be right. There is never, never a time that I have been stopped, and I have been stopped twenty, thirty, forty, fifty times since last year, there's never been a time when I was stopped and the police officer told me, "Well, I am sorry, you are not the one we looking for," you know, "I am sorry to do such and such a thing," and if you are a juvenile, and he picked you up at 8:30, you're supposed to be home at 9:30, he will keep you there talking all the time until curfew time comes and then he can arrest you. And he'll give you a ride, like ride you way over town and let you go. Put you out of his car. I had this happen to me. Take you way off on 41st and Vernon, or Adams, somewhere way over there, and he'll let you go. And don't tell another police officer that that happened to you. If he stops you, "Well, I just got stopped by a policeman, he took me over here and brought me all the way from home," hell, they will take you on to jail. You might get a ride with somebody, explain to him what happened; if you cry something, he might even take you into a café and buy you something to eat, man.

Like the time when my mother sent me up to the school to take lunch for my younger sisters and brothers, and the police picked me up. I tried to explain to him what I was there for, and they take me for a ride, and takes me way across town and drops me off, and say, "Well, O.K., I'll let you go here, you better be glad I'm not taking you down." You'll be so glad that they letting you go, you know, then you realize that you way across town, and "damn."

If they don't like you, don't like the way you dress, the way you talked to them; you always got to have that old Southern "Yes, sir; no, sir." And you can Uncle Tom out, but if you are a man who stands up to your rights, and you say, "No, this is not in the law," well, then, you will go through all kinds of changes, but if you Uncle Tom, you might get out of it.

One time there was a fight, a fair fight, and somebody called
the police; the *Sheriff* came; now they say as long as it's a fair fight,
there's no weapons involved, knock yourselves out, and they went
on about their business. Said, if you can, take it to the gym field.
LAPD wouldn't do that. They'd put you in jail. Drag you in the
car, take you down. And the detective would have run you through
all kinds of talk, that old crazy talk. And put your ass in the tank.
That tank is cold, and the toilet and the face bowl, they are made
together, and the drink fountain is right over the top of the toilet.
. . . You have to shit and piss right there, and everybody that come
there, he piss right there in the main compound, trying to do what
he got to do, no door, no nothing. . . . Then, if it's time to eat, if somebody is doing it [relieving himself], you have to smell it. . . .

Eric: In the station right in Watts, they let you eat in the café
nearby. The cook is picking his nose, scratching his behind, fixing
you a hot dog. . . . The floor is black. If he drops the meat, he picks
it up and puts it right on his hand. . . . He is sweating, and his sweat
is dripping off his nose and . . . all over your food.

Joe: A Negro cop is no better than a white, maybe worse. You
know why: Because they try to establish reputations for themselves.
. . . You see, a rookie will be working, and he is going to be trying
to build up his reputation. And another thing, if you had all Negro
cops in Watts, there would be more dead policemen than you ever
seen, man. [Chorus of "Right."] Listen, because one thing, if you
start them off at twenty-one at the police academy, and you come
out maybe twenty-two, you don't know no more than I do. . . . You
might know judo and karate, and I might know judo and karate;
he got a gun, and I might have a gun. . . . Because they are Negroes; Negroes have been known, down the past and all through
history, to jump on one another. We have been known to do this. A
Negro will fight you quicker than a Caucasian will. And it will start
more fights, more stuff. . . . They start throwing bricks and everything at you; and first thing you know, your money is gone, your
wallet is gone, your gun is gone, you have trouble with your own
head.

[There is a strong conviction among the youngsters that one
type of law enforcement exists for Watts and another for Hollywood
and Beverly Hills. Sometimes the difference is so obvious that even
the most naive observer can't miss it. When there was an incident
in Will Rogers Park, in the summer of 1968, just following the final

jazz concert at Jordan High School during the festival, police cars filled the streets for many days after. Each car carried four policemen, shotguns pointing out the windows. It was, I think, the first time that I had experienced fear in Watts, and my concern was triggered by the police and what they might do or provoke, not by the community.

Though this was an extreme instance, the differences can still be detected any day of the week. The police are more visible as well as more active in Watts. The youngsters are convinced that the reasons are partly economic and partly racial: poor people usually are exploited more often than rich people, and poor *blacks* never even have a chance.

Marvin and *David*: It ain't nothing but a racket, just a racket, so far as the political structure is concerned. J. Paul Getty and Howard Hughes are going to do what they want to do, I don't care what the law is. A main function of the political structure is carried out through the Police Department. Did you notice what they campaigned on last time? Crime. They can get you any time they want to, but if they don't want to, like with Howard Hughes, they'll never get you. Now, these peckerwoods get up there and run for President and say, "Well, look, we want the police to enforce this, we want to enforce that," it's just a racket, man.

Ray: I was real young when I met this particular policeman. He wore no gun. He patrolled the Hollywood and Beverly Hills area. See, I used to live out there.

In other words, there should be an overall understanding between the people and the policemen, instead of, "Well, I don't know you, I'm out to get you." Sure, the city is so big now. But the point is the policeman should be related to the community. Now when a person is hungry, that changes his mind. He wants something to put in his stomach. But in Hollywood and Beverly Hills, there are days when you don't see the police at all. Down in Watts they are everywhere. I mean, the concentration of police in Watts or any black area, there is no comparison of the area out in Westwood and the area where we live.

Earl: It's economics and racism together. Money is economics; racism is whether you are black or white. 'Course if you are black, you ain't got enough money.

I'll give you an example of something that happened to several of us [in 1967]. It must have been between 10:30 and quarter

till eleven in the morning, and we were on the San Diego Freeway
near UCLA. I don't remember the precise time nor the precise date,
but as I was saying, we were on the freeway, approaching the Westwood turnoff, and I was sitting in the back, and I remember telling
Brian not to get off here and let's go on to Montana Street, come
around the back way [to UCLA], but he insisted, you know, 'cause
he wanted to sightsee. We were going north on Westwood Boulevard, and coming in the opposite direction and traveling south
was the police unit, and he passed us, and I kind of noticed that
he took a slight glimpse, and I don't know why, but he did. And
at this time the driver of our car turned, made a left turn on some
street, and I heard him make a comment that the police turned
around, and he was going to stop us. So before I knew it, there is a
man behind us flashing all these red lights, and so I thought maybe
it was just some routine check or something, and the officer approached the car, and he said to the driver, "Where is your license
plate?"

Brian was driving, and I just kind of muttered to myself, like,
"Oh, shit," and . . . I remember he told Brian to get out of the car,
and I remember that Brian came back to the car and got a license
plate off the floor, and I guess the officer checked to see if the car
was stolen, and at this time Brian was showing him all this driver
registration and things . . . to show that it did belong to him. The
officer went back to his car, and he must have phoned in about something, and he found out that the car was clear, and at that time he
asked everyone in the car for identification, and myself not knowing that there was a warrant out for my arrest that had been issued
about a year ago, I kind of gave him my correct name and stuff,
and we were all sitting there in the car waiting.

I was sitting there and I noticed that it was taking him quite
a long time, and he must have received the information that he wanted, and he got this look on his face, and I just said, "Oh, oh!" So
Brian asked us did anyone have any warrant out on him. "No, no,"
everybody said. And the officer just sits there for a long time after
he received his return call, and before I know it, I saw him approaching the car, and he was taking his gun out, he was standing behind
his car; another car approached us from the front, and two more approached us from the side, and then I saw a couple more coming from
down the street.

And he kind of pointed his gun toward the car and . . . tells
everybody to place their hands on the seat, and then he asked everyone to get out. . . . So one by one we got out, and this time he

kept his hand on his gun and his finger on the trigger and tells us to get alongside the wall; and I approached the wall, I put my hands on the wall. I guess my feet weren't far enough apart, so he walked over there, and he kicked them a little more, and I wasn't going to say anything, because he had his gun in his hand all the time, and all the other officers were just standing around, just waiting for something to happen. And by that time, a crowd had gathered. The police asked which one was _____, and I told him that it was me, and he says to me that I was under arrest for felony. I didn't know what he was talking about; I said, "Are you sure that's me?" . . . He had handcuffed everybody but me, and by this time he didn't have another set of handcuffs, and he was calling for this other officer to bring his down, and after he found out that I was _____, he did then take the handcuffs off Eric and put them on me, and he stuck me in the car . . . and they were all ready to take us all down.

Brian asks was it possible he could follow him to the station in his car, so I guess the sergeant agreed . . . and the sergeant was leading the way, and Brian was behind the sergeant's car, and we were following behind him, and we got on over to the police station, and they ran a teletype check, and it was found out that I had a warrant out on myself, and they took me off in all different directions.

I stayed at West L.A. for a day and a half, and they shipped me from West L.A. to the County. I was in County for three more days before my arraignment. My bail was $3,300, and I had a felony. It was a violation of the State Narcotics Act, illegal sale of narcotics, and I was still trying to figure how it all came about, and they cut me loose and I went home. But I did finally go to court, and that was how I found out that this particular guy that was my friend, that I went to school with, he was an undercover agent, so I got three years' probation, and that was it.

Eric: They ended up giving Brian a ticket for this taillight that was in the back. They said it was illegal. They didn't give any ticket for the license plate. Brian could prove that the car was his. . . . The reason they stopped us was that we were black faces in a white community. Right there in front of the bank, the whole scene looks as though we had actually robbed the bank.

During the meantime, standing there in front of the bank, this dude kept passing by in his car, an Oldsmobile or Continental or something. Yeah, he was a Caucasian fellow, and there were whites all around, and they were shouting, "What have they done, what have they done? Why don't you let them go?" The officers within their community were holding us there for no reason at all, you know. They all seemed to be on our side, even while we were getting in the car and leaving.

Marvin: They've still got the same nasty attitude. I was stopped a couple of days ago, out here on Beverly Glen. [*Another teen-ager*: You didn't have no business out there though, did you?] I got all the business there anybody else do. . . . We just looked suspicious, he said; I was with my friend, and he had this little car [the cop] thought was stolen. . . . He said he thought we had marijuana, he kept seeing flames light up and then go down in the car, things like that.

David, Marvin and *Mr. Martin*: Am I a citizen of the United States? [If you are a Negro] you can't move to Burbank. You can't live in Glendale. .... You know you go to jail . . . at six or seven o'clock in the evening [if the police catch you] with them tennis shoes on. The police will figure you burglared. [*Another teen-ager*: I will have to agree because they stop me with tennis shoes on.]

David: I can say this about the Police Department. . . . About fifty per cent of the police in California live in the community that they are assigned to work with in that precinct, and I feel that the people in Watts could be hired as police officers in their own community, because if a person does something wrong there, and he lives in Watts, he can't get away, he can't go anywhere because they all know him. . . . This way you can bring down the crime rate. Let the people run their own community. . . .

[Asked what they would do differently if they were policemen, the youngsters disagree among themselves only on the question of what they think they would do when the law violation concerns a purely personal or private act, such as the smoking of pot. They are unanimous in opposing the *law* outlawing pot, but differ somewhat as to whether the individual cop has, or should have, discretion in applying the law. They recognize that the policeman has a job to do, but have their own separate approaches to the problem of what standards to use in determining how rigidly or in what manner the law should be enforced.]

A Young Adult: From the git-go, I don't ask to be put on Crenshaw [toward the west, though much of Crenshaw runs through the better part of the ghetto], I wouldn't ask to be put in Gardena [a predominantly white community]—I would ask to be put in Watts, because me and the brothers are together down there. All it takes is a little common sense and a little bit of understanding, man. I think we should get enough brothers who think the same way on the police force.

Now, if I was to come across somebody that was holding some marijuana, and I found it, I would shine it on. Marijuana is a part of Mother Nature. If a brother wants it, that's the brother's bag. Now if I knew that you was dealing in marijuana, I'd know there was a reason, I know that you have to survive, I know you have to have a steady income every week because you have to live, and if I was a police officer, I would shine you on, but if you was dealing with pills or something that you might kill somebody or might slip some kind of poison in the pill or capsule, that's different. But I can't see turning no brother in for smoking no bush, man.

You can't tell me to live by the white man's law. You are entitled to freedom. If you can get your grass, smoke it in your house, it's cool. I figure that a policeman has no right at all, not even with a secret indictment, to come into your pad, your private belongings, things that you've never shown people before, things that you keep to yourself, and avail it to the public, which would be the grand jury and a court trial. I feel that the policeman today is not doing his job. I feel that if the community and the police got together and talked about different situations, as far as robbing is concerned or police brutality is concerned, disrespect for the police, it would be a more easy life to live. See, black peoples aren't dumb. We are tired. We are tired of doing things on a list. We've been accepting things for a long time. We have to go to work every day, read off the list, do it. We want to set up our own industry. We want to conform only to ourselves. Whitey can come to us. Ask us things about our own culture. The only way they will find out about us is to ask someone of our breed, but they don't do this.

Earl: The policeman is under oath. You still got to take an oath, this is your job. O.K., so you come across one or two friends, maybe [they] have a kilo of marijuana. What would you do? You got to do your job; [otherwise] you'd be an accessory to the crime.

If they really wanted to stop production of marijuana, they could. Marijuana is hazardous to your health, in the medical field. You may have resistance, but it still endangers your health from the git-go. And it no longer becomes private when you are involving someone besides yourself. Therefore, that gives [the policeman] the right to walk into your pad with that secret indictment. He is supposed to be protecting the public. If he is wrong, then it should be clarified in court.

I would try to understand that people on the street are individuals just like myself. Yet and still I am there to do a job according to these laws, not according to the way I feel, but according to the way the establishment likes them done. It all gets back to self-preservation, man, you can't start thinking about that other man first. Remember you got to live. You gotta go through all this training, you gotta make that living, you have a family you have to support, you are gonna need that money. You are pledged to uphold the law. When you start going these other ways, you are not upholding the law. If the police busted you for something you are doing wrong, they are protecting people.

Ray: As long as a person can do anything in moderation, without causing confusion and chaos, bodily harm, or doing harm to anybody else, [it should be O.K.]. But if it weren't for the police, all these crazy people would have guns and, like, one in every twenty people are going to be insane and you might run into one of them. So we need some sort of force to control it. But, of course, they don't arrest you for what you are doing but what you are *caught* doing.

Eric: My interpretation is that I would confront you in a manner where I would respect you and you would respect me. Try to reach an understanding. I would try to understand a person as an individual.

Of course, if there is money in the community, that makes a difference. We object to the individual [cop] when he confronts you doing the job, but if he confronts you as if you were a human being, as if you were intelligent and on the same level as he was, like you're respectable, he'd still be doing his job and he would have his job.

Wally: You can say you want to be with the bloods in Watts. But you know they are always going to put a white man next to you. (*To Eric*:) See, when that Negro cop confronted you, he was showing off to that white man, he was going to be the first one to confront you.

Just remember that everybody suffers if you let a person get away with things. People everywhere know their own area. If I was the police and I saw someone doing something, it is my right as an officer to protect the public. Like, little black kids see someone walking down the street smoking weed.

David: Just because I'm your friend and you are a police officer don't mean you should let me go all the motherfuckin' time, when you know that I haven't graduated out of high school and you swear every day: "I wish my people would go to school and get an education and beat that white man in his own game." Don't ever let me catch you [if I ever become a policeman] doing it to a high school student.

Now I don't mind a kid getting high on weekends, on Friday or Saturday night, but don't get high when you have to get that motherfuckin' education and read those books, because you know what you are there for. Now with me, I feel there is a certain amount of narcotics you gotta have before I'll take you to jail, but if I had any idea that you were fuckin' around selling to those high school kids during school days or school hours, I might let you go one time if I was by myself, I'm gonna tell you one time don't sell it to them but if I ever caught you again, the second time I'll bust you.

When you become a police officer, as far as I am concerned, you don't use what I call intelligence. I am going to take you to jail for what the people want you to go to jail for. Don't make a damn what *I* want you to go to jail for—it's what *they* want you to go to jail for.

Now, if [a cat is] dirty and you busted him [on Central Avenue], the man will never forget you: one, you are a nigger; two, he don't mind going to jail for something he done; three, it is better for you to bust him than for a white man to bust him; four, he'll know that when you take him to jail, you'll want that motherfucker to learn not to carry that shit on him. There is a place to use it and there is a place to hide it. That's the way every one of them motherfuckers down there feel. If I am wrong, I deserve to be punished. Because in the future, I might hurt somebody that I don't want to hurt. You ask any nigger that's up in age, does he actually mind, deep down in his heart, going to jail for something that he actually done. My point is that there is a time to bust a cat and there is a time not to bust a cat. We don't have a jail of our own. We don't have a country of our own. Therefore, we can't put him in our jail, so we got to put him in the white man's jail that we paid for.

A Young Adult (March, 1969):   The police really put you in the same old bag. I got picked up on Thursday night. I'd been up on 103rd and when I got back to the pad and walked through the gate and got inside my house, the police officers came. One car in front and one in the alley, so I couldn't get out the back. Man, those police officers, they's sly, sly, sly, they get away with stuff now they never got away with before. They can come into your house without a search warrant. They knock on your door and you let 'em in, they can come in and then they can arrest you. That's what happened to me. They just came to the door and knocked and they *said* they heard somebody say, "Come in." That's their game—they say somebody asked us to come in, we didn't have to search for you. You was there. They asked me if I was _____ and they says, "Step outside." So I stepped outside and he says, "You are under arrest." And I says, "I'm under arrest for what?" He says, "Robbery." So he took me to 77th [Precinct]. So I get down there and the first thing the man asked me is, "Where's the money? And where's the gun?" And I don't know what he is talking about because I ain't robbed nobody.

So I go through all kinds of changes. I get a toothache and they take me downtown to the glass house [Police Headquarters]. And don't think the LAPD had forgotten the 1965 revolt because this is the only thing I hear when I go back to the jail every time— all about the revolt. There was supposed to be a sick boy there and the police officers come in there and take him down and beat his ass. They gave me some aspirin and sent me over to the [new] County Jail and then cut me loose on Tuesday morning. They never did have evidence on me.

See, when you get picked up on suspicion, suspicion of burglary, suspicion of robbery, these are all felonies. Then nobody like to hire you. You take nine times out of ten, why should the companies take a chance on it.

And they're still doing this same old dirty thing about stopping your car just because you are riding in the street at one o'clock in the morning. They stop your car just 'cause they feel like stopping it. Yeah, and they'll swear up and down you stole it. Last time that happened to me was Sunday night. We was coming back from Hollywood—you know, the skating place over there. It was me and a couple other of my partners, and my brother, and a couple of girls. And we was riding along on the Harbor Freeway O.K. and we get off at Century and went over to Watts and here they come. And they done got sneaky: they don't have those old black-and-white suspicious looking cars, they got plain ones and they're plainclothes. Well, they just stopped us on suspicion. They said we changed lanes so many times on the freeway, so the police stopped us on that. That's what they said anyway. They just came up right behind us and stopped us. They got one of those funny-sounding sirens.

They should be more educated, more intelligent about how they bust you. They been having this game for so long, it's old. So they told _____ to get out of the car. So now they told everybody else to get out of the car. See, the car is kind of a halfway "low rider," so they think it's got to be narcotics or something. Or it might be stolen.

I know I got warrants out against me, so I say: "What'd you stop us for? What for, man?" Yeah, I say to the cop, "This man _____ is driving. If he's done anything wrong, give him a ticket. You're not supposed to have everybody out of the car. If he's done anything wrong, give him a ticket." He says, "Look, we have all the authority to stop you if we feel like it. We can take you all in if we feel like it." He says, "If you don't believe me, just keep talking." So I shut up. And then he asked me for my identification and I showed it to him: he told me to take it out of my wallet and I took it out. Then they just opened up the trunk and looked all around the car, took out the back seat, looked all over the glove compartment, raked all the trash on the floor. He says, "You got any guns or knives?" I said, "No, no we don't."

Then they searched everybody down. Yeah, they got a new way of searching everybody—they got a new law. You stand up and cross your legs, like this, and your hand behind your head, and now they got another way where they makes you get on the floor, or on the curb, and cross your legs. Man, you can't do nothing then 'cause that aching hurts you so much. And when they puts hand-cuffs on you back there, it's all over, you can't do nothing.

They were just young punks, white guys. They say to the girl, "Come here, baby. Ain't you a CAP?"[3] You know why they pull shit like that? Because their partners have told them about the girls late at night, "That stuff's pretty good." This is one place where I agree with the Black Panthers [about police practices]; the violent part I don't agree with.

Another Young Adult (1969): Things haven't changed really, in law enforcement. The harassment used to be consistent; now, when the tensions are down they harass people, but when the tensions are up they don't harass. Now it's sporadic.

Their so-called "community relations" aren't really relating, not at all to the community in itself. People in the community still feel the police are *harassing*. I don't think the atmosphere with the

---

[3] CAP stands for Community Alert Patrol, an organization which checks on police practices.

policemen really has changed. In fact, the people are more severe toward the police department now because they know the department hasn't changed. I read about some program somewhere where they were teaching the police black history so they'd have a clearer understanding of the black community, but even the attitude of the community toward the black policemen is still the same. And until the situation in the black community is changed, the attitudes will be about the same.

I have a scale for policemen. The so-called rookie, what I call the rookie pig, is at the top of the scale [in harassment]; he's doing this to get experience, he's learning how to harass people. The Los Angeles Police Department is at the top in over-harassment. I don't know whether they hire people from the South or whatever, but they harass you more.

I think, in one way, the people are more afraid of the Sheriff's Department, because they don't harass you; the only time they mess with you is when you're doing something wrong, and people are afraid because the Sheriff's Department is more likely to shoot you. It's pretty much the same with the Highway Patrol.

In the revolt of 1965, I think it was just the idea of a policeman, period. I don't think it mattered if it was Highway Patrol or Sheriff or what. Anyone with a uniform on.

[Some liquor stores in Watts have private "security police," always Negroes, stationed in the store, especially on check-cashing days.]

Joe: This one security cop, he ain't got no more position than I have, ain't no better than I am. The cops drink more whisky, drink more of the whisky than they sell, so he drinks it up, he just drinks it up, he gets drunk . . . and then this dude comes calling me "boy." Walking all over the top of the roof with shotguns and things, they walk all around, all up and down aisles, pushing everybody out of the way, "Come on, get off to the side." What kind of shit is that?

Joe and *Earl*: Getting back to the regular police, I'll cooperate with them if I see somebody killing somebody, I'll turn them in myself. . . . Right, if I see somebody jump on somebody's mama, I'll tell them about it. If I see somebody jump on somebody and beat him halfway to death, I'll tell somebody. . . . I'll abide by the law. Just don't do me, you know.

VI

Pot and Pills

Repeal of the laws which now make tthe possession and use of marijuana a criminal offense would automatically eliminate a high percentage of the "crime" which occurs within the slum ghetto. The
smoking of "pot" (also called "weed" or "grass") seems at least as
common in Watts as is the consumption of alcohol in the higher-
income suburbs. Almost without exception, the young "dudes" will
get an occasional or regular high on marijuana or pills; the older
people probably do not use drugs with such frequency, but no one
can be certain about percentages in this field.

Federal and state laws define marijuana as a narcotic, thus
putting it in the same legal category as heroin ("horse" or "smack")
and morphine. Its possession and use are classified as felonies, and
the offender is subject to a prison term if convicted.[1] The pills (for
example, barbiturates) are designated only as dangerous drugs,
a category of less significance in terms of legal penalties. In mid-
1968, the use of LSD ("acid") was similarly categorized as a misdemeanor, an irony in view of the overwhelming, expert opinion
that LSD is relatively more dangerous to the user than is marijuana.
The evidence so far is that LSD remains predominantly a white,
intellectual, or hippie fad, not generally popular in the ghetto.

In my experience at least, it appears that only a small percentage of the young people who use marijuana ever venture further
into the use of dangerous narcotics such as heroin. Most youngsters
are satisfied with the high they get from pot or "Red Devils" (pills

---

[1] Legislation changing the penalties for first-offense possession of marijuana,
allowing judges the discretion to treat it *either* as a felony or a misdemeanor,
has recently been enacted by the State Legislature.

that get their name from the color of the capsules), and are properly fearful of the effects of using expensive dope and LSD. However, they are enthusiastic about marijuana, strongly rebutting the standard, middle-class, moralistic, and psychiatric arguments against its use.

Pot-smoking and pill-taking have become increasingly widespread outside the ghetto, and a college campus in any urban area may have as high a proportion of occasional users as does the Watts community. The difference, of course, is that the ghetto user is more vulnerable to police interrogation and arrest. The resulting record will identify him as a narcotics offender, the most serious and least forgivable offense from the viewpoint of most employers. Failure to obtain regular employment may induce him to become a pusher, a route on which many youngsters have already embarked.

To an observer, the pervasiveness of pot-smoking, and the depth of the commitment to it, seem particularly strange. The penalties for its use are severe, and the youngsters seem to be challenging the law of averages. Drinking alcohol, on the other hand, carries no automatic penalty, and it also produces a "high." The young people are maximizing their risks, which is precisely the psychology at work. At one point a youngster suggested to me that the title of this book should be: *Watts: The Risk and the Challenge.* "Risk" and "challenge" are welcomed by the youngsters: facing and accepting heavy risks is part of the manhood test which each one undergoes. In this sense, the Watts resident is not much different from the equally rebellious youngster in the suburbs who burns draft cards, joins demonstrations, defies the police, and also smokes pot. But there *is* one significant difference: the suburban rebel has more escape routes and more alternatives. Usually he can return to middle-class status if he chooses, and he is not ghettoized.

The element of risk and defiance in pot-smoking probably increases its attraction for many of the youngsters, in Watts and in Westwood alike. It expresses their distaste for the moral double standards and hypocrisy of the dominant society and seals their kinship with, and acceptance by, their peers. The Watts youngster is typically gregarious, and this may be one factor inhibiting his ability to break loose from the streets and settle down to a regular job. He will miss the companionship of those with whom he has grown up and with whom he shares feelings and experiences. A job, especially one in a place run or populated mainly by whites, may isolate him and restrict his opportunity to "have fun." "Getting high," "having fun," and "grooving" are important to the kids, and the pressures associated with being black and ghettoized in a white, middle-class society give these escapes a disproportionate role in their lives. On the other hand, a youngster will often remark that he has little chance of "getting himself together" as long as he stays in the same environment.

Whenever their interests and motivation are triggered, the Watts youngsters perform with a flair and a perfectionism which is uniquely their own. Everything is pushed to a dramatic extreme, whether it is driving a car, groovin' in a soul session, giving a theatrical performance, playing pool or dominoes, deceiving the police, or getting high. Football, boxing, and basketball are performed with a competitiveness that defies description. They are at their best when their creativeness is challenged, when they can improvise and not merely follow established rules or routines. But these very traits become liabilities in the structured and rule-ridden environment of American business, government, and education.

Their defense of pot-smoking is vigorous and eloquent, but it contains inconsistencies. To the question of whether "weed" improves or weakens their motivation to escape slum-ghetto living and realize their potentialities, they alternately respond that it helps them to adjust to things as they are and that it strengthens their will and confidence to accept new experiences. They insist that "weed" helps their performance in athletic events and on other occasions, an insistence which seems to run counter to some research findings that pot-smoking reduces coordination. Much probably depends on the quantity and quality of the "weed" in relation to the capacity and psychological make-up of the individual, precisely as the effect of alcohol varies according to the same factors.

The legal penalties attached to possible self-incrimination are of such magnitude that candor in discussing the subject deserves to be tempered with prudence. The speakers are nowhere identified, and the transcript has been revised and rearranged so that not even the editor can identify the precise source of any given statement.

Three Teen-Agers: Practically everybody we know uses marijuana. As for pills, like Red Devils, I think there is a limitation: a lot of people don't like the sluggish high you get from pills, because pills make you act crazy. . . . It all depends on the person. A lot of people can take a couple of good drinks of Scotch and won't feel nothing; a lot of people can't take three Red Devils, and other people will get hooked, like, you know, they take nine or ten a day. LSD is for the Caucasians; we don't trip on acid, too deep, too deep. You do find a few people who shoot "smack."

Most people like pot better than alcohol because . . . they get plenty high drinking alcohol, but then that hangover, your head be hurting when you wake up. . . . You get high from marijuana, but you won't be something like a demon, loud-talking, cursing, want to fight, and all that, man, you won't be doing that.

Actually, if a person gets to tripping real hard, you can't tell if he is on marijuana or not; he will be laughing, he's talking, acting funny. The effect depends on the quality: if it's good, you can take just half a one and get a high; but if it's bad, then eight or nine or ten of them, man. You can brew your own: You can make it bad [in this context, "bad" probably means "good"], pour a little vodka on it, and a little gin . . . put it on top of the roof, let the sun hit it for three or four days, bake it, and bring it down, roll it up, and you kill yourself.

You won't go out and start a fire or nothing. It broadens your mind, and it makes you more aware of your surroundings; that's all. . . . It makes you want to be happy, to be gay. You like to trip out for yourself, you're right to have a nice time, and it's good for sex. . . . That's why some trip when the girls are around. And marijuana makes your appetite expand.

If marijuana were made legal, people wouldn't use more of it. That [legalizing it] wouldn't be as much fun; no, it wouldn't be as much fun. It's more attractive when you are fooling the police to get it.

Just like drinking, when alcohol first came about, it was illegal; all right, you get these bootleggers, people done it; all right, people don't take as much as when it were illegal. Now it's sociable like, you know; now they'll be drinking just to have a good time.

See, it costs about fifty cents a joint, a stick, and you can get a matchbox for $3.50; $7.50 for half a can, $10 for a bag, people refer to it as a lid; a can for $15, and then you go into your half a pound. You know, I heard up in San Francisco they give Blue Chip stamps with the stuff.

I remember the first time when I got high. When I first took it, it was rather strong, and I had to get adjusted to this feeling in my throat, and when I had finished the joint and I stood up, I was taller, you know, and I got to walking, I wasn't even on the ground. Then someone could be talking to you, you couldn't hear him.

I'll tell you, you never get a high like the high you get the first time; you never get that high; you always get a different high. It's the greatest thing in your life; it's the greatest thing.

The high is different because the world . . . always changes, and it only makes you more aware of what is happening. But even if you lay off it for awhile, you never get that first high again.

A Teen-Ager: Take me, I smoke half a joint lots of times, and it don't do that much to me; it all depends on the weed. You could be getting high, he might be getting high; he might be mad about something, and I start laughing at him, you know, trip him out, and he starts laughing, and then all of us start laughing. . . . Everything is just fun. But the best high you can get is when everybody is sitting around, you have some jazz on, something comes on that everybody digs, then you go from that, and everybody's tripping, and it be long, and slow . . . and it be like the record never be over with. And sometimes you put a record on, a 45, and it will go so quick you won't even believe your ears.

See, there's no true time either, you never in a hurry unless you . . . takes some bennies, some pep pills, and then everything's going faster, you'll always be wanting to be on the go. You can drink and smoke at the same time, and that's what you call a mellow high. Like, you get a bottle of Ripple [wine], smoke one joint, and drop in one Red Devil, and, boy, you feel as though you bounce; you feel as though you were to walk on the clouds. You know, you staggering, staggering, and everybody you see, "What's happening, man?" You get off in a big bag, and [in sports] you feel you can jump about eight feet high, break world's records; you tripping, man.

Two Teen-Agers: And probably you heard there are a lot of great musicians, jazz musicians, and sportsmen, that takes the stuff. You are thinking better, it will make you act better. You'll be released, man, you'll be released. You accept all your problems you have. . . . You can get off into a righteous bag, you can adjust yourself to any kind of problem. It makes you get away from this, from, like, you don't think about, "Well, I am poor, I ain't got nothing, I ain't going to do nothing." It makes you happy, makes you forget all the bad things. . . . It will get your mind off a lot of things. . . . Like, if you need a pair of shoes, you smoke a joint, you don't even worry about that, [but] if you don't have a joint, then your mind is stimulated to take the shoes away from somebody.

But you are not making people give up [as some of the psychiatrists say about the use of marijuana]. It's just making people more aware of what you are, more aware of the world, making them face reality, the challenge of living, of everyday life. And this makes you more aware of this challenge. It opens your mind to a sense where you feel as though you can accomplish this.

Like, you might not feel like going to work in the morning. You get up, and smoke a joint, you go to work in time. We will buy some any time we can get it and have the bread. Like, say today is Thursday and tomorrow night is the party. I might not get high Thursday, and Friday, I might get high all day Friday, and all night Friday night. Now, being high all day Friday, I'm going to have me a good time Friday night. You can go to a dull party, and you would bring the light. You can be the comedy, you can be the spotlight of the show. Just like in a football game: you get a joint, you smoke marijuana, you quiver, you get down, the ball is in your hand, you runs, you don't know how you got it, but that ball is in your hand. You running over everybody.

It will make an older man feel younger. Yes, it makes him want to tap his feet. It makes a young man want to be older, you look at things as they should be every day. . . . He faces what normally he should face every day, but he close it out . . . because like he has a challenge, "How am I going to overcome this, how am I going to overcome that?" All the time, he can overcome it, if he really get out and try, but there is that certain thing lacking, and [if] he went out and smoked marijuana, I mean it brings that life to reality, and you can see that there is something lacking, and really get out and do something about it.

But, using marijuana, you can adjust to anything that comes to you. . . . It lets you get away from your everyday environment off into another environment; like, say you're used to be down digging in Watts, and let's say you go to a different environment, in your mind you want to adjust to the new environment, yet you feel there is something that is not there. Like you go the west side, and homes that you normally do not see, and you are nervous, you don't know how to adjust yourself. "What am I going to do first?" Marijuana helps you.

It's a very weak person that goes from marijuana to smack; this is something that God wanted him to do, or something he wanted to do himself, because marijuana . . . would not influence you to do anything that you don't normally want to do. You're just yourself, only more gay, more happier, more satisfied with life as it is.

It doesn't affect your driving. . . . You will be more aware, more careful. . . . You can hear clear, you can see better, you can talk better, you can feel better, or anything. People who criticize marijuana are lying because they do not know what they are talking about. I know people that have been smoking marijuana ever since they were ten or twelve years old, and here they are now gray in the head, here they are forty-five, fifty-five years old, and still smoking every day, and never had to go to the doctor. All they had to do is to get a tooth pulled out, from eating them sweets, that's all.

A Young Adult: No one can stop Mother Nature. If you see some-body doing something like smoking pot in front of people that you don't think knows what's going on, then you have the authority— and this is the only authority you have—to come to them and tell them, "Look here, you are wrong." But you don't have the author-ity to put them in custody from the git-go. With marijuana, some people just happen to stumble upon it and it happens and they think it is groovy.

Marijuana can't hurt you. I've been getting high for seven years and ain't nothing happened to me yet. I breathe the same and ev-erything. Now if you are a beginner—at first I thought I was see-ing four things at one time, but after I got to realize it was not but a mere hallucination, something [that] was taking place for a lit-tle while, I accepted it and I learned to cope with it. Man, marijua-na is a beautiful thing. It relieves you of tension and you can't say there is not tension out here, man. You don't have to drop no Red Devils, you don't have to shoot no heroin. You tell me any way that the production of [marijuana] can be stopped and I will cease my conversation.

Sometimes, you know, there is a lot of cocaine-sniffing out there, too, and other things that people might get high on. Okay, for in-stance, the people that have the money . . . to get marijuana. They are the ones that will buy the drug. The people . . . that can't get that little $3.50, or something like this, and they feel that one joint or two joints won't do them any good; well, they start going to any drugstore and get a bottle of Romilar cough syrup. Because if they drink Romilar cough syrup, at least half of the bottle, that'll send you up, too. It's a gas.

See, it's medicine; it's cough syrup for a cold; that has medi-cal value; they can't cut that out.

Grass really wires you up for work, man. I'd be at my work and everybody else is working, we're still looking for something else to do . . . but you wouldn't be messing with nobody. It has made me make new friends. It has made me talk to people that I wouldn't have nothing to do with.

But grass can encourage you to . . . take a drug that is more dangerous. . . . You can be sitting down in a house, getting load-

ed, and let's say you smoke some grass; let's say you've been smoking grass for quite some time. All right, after a while it seems like
"I just want to get higher." So you might decide, "Well, I am going
to try it [e.g., shooting 'smack'] one time," you know, you might
have some buddies that already do it.

Others: That's just you. Marijuana doesn't drive you into a bag
like that. That's just something in you.

The First Three: Hell, the Chinese was using opium. The Indians
use something [peyote] which is the same thing as weed, [but] they
have a stronger quality.

Sure, weed won't change anything or get rid of the causes of
ghetto life. It just makes you more aware of the cause, more aware
of living in the ghetto. You never become unconcerned about your
life, and marijuana only makes you more aware, and . . . makes you
face that challenge. You see the picture better: because of true
focus, it is perfectly centered, but when you are not under the
influence, the picture is foggy.

Like, say, your kids don't have shoes to wear, your kids don't
have food to eat, you know you need this, you know you need that,
and . . . that will cause a person to go out and steal and rob, because
a person will have the feeling, "What am I going to do?" then your
mind began to drift, and then you figure, "Oh, maybe I can go over
here and take this, beat this chump out of some money." But you
got marijuana, and it makes you think, "Well, I can go over here
to the County aid office and get some money. I don't have to have
all this here, I don't have to take all this, I don't have to lay up in
this house and take all this here business." You can go over here
and ask somebody. Normally he would feel ashamed.

You don't even have to have money to get marijuana. You can
walk out through the alley and see a plant growing, just wild, waiting, that's right in Watts.

Or somebody might put in $5, maybe someone else $1, you
put in a quarter, and you get a bag for $5 or $10. That bag will last
two or three weeks, divided over everybody equally. . . . Friday
and Saturday night, everybody got their poverty money in their
pocket, everybody got $1.27-an-hour check, you understand, they
can buy a can of beer, and other stuff. So you will all get together,
and have a party, and get high.

In the summer of 1966, about two dozen teen-agers from the
Watts area came to UCLA for an informal discussion of "narcot-

ics." Some of their individual or collective observations are print-
ed below to permit a comparison with the views expressed by other
young people in the previous pages of this chapter.

It's true that there is a lot of pushing of Red Devils and marijuana at the high school. Some students come to school with no inten-
tion to learn but simply bring Red Devils and other stuff and deal
them out in the school. The school authorities know about it, but
most people who are caught don't give away any information about
the big dealers.

I don't see why marijuana should not be legalized. Alcohol is worse
than marijuana. Legalize it with control, like alcohol. Most people
take marijuana because it is a different kind of high. It is not as
dirty as drinking. Many don't want to go through the hassle of swal-
lowing alcohol. It is better than cheap wine. Cheap wine is bad for
your whole body.

You forget your worries. It is one way to have fun without spending too much money. Every weekday you get up early to go to school
and do what you should; when weekend comes, you want some re-
laxation.

Marijuana just makes you enjoy life better. You can still do what
you should, only every time you open your eyes, everything is more
beautiful. Sometimes your speech is effected, as though your tongue
is too big. When you are high on marijuana, you are more careful,
for example, about driving, because you don't want to get caught.

To take marijuana is not to get away from your problems, but
just to enjoy yourself. A lot of times, there is nothing else to do.
Marijuana brings out what you want to be. For example, often you
are shy; by taking marijuana you are not shy any more.

[If you want to outlaw things like marijuana and alcohol] then you
will have to change the whole civilized world, for in this world, drinking is a social custom. Can you pull the real change? I think it is
too late to change the society. In America, we started wrong. We
have a certain age for drinking, a certain age for smoking. In Europe,
everything is open, and people don't get drunk as we do.

In other words, if you put these things where you can get them,
you may not want them as much. Marijuana only gives people a
good time. You cannot wait for the world to be perfect to have a
good time. Sometimes some people need something like marijuana
to help them to struggle in life so they eventually may succeed.

VII

The Schools

One senior high school—David Starr Jordan—and two junior high schools—Edwin Markham and Samuel Gompers—enroll the teen-agers of Watts, and nine elementary schools serve the younger children. A short distance to the west, a brand new senior high school, Alain Locke, has now risen. The racial composition of these schools is typical of the pattern in all of the south central ghetto schools: the student body is overwhelmingly Negro, with a small percentage of Mexican-Americans. Jordan has been the focus of bitter controversy in recent years, for it is situated on the eastern boundary of the ghetto (surrounded by junkyards and industrial plants which produce a never-ceasing din), within a few yards of the lily-white community of South Gate. In the early 1960's, a few token students from the Watts area "integrated" South Gate High School for the first time, and some were taunted and pelted with eggs. Despite the aggressive efforts of the American Civil Liberties Union and other organizations, *de facto* segregation was probably as pervasive in the Los Angeles city schools in 1967 as it was ten years earlier. There are, of course, notable exceptions: a private organization led by the wife of actor Burt Lancaster has arranged transportation to bring youngsters from the middle-class Negro ghetto to elementary schools located in posh Bel Air and other west side areas, and a few other non-ghetto schools enroll varying percentages of Negroes.

The outstanding result of recent "civil rights" activity in the educational field has been an improvement in the facilities of schools within the ghetto. Jordan High School, for instance, has obtained a new auditorium and other physical benefits, and a new junior college serving south Los Angeles has been constructed on Impe-

165

rial a few miles to the west of Watts. The faculties are integrated, but Anglos remain in the majority.

Representatives of the black community and the school bureaucracy continue to debate the question of whether an excessive number of inexperienced or otherwise inferior teachers are assigned to ghetto-area schools. The statistics are confusing at best, but there can be little doubt that the quality of education received by Negroes is substandard compared to that offered to white, middle-class youngsters in western Los Angeles or the San Fernando Valley. About half of the tenth-grade entering class at Jordan will drop out.

Both the youngsters and the adults are resentful of the differences they perceive, and their perceptions are remarkable. They readily detect the subtleties in teachers' attitudes and expectations, even when they have had little chance to directly observe conditions in white schools. They feel that most teachers and administrators in the ghetto have little confidence in the potentials of their pupils unless and until the youngsters become carbon copies of the average, white, middle-class child. The schools, with their endless regulations on haircuts, dress styles, and appearance, are insensitive to the emotional needs of the youngsters and the growing sense of racial pride.

A persistent theme expressed by the residents is the demand for greater community participation and influence in the educational process. The adults, in particular, are not unaware of some of the special problems any school will encounter in a low-income ghetto, and they seem reasonably objective about the home-environment deficiencies which will destroy a youngster's motivation. Even so, they judge the schools harshly, detecting a failure, perhaps an unwillingness, to build a rapport with the students as a group and with the wider community. The assumption that greater community control over school affairs is the answer may turn out to be oversimplified, but it is commonly expressed and is already being tested in the city of New York, with the support of the Ford Foundation.[1]

"Community control" hardly constitutes a panacea. The complexities of financing, curriculum development, teacher training and recruitment, morale, and administration will not vanish in a decentralized system. Indeed, in some cases, like financing, they

---

[1] There has been, however, a great deal of difficulty over decentralization in New York. The long teachers' strike in the fall of 1968 was a direct result of the clash between the professionals in the educational system and the residents of the ghetto. Feeling still runs high at the present writing.

may even become more difficult. The advantage of decentralization lies in the process itself, which can give the community some
sense of participation, power, and responsibility. Christopher Jencks
observes that while there is no evidence that "community control"
will solve the inner city's educational problems, it will at least cool
the tensions.

> So long as militant blacks believe they are the victims of a
> conspiracy to keep their children stupid — and therefore subser-
> vient — the political problem will remain insoluble. But if we
> encourage and assist black parents with such suspicions to
> set up their own schools, we may be able to avert disaster.
> These schools would not, I predict, be either more or less
> successful than existing public schools in teaching the three
> R's. But that is not the point. The point is to find a political
> *modus vivendi* which is tolerable to all sides.
> The development of an independent black school system
> would not solve the problems of black children. I doubt, for
> example, that many black private schools could teach their
> children to read appreciably better than white-controlled pub-
> lic schools now do. But such schools would be an important
> instrument in the hands of black leaders who want to devel-
> op a sense of community solidarity and pride in the ghetto,
> just as the parochial schools have worked for similarly placed
> Catholics.[2]

Unlike the prevailing system, decentralization offers some
latitude for innovation and for a broader insight into the needs and
problems of the community. Its real merit has been suggested by
Rhody McCoy, administrator of New York's decentralized Ocean
Hill-Brownsville school district: "Everything else has failed. We
want the right to fail for ourselves."[3]

However ironical it may appear on the surface, it is natural that
the demands for decentralization will be opposed with some vehe-
mence by many of the "old radicals" — the trade unionists and the
veterans of the struggles of the 1930's and 1940's. Their accom-
plishments are reflected in the elaborate rules and "due process" of
the collective bargaining contract, the seniority lines, and the grievance procedures, all of which protect the tenure of the members
of the system. Their economic security is precisely what the move-

---

[2] "Private Schools for Black Children," *The New York Times Magazine*,
November 3, 1968.

[3] Wallace Roberts, "The Battle for Urban Schools," *Saturday Review*, November 16, 1968, p. 117.

ment for community control and innovation directly threatens. The major obstruction to the new movement is the experienced professional, whether in white- or blue-collar, who has been locked into a position of power. He is protected, often by the fruits of an earlier radicalism, and his security is inconsistent with change and reform.

Any close observer of big-city institutions can detect the depth of the professionals' power and the strength of their capacity for survival. Sheltered by seniority, comfortable in a familiar pattern, they can be found in key positions of influence throughout the schools, the police departments, the welfare agencies, and the other vital public institutions. The changing tides of politics, or a different school board, or a new police chief seldom affect them. Civil service, or "tenure," or union rules, have built an impenetrable wall around their jobs.

It is, perhaps, too tempting and too easy merely to condemn the system which protects them. "Due process" can only be expressed in rules and procedures, which are at once the essence of bureaucracy and the heart of civil liberties. The alternative, clearly, is the arbitrary and even capricious exercise of power by a government or an employer. The difficulty is that those outside the "system" can hardly respect a process from whose benefits they have been excluded. The case of the professionals for "due process" in the local schools will be meaningful only in the degree that they have themselves accorded full protection to the rights and prerogatives of the students and the parents. As the experiences depicted in this chapter illustrate, the teachers and the administrators rarely grant "due process" to a youngster accused of disciplinary infractions or misbehavior of any kind. If they are inclined to respond that they could not otherwise run an effective class or school, the community can logically rejoin that, in like measure, it cannot get the quality of teaching and administration it seeks when it is prevented from displacing the professionals who are the source of the deficiencies. What is sauce for the teacher or vice-principal would also appear to be sauce for the community.

One concrete result of discontent with the public schools is a movement to construct a new unofficial school system outside the jurisdiction of the local Board of Education. Most vocational training programs in the south central area offer remedial courses; community organizations and college students administer tutorial projects; militant groups sponsor "Liberation Schools" to teach black history and other subjects; and in 1968 the Los Ange-

les Urban League unsuccessfully tried to develop "Street Academies," modeled after such a program in New York City, which enlist
school dropouts and pushouts and other ghetto youngsters and
offer courses or counseling designed to meet their special needs.

In late September, 1968, a group in Los Angeles announced
the formation of a Black Community Local Board of Education,
because, it said, the city school system "has failed to educate our
children and to erase the blight of racism. . . ." The entirely private
Board will represent those in the black community who are dissat-
isfied with educational policies and seek greater recognition for community demands. Its major sponsors have been a thorn in the side
of school administrators for over a year, generating some turmoil
at Manual Arts High School in the western part of the ghetto and
causing the reassignment of Manual Arts' principal. Late in 1968,
after student strikes and much pressure, the Board of Education
named a black in place of a white as principal of all-Negro Fremont
High School. Community agitation had earlier been responsible
for the assignment of a black as principal of Jefferson High School,
another ghetto school. In early 1969 more student strikes and boy-
cotts hit many of the ghetto schools, in protest against school policies and, especially, the activity of police on campus in certain
cases. Ironically, the discontent has spread to the normally quies-
cent Mexican-American community, and some of the most vigorous attacks on prevailing school policies are coming from that quarter.

Even the McCone Commission report, a modest and moderate document issued by the governor's special riot investigating
commission in late 1965, leveled a strong criticism at the school
system:

> The schools in the disadvantaged areas do not provide a
> program that meets the unique educational needs of culturally
> disadvantaged children. Although special remedial programs
> are offered in an attempt to compensate for deficiencies in learn-
> ing, the *basic* organization and orientation of schools is the
> same in advantaged and disadvantaged areas. The same ed-
> ucational program for children of unequal background does
> not provide an equal opportunity for children to learn. (p. 58.)

In the following section, several teen-agers and adults give
their own spontaneous impressions of the local school system, and
indicate the sources of their discontent. Most of their comments
were made in 1966 and 1967 and there have been some administra-

tive and personnel changes since, but my observations suggest that nothing fundamentally has changed. In some cases I cannot corroborate their criticisms on the basis of personal knowledge, but for the most part, I can confirm that what they say is true.

Richard Townsend and William Armstead, each sixteen, offer a pre-riot description of educational problems in Watts.

There are, for the most part, two junior high schools, Edwin Markham and Samuel Gompers, and one high school, David Starr Jordan, serving the community of Watts as institutions for secondary education. Unfortunately too many students do not realize how important it is to receive this secondary education. For various reasons they become uninterested in learning through school and sooner or later they become what is now known as the "high school dropout." It is true, however, that a small percentage of them incur various problems, generally pertaining to the family, and use this as an excuse, one which is accepted by most schools, to end their formal education. Too many students make up excuses just to put an end to what they might describe as a rather boring and worthless experience. The reasons for this disinterest in the student usually begin in the home. There are many possible reasons for this:

1. Too often parents find themselves so busy and so involved in everything else that they give only little, if any, time and attention to their children. The child usually finds himself in a lonely little world of his own, searching and reaching out for something, anything, to compensate for it. School and his studies usually are not his compensation.

2. Many parents pretend to be interested. These are the ones who take a passive part in their child's education. They tend to give encouragement by mild conversation and are reluctant to do anything more, but some students need more than this. These parents take education too lightly.

3. Going from one extreme (statement #1) to another, there are those parents who are too harsh. By harsh we don't mean that too much emphasis is placed on education, but instead that the emphasis is in the wrong manner. If students, or anyone as far as this is concerned, are given the strong feeling that they are being forced to do something, some kind of a revolt is bound to take place. Family problems will probably result and it is likely that pretty soon the student will become discouraged and drop out of school.

4. In many cases broken homes or large families are factors that lead up to disinterest. There are many times when par-

ents have so many children that they can't give the proper time to each. This is often the case when one will use the financial excuse in order to drop out of school.

5. The female populace of the high school dropouts usually drops out because of pregnancy. This also usually stems from uninterested parents who are too harsh. Uninterested parents usually have this attitude either because of their lack of educational attainment or because they just don't care. Others don't really realize the importance of receiving an education. . . .

Recently the high school dropout has become a major part of the unemployment problem of the nation. This is . . . very evident in Watts, a place where the majority of the population is made up of teen-agers and young adults. High school dropouts find it very difficult to get any kind of work, especially since most jobs nowadays require a high school diploma. Most of them become disappointed because of this difficulty and discontinue looking for employment. Another problem that a number of them face is that they are considered under age and not part of the labor force. All of these factors lead to juvenile delinquency and crime. Many of these delinquents will become the unwanted class of our society, namely, the criminals, habitual drunkards, hobos, etc. . . .

Some of the Watts youngsters, representing the range of academic achievement levels, reflect upon their own experiences in the classroom.

Jerry: The first school that I ever entered was Russell Elementary School, which is located on Manchester Avenue, right outside of the Watts area by the map, but as far as the people are concerned, it is in Watts. The second school that I attended was 102nd Street, which is located in Watts, we may say the main section of Watts. I graduated from 102nd in 1956, and attended Jordan High School in the seventh grade. After staying in Jordan a year, they opened up Markham Junior High; I attended there for two years, and graduated in 1959, and went to Jordan. I attended there for two years, three years, but you might say two; I skipped a grade. But I still didn't agree with the education that I was being taught, mainly because all my life since I was eight years old, I want to learn something about all people, not just one. As they tell me in the history book about way back in the sixteenth century about the Jews, the Caucasians, but they never mention anything about the Indians, or the black man's history. This is what I wanted to learn; I wanted to learn about everyone's history, not just one race.

When I was eight years old, I figured, well, out of all the books that I had read at that time, I was only learning about one race. But at that time I had stopped going to church at eight years old, the same way in school and in church. The Bible will tell you a certain amount. They say that God said this, God said that. Now, to my belief, I do not believe in the Bible, because it has been tampered with, as far as I am concerned. But I do believe there is a Supreme Being. This is just like a history book; that is all the Bible is; it will tell you what it wants you to know and no more. But I know that something had happened beyond the time that I learned out of this book. This is what I wanted to find out in life. What was it? What had been done before that time?

It seems as though it has started to improving just a little bit. They did bring in Negro history in 1964, but at the time I was in there, there were no improvements, no change in any kind of way. [The new book] is mainly on people who has contributed something: for instance, Sojourner Truth . . . Crispus Attucks, the first escaped Negro slave, a leader of the Boston patriots, he died, well, he died for freedom. . . . This is about mainly what they would put in there; what someone has contributed: like Jackie Robinson, first Negro professional baseball player . . . George Washington Carver . . . Booker T. Washington . . . Phyllis Wheatley . . . people like this. . . . But what about the rest of them; this is what I want to know. They told me as far back as the fifteenth century on the Caucasians; they didn't tell me back in fifteenth century on my people, when I know that . . . a person of a dark race was the first person on earth. I don't believe in the Bible, but this is what it says in the Bible. Tell me about him . . . don't just tell me about one.

Chuck and *Fred*: The names of Negroes that does something for the United States, has contributed something. This is what they teach you in Negro history. But all this is about the only kind of Negro history they would teach you, is what your mother, what our mothers and fathers, would tell us about. People that they heard had done something. As far as people that hadn't done that much, but they had contributed something, they don't mention them. They only mention the ones that white men are familiar with. . . .

As far as the good teacher is concerned, if you have a problem concerning something that you are doing, in a particular class, he sits down with you about five to fifteen minutes, and explains the problem to you and shows you how to do it so it can be done correctly. The bad teacher, now you ask him to explain a problem to

you, he doesn't have time, you know, he just writes up on the board
what you have to do, do it. That's it. He doesn't explain it to you.
This is what I feel. . . . I would say approximately twenty-five per
cent [of all teachers], they really care about a student. There *is* a lot
of teachers that shows favoritism.

Jerry: As much as I saw in the administration, it didn't matter
whether the teachers were white or Colored. They all got treated
the same way by the students. They all responded, they respected a Negro just as much as they respected a white; they respected the white just as much as they respected a Negro. . . . It is really a matter of love and understanding and patience.

    I don't have any observations about [teacher turnover and
qualifications], but I can say that I found out over the past years
that the teachers that do teach at Markham and Jordan are teachers that think they want to teach at these schools. They picked these
schools to teach at, but . . . some of them find out that "Well, maybe
I'm at the wrong school," and therefore they give them some kind
of transfer. But the ones who stayed there are the ones who want
to be there to help those kids . . . who really want to teach . . . and
you don't know who they are until they have been there a certain
period of time, to your own knowledge of how many years you think
they should be there.

    Many Americans are probably convinced that the typical class-
room in a ghetto school is a reflection of the "Blackboard Jungle,"
chaotic, undisciplined, even dangerous. Some of the teen-agers here
comment on the accuracy of this image; their impressions are not
wholly consistent with one another, but it would appear that the
problem is more likely to be apathy and frustration instead of aggressive hostility.

Jerry: The only time you get some mishaps in the classroom is
because the teacher brings it upon himself. I have been in many
classrooms, and I have never saw where the student just ups and
does anything wrong. Maybe a student might be trying to figure
a problem out, and the kid is just sitting there, just sitting there
trying to figure the problem out while the teacher is getting the
impression that he is not doing his work; therefore, the teacher will
go over and get on the person's back, and they [the teachers] don't
even understand why they [the students] are just sitting there. He
doesn't go, the instructor doesn't go over and ask them, "Do you

have a problem?" They would call you up to their desk and something and . . . send you to the referral room in junior high school or to the boys' vice-principal or the girls' vice-principal in high school. This is where they'll send you; they won't ask you what is your problem. If you give him any back talk, why you are sitting there, it is not doing anything but making it worse on you. When you go to a vice-principal of some sort, well, maybe they are going to suspend you, for what reason you will always wonder, why am I being suspended? Why? For what reason? I haven't done anything. But today I might have done something just because I am trying to figure a problem out and the teacher didn't ask me what was wrong.

Chuck: From my personal experience, I think the teachers' discipline is just a little bit too much, simply because the classes, for one thing, are oversized, there's too many people in one class; so therefore the instructors . . . don't have any time to take off during the class to explain the assignment or the work they happen to be doing at that time. First of all, teachers put the assignment on the blackboard, and just rattle off what she goin' to do with it, and what time she wants the assignment due, by the end of the period or maybe she wants it done for homework. She never takes time to explain it; just a person sitting back there in class won't know what is going on; he's trying, but he can't get any help from the teacher or anything, so he just sit there, he's puzzled. But I think that the teacher should just try to understand . . . I wouldn't say all the people's problems, but just to understand what is going on.

Jerry: The only time that you get a discussion is that you might study about a certain part of history today, and two or three days later the teacher come back and ask you, tell you, let's have a discussion on it. By that time, well, you have forgot it; all you want to do is do the work, turn it in, get a grade on it. But the point is if she wants you to memorize something, she should have her discussion right then in the classroom, after you get through. Give a certain period of time to work on a problem, then have a discussion on it; this they do not do. They will have a discussion two or three days later. . . . Then your mind will be on something else that she gave the day before. You don't even think about what she gave you three days before that. I think you should have a certain length of time in the classroom to have discussion period every day.

Fred: I remember a class I had; it was a science class, my teacher . . . had us to read a whole chapter within three days. Every Thursday we would have a discussion on this chapter, and the only time that we would have a discussion was when we read the chapter; and a lot of times that we read the chapter, answer the questions, and then when we were supposed to have a discussion, and there is something going on: either we see a movie, or we have five to ten minutes' discussion. We'd never have a whole period of class to have a discussion on one particular subject. The only time that we really had a pretty good discussion is when we were on the subject of narcotics. This is the only subject that we have had and spent the whole day in, this is the only time.

Wally: When I was at Jordan [in 1965], it seems there was a lack of communication . . . and I guess the teachers were going the wrong way of teaching. Like teaching this person something he already knows.

I mean, teachers do this same scale at the same level and continue at the same level throughout, all the way till he graduates at the same level. You don't progress, and once you transfer to a junior college, there is a little difficulty, you have the problem of keeping up with your grades.

That's one thing I noticed when I transferred to Trade Tech [Los Angeles Trade Technical College, a junior college]. And they made it easy for me; I went into a training instead of academic course, and I got used to that training; then I got acquainted with the books, and I transferred to sociology, and on my own time I go to the library, I got some books at home, and I read.

At Jordan, they just counseled me on my grades. At times I was falling down, they called me in and told me that, "You understand you are having a little difficulty with your grades. . . ." I said, "No," and my counselor would give me a date to pick that grade up, and if it is not, I should be dropped down to a lower level. So I maintained the same grade level until I graduated.

In my second year, they asked me different questions, what am I planning on doing after I finished high school, was I planning on getting trained on the job, or continue my education. And I was undecided until the last part of the semester. When I first graduated, I tried out for a job, but it was difficult for me, because I was inexperienced, lack of skill in that type of work I was doing. . . . I was working as a recreation leader.

I went to Trade Tech, and . . . I was just sitting there one day, and I was just thinking: the trade I'm in now, there is no difficulty, there's no hangup behind it, and I can close my eyes and do that type of work.

A counselor called me in and said, "If you ever decide to change your course to academic, you know that . . . if you started on sociology, you could continue on with your education," but he told me it will be a little difficult to continue my education on with that type of training, because there are not too many state colleges and universities that have apprenticeship programs. So I say, "Well, this is the time that I want to continue my education," and the only way to continue my education is to transfer to a field that could help me out, that could improve my society or my environment. That would be some kind of social work.

Dick: They actually tell you how long you must wear your hair, although there are no guidelines to distinguish whose hair is too long. It depends on the administration's choice as whether you are favored among the administration or not, as to how long you may wear your hair.

All those who are in sports are the cream of the crop as far as Jordan High School is concerned, for the principal himself [1965-66] is an athletic individual. He was the head referee at the Rose Bowl game. One thing he cares about is getting a good basketball, football team, or track team for the semester. Those are his main interests.

Well, the students dislike the rules horridly, but there is no way they can get around them because they are afraid to speak out. They deplore the rules; they can't stand them; they feel they are too strict. You know, they just don't go along with the wills and wants of the student body, or what they would consider as good taste.

Jordan is a wee bit worse [than other schools]. It is more rigid in our school. Other students at other [i.e., Caucasian] schools, they have more leeway because, you know, at so many schools, the principal and the students' parents may be close friends, something of this nature, somebody may be friendly with somebody at the Board of Education, so therefore they have to be cautious on the demands they make on the students, so they can't just throw them out of school right quick, make them cut their hair off, or take the hems off the young lady's skirt. . . .

There is no large disciplinary problem in our high school. Last semester at Jordan High School, and I attended it, we had exactly two fights the whole semester while we were there. And the only problems . . . were . . . personality conflicts between the teachers and the pupil, and there was no loud and unruly going-on. We found that the Caucasian schools we observed, they do more adolescent stunts and tricks and play more pranks on the administration and teachers than we probably even think of doing.

In the vice-principal's office, he has a set of handcuffs, and the dean of boys, he has a set of handcuffs. [They use them] just when they feel there is some student who they wish not to attend there any more, and he feels that he would like to attend there, and someone in the administration will try and bodily remove him from the campus, and then they use the handcuffs. They call that the restraining measure where they will handcuff the individual and virtually drag him to where they will wait for the police to come.

George: The "social adjustment" [transfer] is when they decide they will put you on a social adjustment program; in other words, a "social adjustment program" is when they take an individual from one high school and place him in what they consider a "different" environment; they try to put him in a strange environment, where the individual might—

Dick: —better himself, not realize that usually when the transfer is made, he's usually sent to a school where they have a large majority of social adjustment transfers. Then it turns out the student comes back to the high school again, he is embittered in the first place from being ousted from his original school, and when he gets there on social adjustment, he becomes what you might call slightly adjusted socially, but it's on the negative side. . . .

George: Riis is more or less considered a school for people that are hopeless, beyond themselves, you know; you can't control them. For instance, let us say I was on social adjustment to Fremont, which is very true. O.K., this was some time ago, if I had gotten kicked out from Fremont, and I had to go to several other schools, and then the last school I went to, they kicked me out, the only place for me would be Riis or that place where the bars are.

I am not going to try to use no very big words, anything like that, even though I can; I am just telling you basically what the scam is around Jordan High. To me, Jordan High is an institution of brainwash. The teachers, they more or less have somewhat of an understanding with the administration, and like if a teacher insults you, you're supposed to sit down and take it. Like this teacher insulted me, you know. We were doing a problem that, in order to work this problem, you have to subtract; so I didn't rightly understand how to do the problem. So I asked him to give me an exam-

ple. O.K., his example was if I had a pie, and I want to take some
of the pie away from the whole pie, what would I do. Okay, since
he was using pie, I said, "I would merely eat some." He tells me
to get up and leave his class and don't come back until he tells me
to. So I jumped up and I said, "Yes, O.K., I will leave your class,
mister." And while I am walking out of the door, he sends a referral down on me, just a gas, and when I got kicked out of Jordan,
boy, that was a gas, too. I was insulted by a teacher named Mr.
——, and so I took some very serious actions toward him, like letting air out of his tires, so they found out about that. I think that
some Uncle Toms at Jordan told them that I did this.

I would consider [three teachers, a Negro, a Creole, and a Cau-
casian] good teachers. [The Caucasian], he doesn't look at you because of your color, you know. He looks at you as a human being.
I mean, like if I was white, and this brother and I were in trouble,
he would help me just as much as he would the brother, see. This
is just how he is; he believes in equalization, I guess; that's one of
my own words.

Dick: Let me tell you, the mentality of [one administrator] is so
low that we used to get in conversations, I used to make up words,
and he wouldn't know exactly, he never knew what I was saying.
You know, he would be doodling while I am talking. I guess he was
trying writing the word down and see what it was after I left. . . .
And I was talking to the dude, and I just commenced to blow on
him, and after a while, I was thinking he didn't know half what I was
talking about. So I got to tripping the dude.

Steve: Jordan [High School] is all right, with the exception of
a few teachers, you know, kind of got on your case. Don't anyone
like to do a whole lot of work, but when a whole lot of work is put
off on you and made fun like, it is all right; but when the teacher
just give you some work and say, "Do it," without explaining it,
then you come into difficulty. They usually say, "Well, read the
stuff and do it."

Sam: That's mainly why, one of the reasons I never did check
with school myself, because teachers never did try to explain anything to me. They'd write some upon the blackboard, you come into
class, they got it on the board. . . . Here you are, trying to do some
work, and you don't even know what it is; you just know it is on
the board, and they come back, talk to you about nothing. School
is what you make it. . . . I think school should be run a whole lot

different than they have run. I mean, for one thing, they mess around in your personal life too much; they want to know things, families, what happened to your great grandma, all this different thing. How many relatives you got . . . and I don't see that it takes all that to go to school.

I know how Jordan is; it has its downfalls and it has its upfalls; like, people put down Jordan about different things, I know for truth, Jordan is a nice high school. It is just that a lot of changes have to be made in the school, you know. Like, it boils right back down to parents and teen-agers, it's the same old thing. They don't want teen-agers telling them what to do. . . .

Steve: A lot of people don't like teen-agers to give them suggestions, the way we think things are, and taking theirs and combining it, and maybe you come up with something good. They just ignore ours, and take theirs and use it. "I've been in this world longer than you have, and I know more than you," and all this different stuff; but still, I might be only seventeen, eighteen years old, there is still a lot of things that I know that you don't know.

At Jordan, right now, you know these naturals that you wear? They can't wear their hair long, they have to get their hair cut. . . . Well, they say it looks bad for a high school boy to go to school with so much hair on his head.

George: There is another thing, if you don't get it cut, they'll try to cut it themselves. . . . Yeah, they will send you to the VP's office and all this stuff, have the coaches cut it.

Sam: Another thing, you know, they'll send you to the coach for swat. When you get into high school, I don't think he should go into a class and take the swat, just like junior high school. That is what make a lot of kids drop out of school right now, today. There is pressure on the young kid's mind, see, because I had this pressure put on my mind when I was going, and I know. Nobody's going to go through that because, you know, "Change clothes and strip, get in your white tennis shoes, your white socks, your blue shorts, and a white T shirt," if you don't have this, now, you get five swats for your shoes, your socks and your pants, and your shirt; you get that many swats, see. . . . At the time I was going to junior high school, this young Mexican-American was going to school with me, he was my friend. And we had this teacher, this white Caucasian teacher, and he made him climb up on this ladder, made him actually bend over the ladder, and gave him five swats. Not just using his hand, but taking a board.

Sometimes they have these great razor straps [*sic*] built. Big, long belts made of cowhide or something, and make you bend over, grab the seat of the chair, grab the chair, bent over. And this stuff actually is brutality, man. This is one reason how Colored kids grew up to hate white people, because all the time, it would be white people doing this.

Steve: It's like this CCC [Community Conservation Corps] program that I am in. . . . It stinks in some place, and it's groove in another; like I said before, in relating back to adults, they won't take your suggestions. You give them a suggestion, and they won't accept it.

Chuck (December, 1968): There's still a lack of communication between the students and the teachers. Like ———— [a prominent administrator], he's black, but yet, the students say, he *thinks* white. He has a job to do, he has responsibility on his back, so why not somewhat equal things? Like, come down; if you can't reach the student from where you are, why not come down? There, if you meet on equal grounds, there's always things that can be solved. But it seems as though he don't want to make this step. So there is a conflict.

Things used to be hectic on campus. But we weren't having the problem they are having now. We just caught the beginning, and now they are catching the middle part or the ending part.

I got aware of things in about the summer of 1964, when I was involved in a black militant group. I became exposed to Negroes like Harriet Tubman, Malcolm X. You know, at one time I thought Cleopatra was white. This was the time when everyone started to think the same, things they wanted to see changed and never changed. Everything has an exploding point and that's what I say mainly caused the riot: an explosion. Like, a wound can hurt only so long.

Like, when I was in my last year in high school and I had sprained my ankle, and the coach told me, "Come in tomorrow, maybe afternoon, but if you can't make it, call me, I'll fix it up." So I called him, went to school at 11:30, so the principal sees me come in and he says, "Chuck, where you comin' from?" I says I'm comin' from home. My foot was bandaged, you know, and I was telling him what was wrong, and he tells me to come into the office. So there was quite a few there, I think there was four sittin' on the bench, and he told me to sit on the bench. So actually there wasn't room enough for me to sit on the bench, and I told him there wasn't room. So we got into static, you know, we was exchanging words. I admit the situation could have been cooler if I had somewhat accepted his statements, but what he was saying to me was actually downgrading my character, and I wouldn't accept that. He spoke in terms of the "great power," you're black, I'm white. Well, I was going through the stage then where I felt as though I was equal to anyone else, and I still feel this way. So, if he can approach me in that manner, why not approach him in the manner in which he approached me?

Jerry (December, 1968):   If black people had any sense at all, they would do the one thing that the white man didn't want him to do, and that is, to go to *his* school and get *his* education, and use those same tactics that he used, use them right back at him.

The teachers told us all about Christopher Columbus, but they didn't tell us about the black man who was his navigator. And it didn't make any difference if the teacher was black or white. You know, when a nigger's making as much money as a schoolteacher makes, you got to go up on that hill [where the Board of Education is located], and when you go up on that hill, you got to go with the system. The game is the same, but the name changes. And not only the name, but the color changes also.

You know, there is a lot of difference in calling one Negro a "house nigger," and then calling another an Uncle Tom. Now the Uncle Tom, believe it or not, would kill his own mama, if it's money or anything else that is gonna benefit him and himself only, but the house nigger he's a little bit more lenient. He will take under consideration that he was in the field before he got in that house, although he is trying to go all the way up there. He's not gonna give his mother up.

Paul Williams (1969):   When I was in school, I had to read what was suited for me. The minority of students were put in "advanced" classes, which were the same as the grade level. In other words, the "advanced" students in the twelfth grade would be reading at the twelfth-grade level. The majority of students would stay behind. Once you go on into the junior colleges or the university, you are stuck with this handicap.

Now, in 1969, the books are different, and it does seem like it's easier to read, and you probably have improved methods, but in high school I think the situation is still mainly the same. I know the atmosphere hasn't changed. The psychological effect on black students hasn't changed.

See, the black teachers are the teachers that are really sensitive to the problem, that can relate to the students. As a junior college student, and even as a high school student, I found teachers that I could relate to, that showed me the connection between them, or their relating to me, and what they are trying to teach me. Just to use one example, Mr. _____ [a teacher in junior college] teaches black history and, as an image in the classroom, can relate to you more because for one thing he was raised in Watts and so he has the same experience as other blacks. As far as high school is concerned, Mr. _____ and maybe two or three other teachers have this relationship of, say, the same experience. It seems like they have lived in the same situation and can relate to you and can understand your problems. It's not that they gave you any more slack, but it seems like they have more insight, on the psychological effect.

But the majority of black teachers today still seem to be orientated towards middle class and even seem to be more white than the whites themselves. If we only have the same amount of teachers that students can relate to, the situation still hasn't changed. You have just one or two or three teachers in there that are keeping the morale of the students up or giving the students something to relate to. And it seems the teachers that they can relate to, they seem to be dropping out. They seem to be going either to the junior colleges or to the university.

We need a new perspective. The black students and Black Student Unions have a different perspective where they can look at the problem. The administrators and the faculty, who are somewhat established to some degree, have a set process of teaching so they have only a certain insight into the problem, but you put together a combination of all these [viewpoints] and you can modify the situation.

The black movement has affected me a hell of a lot. I found out I got a lot of insight and awareness, so I know how to deal with myself, and I think the black movement has had the same effect on other black students. Now I think if we start at a lower level, say at junior high school or even grammar school, teach them a little history, so they can have confidence in themselves. Most people need somebody to look up to and most black kids don't have these images. When I went to high school, these situations, these pressures, came up, and I found that psychologically I just wasn't prepared, and then this black movement came along and it gave me a boost.

If I was administrator, say, at Jordan High School, and I had to change the whole structure, the first thing I would do to ease tensions would be to erect a community advisory board, to advise on the question of [bringing] the police on campus. If the parents and community advise that the police be on campus, then they would be brought in. Another thing I would do, on the hiring of teachers and instructors, is to have the teacher interviewed by some black students who have a certain amount of insight that can help solve some of the problems. If you have a BSU president or vice-president that seems to have some insight, take his viewpoint, the viewpoint of representatives of the community, the principal's viewpoint, my viewpoint. Just don't take it on the relationship of administrator to faculty, or faculty to faculty, but take it from the viewpoint of students, faculty, everyone concerned, and maybe there you would have a conglomeration of maybe the closest to a type of teacher you would need to stimulate and motivate the student's interest in learning.

The first thing I would do is try to stimulate this interest in learning, on the level of communicating with him more on the things that derive from his interests. In high school, you're interested in something, but I don't think they pinpoint it as well as they should. I think if they did more research in high school, more counseling in the black communities and black high schools, then black people would find their interests. Mr. _____ [a college instructor] did some research on counseling; he took this chart of a white student and found it was filled out to a "T," personality tests, interests, aptitude tests, everything. But this black student from San Pedro, his chart was clear, the counselor hadn't done personality testing, hadn't done anything really to evaluate the student.

The Black Power revolution should stress the value of education so it can do what the "White Power" revolution does: get the people to let their hangups loose so that they can function, they can do their own thing. The black man's brilliant; we could be scientists, on down. We could get ourselves together and rule the world. Black Power, to me, means to motivate black people to stay in school, to give self-identity and self-ambition, to keep pushing.

The big hangup is in the educational system. We've had too much miseducation. I'm talking about getting educated in the form that consistently makes you sit up and study maybe, or makes you consistently stay on the job, this striving. I'm concerned with motivating people: a lot of people just don't concern themselves about going to school. Maybe they spend their time groovin', just living from day to day or hour to hour. You've got to have this drive.

I have changed some details concerning the following incident which occurred in 1968, but the essentials are correct. I am completely convinced of the reliability and veracity of my informants, having known them well for some years.

Speakers: One day some pupils came in tardy and Mr. Johnson [a white teacher] asks them why they were tardy, and he said, don't do it again. Charles [a pupil] said he couldn't make it on time because his room was way over there in 101 and he said, "I couldn't make it over to room 36 in time." Then, a later time, the boy came in on time, and Mr. Johnson say, "Good for you, Charles." Charles said, "The reason why I was on time *this* time was I asked my teacher could I come out *early*." He [Mr. Johnson] said, "How come you all laugh so much?" And Charles said, "That's the truth—I even got my pass." And then Mr. Johnson said, "Your mama!" Just like that, we didn't know what he was talkin' about. He said, "All you black niggers go back to Africa where you came from." Arthur [another pupil] said, "I didn't come from no Africa." Then Mr. Johnson said, "You shut up, your mother look like a damn— — —." He told us to go out and we didn't do nothin' and then he said, "How you people act, just like some kind of wild animals in the jungle." Arthur said, "I came here to learn, man, and if you don't want to teach me, I'll get my credits changed," and then we went to the vice-principal and wrote down what he had said.

Then we went back and he continued saying about "your mother" and all this. And then Mr. Terry [an administrator] talked to him, and he say he wasn't going to do it no more, and then the next day he didn't stop, he just keep talkin' about "your mother." And Mr. Terry, the reason why I don't like him is because he don't want to see into it because he believe Mr. Johnson. He say, "Yeah, I believe some of your mothers do run wild." Arthur said, "My mother doesn't run wild." Then he said, "Uh huh, yeah."

Several mothers of children in Watts-area schools reflect on school policies in relation to appearances and related issues.

Mrs. Harrison, Mrs. Richardson, and *Mrs. Smith*:   In some of the high schools a student is not supposed to wear a natural, and the vice-principal or the coach or somebody will keep a pair of clippers or scissors in the office and cut hair when it gets too long.
They couldn't touch mine!
I started my daughter to wearing a natural, because I am de-

termined that when she grows up, she can make it her own way. Now the children, of course, this is so unusual that the children sometimes have little comments to make; well, you can excuse a child. . . . But I am waiting and hoping that I will hear just one comment from one of the teachers.

Mrs. Smith: They will never say anything. Over at Gompers [Junior High School], quite a few of them wear naturals. Like, I told one the other day, if she didn't comb her natural right, I was going to braid it up for her, because she didn't even comb it. . . . Now some of them are so particular about theirs, and my father loved his. . . . My older boy was telling me that one of the mothers came over and was telling another lady's daughter that she didn't like her daughter running with her because of the natural, so I called the mother into PTA meeting and explained that as long as the child's hair is neat and is what the parents like that child to wear, you have no right to condemn it; let her be an individualist if she wants to.

I know one fellow wore make-up over to Horace Mann [Junior High School] to see what the vice-principal was going to say. He talked with him about his natural, so he wore make-up, he put it all on. . . . The vice-principal didn't say a word, nobody said a word, it went a whole week, then another group started; they wouldn't say a word, but when their natural group break out, they start complaining again. So it's half a dozen on the one hand and six on the other.

Mrs. Harrison: One thing they don't want the Negro to do is to regain a race pride.

Mrs. Richardson: This is not only between . . . the races, but I noticed when I started to find myself, I had trouble with my own relatives, my mother. You know, when you start to change, they don't understand this, and they want to try to bring you back around to their way of thinking. They don't want to let you to get to know yourself.

Mrs. Andrews: The teachers don't take up the time with the kids as they do with the kids in Beverly Hills, Hamilton High, or Dorsey High, or some of those types of schools. You get the Caucasians out here, they do not understand Negroes, and do not try to understand. I think that the Board of Education, if they are going to have a new teacher to come into this area, they should have them to come in and live before they start teaching, to understand what's going on, and then they will understand the frustrations and the problems, and maybe they can cope with them better.

All right, then you've got our people that used to eat black-eyed peas or red beans and rice, and then they got themselves a job as a teacher, and most of them take jobs as teacher because it does pay good money. But after they come into their own neighborhoods, they're the very ones that know what our frustrations were because they had them at one time themselves, and they look down. Instead of reaching down and help pulling up their people, they will stand off there with that white man and do the same identical thing that he does.

Now I am not saying that ninety-nine per cent of the teachers are terrible, and that the parents are not responsible for a lot of the attitudes that's in school. It revolves around the students, the parents, the teachers; there's a lot of blame to be put in lots of places, but I still say the Board of Education is lousy, and when it comes to the education of the Negro, you can come down South and get taught better than you can in California. . . .

I know this because my kids have went to school in this area, and my oldest girl is twenty-three now. They do silly things, like over at Gompers, my niece didn't have on the right kind of shoes, is that anything to keep her in the office all day to make her lose her classes? [In] the first place, if she didn't have on the proper shoes, then the vice-principal should have notified my sister and told her, "We have certain rules at this school, and this is not proper attire," and take it up with the parent, because my niece is new at the school, but why punish the child. Now if a child get out of order, I can understand. But because she don't have on the proper stockings or socks or shoes; you know the kids still ain't wearing the proper clothes because they're still wearing miniskirts, and what could be worse than a mini, as far as I am concerned. So what does the shoes matter? I'd rather have my daughter wear a pair of sandals to school than wear a miniskirt.

They're supposed to be teaching the kids reading, writing, and arithmetic, not what they wear, because maybe that's all that child had to wear. Did they try to find out whether this child had the proper shoes at home? They don't try to find out anything; Miss _____ did know what programs my niece had; she didn't know whether she had ever been absent from school. When they got something against you . . . then they can bring out their programs, that she did this on such and such date, but they didn't have anything to say about my niece. . . . So I told her, she just has to go up to school, but do it in an intelligent way.

I wouldn't say that the pupils feel . . . that the Board of Education is neglecting to give them the proper education, because . . . you have a lot of kids that are not interested in school, their parents have never backed them up in making them understand how important education is. It's only the parent that's really interested in their child feels that the Board of Education is not giving the children in the ghetto areas the opportunities that they should have. I mean because they have got a thousand bad kids over here and five hundred [good kids] over here, why should the five hundred suffer because the other thousand don't care? The only way we're going to be able to get what we want is . . . to go down to the Board of Education. But as long as we sit around and talk about what they're going to do, and don't do anything about it, we're always going to have this problem. And then sometimes I think that . . . the Board of Education don't even know a lot of things that go on.

Maybe [the teachers] do have the same qualifications [as teachers in Beverly Hills], but their attitudes is different. Of course, I realize that the teachers have a difficult problem, because they have a parent that will not cooperate, pupils that do not cooperate, but what makes me angry is that they think every pupil in that school is the same. . . . I had to go down to Jordan about five years ago about my daughter. She was trying to tell a girls' vice-principal or something about going to Fremont, and the woman called her a liar, so I had to go down there. . . . I asked her, "Did you call up to Fremont to find out whether she was telling the truth?" And she said, "No." Then I said, "Well, then you had better get on that damn telephone and call right now". . . . And then when she got on the phone, she came back, then she wanted to apologize. I told her, "Seems like to me, you think that every Negro that walks through that door is a liar and a cheater, and they don't want any education; they are all the same." You cannot put people on that kind of basis just because they live in a ghetto area.

When you go up to the schools . . . they talk down to you before you open your mouth. They don't know whether you are educated, illiterate, or what have you, but they all talk to you just like you are a little child, and that you are completely ignorant; and then they put in these great big old words, but it just happens that I know what they're talking about, and I don't like that attitude. I've always said, "If my child don't act right, I want you to let me know. If they need a spanking, give it to them," but they [school officials] waited till things happen; like they suspend my daughter, [when] the teacher [was] choking my daughter, so she scratched him and she kicked him and she did something to him, and they want to put her out of school; but I told them and I told the Board of Education that if they expel my daughter, I was going to take it to the highest court. Now when my child don't do right, I am not going to take up for her, but I will not tolerate a man over six foot four choking my daughter. They have rules for . . . the students about the teachers, but what about the teachers when the teachers do wrong against the pupil, because they could handle it in a different way. He didn't have to choke her, and he was a Negro himself. He could have appealed to her, the better side of her, but he just tried to be like Mr. Charley and drag her on into the school and made a big mess of it.

Mrs. Fitzgerald (a PTA president): You know, I have come to the conclusion that so long as they [the girl students] don't wear bikinis, if they covered their nakedness, I would be just kind of satisfied if they would have the proper instructors, and if they could have people that are concerned about them. . . .

I think that the attitudes of the teacher and the attitudes of the parents have a lot to do with what's happening to our youngsters. . . . Now let me explain to you what I mean by the attitudes of the teachers. Shortly after the uprising in 1965, they had . . . discussions, and a couple of my daughters were called in, and they would ask them what do they think can create a better relationship between the teacher and the student. And one of the girls, she's kind of outspoken, she thought that the teacher should be seen in the community, not just there on his working time, that he should be seen back in the community by the students, shopping at the markets, or visiting some of the local businesses, or going to maybe a church once in a while, not only just coming in to work, because the children get the feeling he is only interested in his job, he has come in here for employment.

I think that [living in the area] would be of a great benefit to the teacher to know the students as well as it would give the students a chance to appreciate him. But if this couldn't be done, just like this student was saying, if he would sort of take advantage of the markets, the businesses, or social activities once in a while, the students would still be able to appreciate him as being involved in the community more than just in his daily employment. But this counselor, Mr. _____, said to this girl right before the other students and teachers and so on, "Why, I can hardly wait till three o'clock so I can get out of here; I wouldn't be caught in here for nothing other than while I am on the job." When the kid told me this, and she looked hurt because she didn't know whether she had done wrong by suggesting the high and mighty teacher come back, maybe was she out of place, well, I don't usually express my feeling before my children, but I hit the ceiling. I said, "I wish the son of a bitch was good enough to work somewhere else," you know, that he wouldn't have to come in here if that's the way he felt about it. And many times now these attitudes [are] pushed off on the kids. Another teacher told her, "Why, you're just bums, the students are not like this where I live." Well, it's too bad he couldn't work where he lived, instead of trying to bring our students up to what he felt was proper for their morals and their ethnic values and so on.

You know, after all, teaching, to some people, is a job, and is not a profession; it's not a dedication, it's a means of making a living. I feel teaching should be a dedication, and I feel that in many instances we do have some teachers in both ethnic groups that are dedicated, but when teachers make statements like that former counselor made, I think that this does a lot of harm. . . . Then we have had vice-principals, administrators, and so forth that have been known to talk in low, cursed tones to the students, calling them names regarding their ethnic group, low names. . . . They would deny they have done this, and maybe this student was in trouble lots of times, and nobody was supposed to believe him. But . . . even girls have been called "black cows," and things, by teachers there at Drew [Junior High School].

[A mother and her daughter discuss the possible value of augmenting regular school personnel with special teacher and counselor aides drawn from the local community. (This proposal is an integral part of the "New Careers" movement which now receives national attention.)]

Mrs. Fitzgerald: I definitely think that a ghetto person could get over to the kids better than the professional can, because if it's a dedicated community person that is sincerely interested in the youth and in what he is trying to do, the youth is going to have more faith in him, and they would respond better, they would have respect for this person. It is a fact that somewhere we're missing the boat, because the students don't have any respect for the teachers, they don't have any love for the school itself; why do you think they keep breaking in and just tearing up; they are not taking; ninety per cent of these break-ins are not done by professionals; they were done by the students. The egg-throwing, the ink-throwing, the breaking of the ash trays, deliberately destroying the teachers' lounge, you see, that's because they hate certain of these teachers.

And, about the parents' attitudes, not enough parents are concerned about what's really happening to their' students at school until maybe they are involved in a major thing. For example, they don't come to see if their children are cooperating . . . with the school administrators and with the teachers; and also they might jump up and speak . . . resentful about different things. Number two, the parents [are] going to have to be educated, toward how to not let their attitudes reflect back through their children. You know, a child can come home and tell you how he's been kind of humiliated and hurt; well, you'd better try to encourage him, because he has got enough hate in him already without letting him know how you feel. It's time then for the parent to go in to the teacher and try to work it out with the teacher and try to let him know you are concerned, and you are watching his steps.

We could prevent all these tensions, the dropout, if we had persons from the area working with the schools. The principal asked my help here this fall. He wanted to know what could I do, what could I recommend could be done to help solve his dropout problem, because with the enrollment of a little over 1,700 students, he was having daily absenteeism of 400 to 450 students, and he asked if I could get some mothers that could give some volunteer time in trying to call these various homes, because he wondered if the parents really knew that they were absent, and because he said it was just too big a load to put on the attendance office.

But I think it needs to be subprofessional work, [for] a community person with a livable salary from the Board of Education, somewhere from $4,000 to $5,000 a year.

Shirley (A Student): I feel definitely that [an indigenous counselor's aide] would be better, because I don't trust my white counselor at South Gate [High School]. He tried to give me a homemaking major, he said, "Well, I think you ought to take homemaking; therefore, you take clothing and foods," and all that junk that I get at home. I told him I didn't want it, I want an English major, and that's what I got.

Our friends at Fremont [High School] say they don't tell kids about their graduation credits till about maybe a month before graduation, and then it's too late to make up; but knowing from my own experiences, I don't think the counselor [will try] to give you as much as you can in the three-year span, because . . . I read up on what I need to graduate and what I need to take the course that I am taking, those counselors could just give you anything.

You see, if it's a Negro person, a person from your own area [that is serving as counselor aide], if they knew what you needed, they knew the counselor was trying to just put something over on you, they will try and help you and let you know what you needed, try and give you what you needed.

Mrs. Fitzgerald: One of my daughters went to South Gate, but she had trouble with chemistry, and so she wanted to bring this "D" up in the summer. So she went to Fremont to try to enroll. Well, they said the class was overfilled. . . . Now, she was a science major, and when I walked in, she says, "Mama, the counselor gave me sewing and bookkeeping, and I don't want them; I am a science major, I don't need sewing and bookkeeping." Se we were able to get [her] into Washington [High School] where she was able to take chemistry. They were overrun, but they opened up another class. She made a "B."

Mrs. Andrews: Get the smart kid to help two or three others in the class. When my daughter was in the fourth grade, she was an all-"A" student; they took a group of kids in that class and had my daughter to help teach them. In the first place, the class was overcrowded, and it worked out.

Better still, we have a lot of people that went out . . . and something happened that interrupted their education, so . . . if they have teachers' aides, why are they not putting them in school to help the slow students or help the teacher when the classes is overrun, at least the kids would get a better education.

Because now when I went to school, even if the class was overcrowded, teachers did not get married, so their whole life was revolved around pupils, bad and good. Here, if you bad, they don't even try to help you make good; they push you aside; like at Gompers, if you have a fight, they send you to another school. . . . Why do that? Is it helping the kid any?

I think that if something happens at that school, it should be straightened there, don't send them to Markham. If kids in Markham bad, don't send them to Gompers. What is it proving? Not a doggone thing. It is showing that the Board of Education and the teachers are not doing their job, and some of the parents are not cooperating together. The Board of Education and the students get together and get an understanding, understanding beats the world; we ain't never going to have nothing like Beverly Hills, and all them other places are always going to have the best.

Mrs. Gray: You have forty-five students in this class here in Watts; you have forty-five students in Beverly Hills to one teacher. Maybe you have thirty-five slow students here in Watts; maybe you don't have but fifteen or twenty slow ones in Beverly Hills. . . . What they need is more teachers out here.

Mrs. Osborne: You will have to double your amount of teachers to the students, because you have that many slow students out here. . . . If we can get to where we cut out this half-day session for those school kids to where when they go to school, they can learn something. You can't learn anything in a half a day.

Mrs. Gray: Everything depends on you, on the way *you* feel. You have heredity, and you have environment. But it is the individual's personal response to his environment; it is the person's response, his reaction to what he has.

Mrs. Andrews: I don't go along with that. I mean, I could come from a home, [where] maybe my parents' education wasn't important to them, and it could, if I am weak, rub off on me. But if . . . there is something born within me, no matter how illiterate or "no-careish" my parents are, but I got that flame burning in here, I am not going to let nothing stand in my way, so you can't condemn ones that don't feel like you and me. What about them, those are the ones [that] need the help.

A girl expresses some opinions about the quality of education she received in the ghetto schools of Los Angeles.

Shirley: I don't think the teen-agers are getting the same education [as teen-agers get in other areas]. Because they put any old kind of teacher in there, a teacher that they don't want out in areas like Hollywood, Fairfax, like that; those teachers they put up there, I don't think they really care, they will throw anything at you and want you to take it and don't say nothing about it.

The education is better at South Gate because . . . the white people are going to give their kids the best, and they are going to demand the best teachers, and they can't give me one teacher in the same classroom and give the white kids another one, so I got to be getting the best.

The teachers should come in and get to know the people and

get to know the area around the people before they become teachers. Yeah, and go to church with them. And if not, even if not shopping, go around and talk to the people and talk to the students. . . .

Much discussion has been focused on the so-called dropout problem in ghetto area schools, and it is clear that the official dropout rate in *de facto* segregated schools is from two to three times greater than the corresponding rate in other schools. What has not been so obvious is the fact that many of the dropouts are actually *pushed* out of school, and hundreds of pupils in minority areas are transferred from one ghettoized school to another whenever school officials arbitrarily adjudge them to be "social adjustment" problems. Sometimes a youngster will be sent to a special school, limited to children who have been evaluated as severe behavioral cases. The dropout rate at these schools is, of course, phenomenally high.

Jerry: The classes . . . are overfull, and at the same time that the instructor is saying the class is too large, he can't instruct the whole students . . . the student is saying at the same time, "I can't learn anything; there's too many people in here. There are too many. You never will get enough time to get around to help me. Why should I stay in here; I might as well check out of the school." This is what they would do; they would check out.

Fred: A lot of times . . . if you don't like this certain class . . . for instance, if you have biology, there is a certain teacher I don't like, so I'm going to ditch this class. A lot of times they [the students] go to class but they don't do anything; they just sit down and either mess with the young lady next to him, talk to 'em and disturb the class, or just sit down and go to sleep in class. You find more students, there is an awful lot of students that go to school, they just sleep in classes they don't like.

There is an awful lot of transferring. . . . They only transfer you if you, say, miss a certain class so many weeks, like you've been to school, but you just didn't go to one of your classes. They just let this go so far, it all depends on the referrals you have. If you have a lot of referrals, and give the teacher a lot of trouble like this, and been suspended more than one time, they get tired of this mess, send you to . . . another school, like Fremont or Jeff [Jefferson] or some school like that; but in junior high, if they can't get along with a young man, they send you to Riis, all boys' school.

Jerry: I'd like to say about transfers: as far as Fremont, Jefferson, Washington, and the rest of the schools around here, with the reputation such as they have, they will send the kid to, and here is South Gate right around the corner, they won't even send him there. This is what I want to know, why is it that they can't attend any schools closer than Fremont, Jefferson, and Washington?

Fred: I remember, I can't recall the exact year . . . when about ten students from South Gate were going to come to Jordan to go to school, and about ten kids from Jordan were going to go to South Gate to go to school, so we had about seven kids from Jordan who signed a petition that they would like to go to South Gate. All right. They went to South Gate; they had to go through a whole lot of changes when they went there, too. I remember a young lady, her name was Sandra Dyson, she started in South Gate and she had eggs thrown all over her, she had been spit at, talked about, yet and still, she still went there, and this is why they thought that if they would send white kids to Jordan, the same thing would happen to them, to the white kids at Jordan. This is the reason why they don't send them to South Gate, 'cause there won't be nothing but a whole lot of violence.

The proximity of all-white South Gate High School to all-minority Jordan has long been an issue in Los Angeles. The discussion of school transfers inevitably raises the question of how Negro youngsters feel about attending an integrated school.

Fred: There was an awful lot of talk about it. They even had students going to different students' homes and talking to the parents to see how they felt about integrating Jordan and . . . well, this is what they asked, "Would you let your son or daughter go to an all-white school?" . . . As far as I am concerned, I would like to go to an all-white school to integrate, because I feel this: I would get a better education there. Although I know that I would probably have to go through an awful lot of changes, I might get beat up or jumped on or something like that, but I would still go. . . . I even asked the principal, could I go. He didn't give me any answer.

As far as teaching is concerned, yes, South Gate is a better school. They don't have second-rate books, like you are in the seventh grade, they aren't going to give you no fifth-grade book to read. This is what they do at Jordan, you know.

Jerry: In Jordan, this falls on the instructor and administration, because if they wanted you to get an education, they could get you the book. We wouldn't have the second rate, we would have the first rate, just as they have.

Fred: Why give Negro students secondhand books, like I am in the eighth grade, and I get a seventh-grade book. Give me an eighth-grade book, just like because I am in the eighth-grade level, how come I can't learn the eighth-grade level, but instead they give you secondhand books, a grade lower.

Chuck: I am going to tell you why I think white schools are more up to date, more or less. They have covered what is to be covered, simply because the faculty and the students are all pulling for the same thing. For instance, like at Jordan High School, you are running for president, secretary, historian, a position at the attendance office. Finally you gets into office. So after all, in your campaign, you can explain to students what you'll accomplish, yet and still the administration is backing you while you are running, but when you get into this office, you get to telling the administration about your plans for betterment of the school; they don't even want to hear, so by this way the students themselves actually don't have a voice in the way the school is being ran or anything that is pertaining to the school. So I feel that the school administration should at least give way to students, take their voice, sometimes don't decide everything for yourself.

And another reason is that the textbooks at Jordan, they are from Caucasian schools mostly, the books are older. Something else about the school that I disagree with is the way the school is being ran, mostly because, say, the principal is athletic minded, all he want to hear is something about athletics. . . . I feel that sports-minded young men don't have to be all that smart, for him. If you good in the sports, he fights for you, and if you just out for the sports, I am not saying you have to be an Elgin Baylor or Jerry West or somebody like that, he will do everything he possibly can to help you out. You could be failing your classes, he go talk to your teachers so you can play; this has happened. The school needs, first of all . . . remodeling, an up to date building, because the building there has been there for thirty-five years or longer. Most of the buildings are decaying inside, walls are cracking. That's another problem, entirely different, but yet and still I think the administration and the student body should come together as one unit, understanding each other for their points, all they have to do is to agree on certain things.

Fred: I think . . . the students at Jordan, they want to learn; they want to accomplish something in life; I mean, they know this, they know that they are getting second-rate books and things of this nature. They don't want this; they want first class just like the white man can get. How come we can't have it; this is what they're saying. There wouldn't be very many, I don't think there would be too much dropouts and quitting school and things like this if we had first-class stuff in school, first-class equipment.

[The administration doesn't give the school a first-class educational setup] mainly because probably they don't even care; they probably think the only thing Negroes is good in is sports. Why try to put something in their head.

Jerry: May I say something on that. This might sound as though I'm prejudiced, but, believe me, I am not; but the only way I can see that they have been giving us the second-rate education is because they know, the whites have realized, where we can't beat them. Negroes can't beat the whites by shooting it out with them, you can't beat them by athletics, something of this sort, but we can beat with their own education. If they learn us their education, then we can beat them. Until they learn us their education, we will never beat them. It is just like, who was it, Thomas Jefferson, "All men are created equal."

Lincoln said, "Stand with the man who stands right." This was not even put in the Declaration of Independence. But I think it should have been, because you get the meaning, to stand with the person who stands right. If we all can stand right, we all could be equal, but until we all stand with the person who stands right, we will never be equal. Until then, we will never get first-grade education the same as the white. . . .

As far as I can see [control over the school system] is what the majority of the mothers and fathers and kids in that community want, because if you notice, if you go in Watts, the parents of the students that attend Jordan can't, don't, have any say-so on the Board of Education. If you go in Huntington Park or South Gate or Lynwood, you know, or Inglewood, the people run the Board of Education. The people run it, not the administration. This should be done at all schools, not just certain ones, or a certain amount, I mean; all of them, from grammar school all the way to college and university. And it should never change; if it should be ran by the people, the people only, then everything would be just fine.

VIII

Welfare

Although there are no official figures relating to that narrowly defined area, probably close to half of the population of Watts (including children, of course) is "on welfare." The four housing projects, containing about a third of the residents, are heavily populated by families headed by women separated or divorced, or otherwise lacking the support of a husband. Until 1962, the provisions of State and Federal law denied relief (then called Aid to Needy Children) to family units in which an able-bodied and employable man was present; the man must have been absent or incapacitated before his wife and children were eligible to receive welfare assistance. After a change in the basic law, families with an unemployed male head may now obtain federally subsidized aid, but only about ten per cent of the households getting assistance in Los Angeles County fall in this category (retitled Aid to Families with Dependent Children, AFDC). Broken homes remain the major recipients of "welfare."

Family aid in this country has traditionally been conditioned on the premise that the household cannot obtain an income (or gifts) from any other source, and that the status of the aid recipient must be constantly checked to make certain that a man with cash in hand is not somewhere in the vicinity. If a man is discovered, the welfare budget of the household must be "re-examined." Income from this competitive source will be deducted from the semimonthly checks provided through the local social-welfare agency. Though the 1967 Social Security amendments passed by Congress liberalize the amount of *earnings* which may be retained by an AFDC household, without a corresponding reduction in welfare payments, the other restrictions remain firmly in effect.

The Puritan ethic thus requires the social worker to be a part-time policeman and spy. Though a major part of his or her responsibility is to ascertain the needs of the welfare recipient and adjust the budget allowances accordingly, much time must be spent in guarding against the "immorality" of a hidden or extra income. The life of the AFDC family is strongly influenced and regulated by moral judgments expressed in legal and legislative form.

Particularly vexing are the apparent inconsistencies in policy among "welfare" offices. In 1967, the Social Workers' Union and the American Civil Liberties Union in Los Angeles cooperated in a survey of case workers to ascertain how practices varied on such major items as emergency food allowances, allowances for special household needs, and administrative support for workers' decisions. The findings showed wide variation from one supervisor to another, and from one area office to another. Some honored requests for special allowances most of the time, while others regularly denied them. The contradictions serve to remind welfare recipients that their lives are controlled by the personal judgments of certain key bureaucrats.

The 1967 amendments reflect a growing legislative irritation with the existing welfare system. The net result of the "freeze" on additional Federal support for expanding welfare rolls, the liberalization of job-earnings allowances for AFDC recipients, and the establishment of the Work Incentive Program (WIN), is a further pressure on employable heads of households to enter training and employment. The assumption is that a high proportion of welfare recipients are employable, a dubious assumption indeed. The predominance of broken homes means that the chief target group of these efforts consists of women with families, and where small children are present the new thrust would require their absence from the home much of the time and the entrusting of their young ones to institutional baby-sitters, such as day-care centers. This further weakening of an already weakened family structure can have psychological and sociological results not even envisioned by the lawmakers. Nor is it clear that the legislation takes cognizance of the difficulties in employing those with an inadequate basic education, particularly in jobs which are reasonably durable and pay a net income at least equal to the modest welfare allowances.

The "liberals" are equally disenchanted with the prevailing welfare system, and some of them (with a few unexpected allies such as the University of Chicago's Milton Friedman, the redoubtable conservative economist) press for a guaranteed annual income instead. On both economic and sociological grounds, the more ar-

ticulate among them question whether it is wise or realistic policy
to try to force welfare recipients into the labor market. But their
own prescription has its own built-in psychological disadvantages,
as I shall argue in the concluding chapter.

The "conservatives" are incensed by the large size of welfare
families and the high birth rate in low-income ghetto households.
Illegitimacy fires their moral indignation to an even higher tem-
perature. Yet there is a fascinating contradiction here: policies encouraging the dissemination of birth-control information and devices receive far less support from "conservatives" than from "liberals."

Three of the women whose views are reflected in the following
section have had long experience with "welfare," but their educational levels and their general sophistication are probably above
average for AFDC recipients. They have all been associated with
the sort of community organizations and governmental programs
that expand their knowledge of the system. Each is seeking, by
further education and by employment, to break away from welfare
dependency, and they note the weird inconsistencies in prevailing
practice which, on the one side, encourages this movement and,
on the other, places barriers in its path. Their experiences on "welfare" are similar to many others that I have observed elsewhere
in the Watts area. Though most of the following statements were
made before the passage of the 1967 amendments, and there have
been some administrative changes in the system since, the general
tone of their discussion remains as applicable today as it was then.

The allowances available to mothers on AFDC are determined
on an item-by-item basis by the State Department of Social Welfare,
under very general guidelines laid down by the Federal government,
and administered by a county agency set up for this purpose under the direction of the Board of Supervisors. Social workers employed by the county determine whether an applicant is eligible for
aid and, if so, the extent of the need. Despite propaganda to the
contrary—circulated in part by such respectable sources of misinformation as the McCone Riot Investigating Commission—the vast
majority of welfare recipients in Los Angeles County have resided
there for many years. Once on "welfare," the mother is subject to
the whims and value judgments, good or bad, of the case worker
assigned to her, and the legislators who enact laws governing welfare policies.

Mrs. Harrison: When you are drawing public assistance, your
whole life is legislated by the Bureau. And your social worker is

your legislator. When she tells you or makes the recommendation that you move, if you don't move, then you are uncooperative. And if you are uncooperative, then you don't get a check.

The social worker can take a pen and paper and write you in or write you out at will. You can challenge it, but it takes a long time.

Mrs. Harrison and *Mrs. Richardson*: A Negro case worker can be worse than a white. I don't know why exactly, but we feel that it is for several different reasons. First of all, it could be because the Negro social worker has a nice job, and lives easy, and could care less, because she has, so to speak, "made it." In other words, she feels like that you should make it yourself.

Now, if this could be one reason, then another reason could be also that because they are in the Bureau, they kind of have to go along with the Bureau's policies, if they want to keep that job. We feel there is some pressure being put on them to be more strict with us; they can get away with it better because they are one of us, whereas they can kind of convince us that this is the law, on the basis of, well, I am a Negro and you are a Negro, and I am telling you this is the rule. They feel we will accept it better coming from a Negro than from a Caucasian.

Dollars-and-cents wise, I don't think the social worker has much power, but then there are so many other things that a social worker can help a client with, rather than dollars and cents. Like referrals. Maybe you got a problem, the social worker should be equipped to give you some information about a resource, but because their case load is so heavy, they just don't have the time and, as I said, some of them could really care less.

Some of them really don't see what you see as a problem, as being a problem. For instance, I know a lady that has a child that the mother doesn't feel the child particularly needs any psychological help, but the school has recommended that the child have some psychological help. And then, but the social worker there again says, "Well, there is nothing wrong with her; she is just bad; all she needs is a little punishment," you know. This is the way it is dropped.

All three: The social worker keeps up with anything different in your house. On the one hand, they will criticize you because your house doesn't look right, it is dirty, it is untidy, it is this and that, and all the other things; but they come back again, and you got out a new piece of furniture, they want to know where you got it, how much it cost, how did you manage to get that much money out of the amount of money you get from the Bureau. If it were given to you as a gift, who gave it to you, and what is his intentions toward you.

   If you can stretch what you get from the Bureau to the point that you can have something halfway decent, you might even be cut down. Your budget might be cut. My girl friend, they took $10 out of her check a month. She has one child, and when the child reaches age seven, you are supposed to get $2 or $3 more difference at the ages of seven and thirteen. When this child reached the age of seven, she [the mother] bought a washing machine. Then her worker came out and the next month when they gave her the raise, he came to see if she had got it. Then he saw the washing machine when they brought it in, so the next month, that $10 was cut out. But in my case, I bought a new stove, with one oven on top and another on the bottom, and my social worker told me they could not allow me the $60 for a used stove; she would allow me $40, since I had bought a new stove. And if I could manage, it was quite all right. She didn't even put it down in her notes. She said if you can stretch it, you go ahead. It was too late, because I had already gone ahead.

Mrs. Harrison: They used to have the practice, I haven't run into any more of it recently, but they used to have a practice that if they came and you have a new piece of furniture, say, a television, or a nice record player, or something like this, and if that had been a gift from someone, they had to know who this person was, where this person bought this item, how much it cost, and if it cost $200, this was considered that you had had $200 extra income, and they made a deduction from your check until that $200 had been taken out.

Mrs. Harrison and *Mrs. Smith*:   Definitely, the workers have too many cases. Sixty is the case load. That's too much paper work, and too many problems that this one person has to be concerned with, and they cannot function properly. But each case worker, they need a case worker assistant to help with their paper work. They can help talk to the parents to find out more information while the worker is computing the budget, they can assist them computing the budget, and so many things they can help them with, because majority of the time another person can communicate better with the case worker and the client than the case worker can with the client herself.

   Welfare recipients detect some improvements in policies and attitudes of the Department of Public Social Services (formerly the Bureau of Public Assistance) since the anti-poverty program has been launched, and special organizations have been established, to assist the poor and increase the flow of information. In Los Angeles, the Neighborhood Adult Participation Project (NAPP) performs the function, in part, of enlisting low-income persons (predominantly in Negro and Mexican-American neighborhoods) in programs designed to better the relationship between agencies and the poverty communities. The NAPP program, controversial in several respects, has recently been shorn of its militant aspects and converted into a job-development effort.

Mrs. Smith: Things are lots better with the Bureau of Public Assistance since NAPP has come into existence, because they are able to function more, and NAPP can give the case worker a lot of help and information that she can feed back to the community so that the case worker can study the cases much better and function more with the people.

Mrs. Harrison: If the recipient comes in with a NAPP aide, she gets what she is properly due. But if she comes in by herself, I am still sure that she gets quite a bit of runaround and quite a bit of information being hidden from her.

Mrs. Smith: [The staff at the Bell office] didn't know whether we [NAPP] were sending people or what. So the attitude on the whole in that Bell office has really changed, because usually when you walk in the door, they would just stand up and look at you, and take your name and your social worker, and tell you to sit there. And you sit there from eight o'clock until two o'clock without any service, but they don't know who you are. One day I went in, and I just used the client's name, I did not say I was from NAPP or anything, and I sat there from eight o'clock until 9:30. At 9:30 I put on my badge that says NAPP, right away I went in, and this is where I exploded.

Mrs. Harrison: In the past, I've had some excruciating experiences with social workers on home visits. Once a social worker came to my house, around two o'clock in the afternoon, for her home visit. Then they were supposed to come once a month; now it's every three months, they don't usually get around to it; even when they were supposed to do it once a month, they didn't get around to it. But she came in, and I had company, and it was a couple, man and woman, and we were standing around talking, I don't know what we were talking about. But, anyway, I knew she was coming, and I was prepared that when she came, that these people would excuse themselves and leave, but she came in and I introduced her to the couple that was there. And we weren't finished talking, so they weren't going to leave right then; they went over to sit on the couch, and the social worker and I were going to go to the dining-room area there and transact our business, you know, make out this annual affirmation. So as we talked, we got along pretty good, but now when she was ready to leave, she come back to my living room, she stopped there and started talking to this couple, now she wants to know what are their names, where did they live, and what is their business visiting with me, how long have they been there, and when do they plan to leave, do they live there, can they show proof of their records. . . . Now, at that point, I needed the check, and I knew that my relation with her was the only thing that stands between me and the check, so I let it slide, because if I object, she is going to say that I am noncooperative, and I am not going to get the check.

Mrs. Richardson: During 1961, 1962, and 1963, I lived in a one-bedroom apartment and paid $65 a month for rent. Well, in my budget, I was allowed $61 a month rent, and I had a worker who recommended that I move into the [public housing] projects, and I told her I didn't want to. So on the third visit, she pressed the point, and she told me if I didn't move that she would cut my budget, which she did. I was receiving the maximum grant for a family of two, $149 a month. She cut the budget, she requested the cut, and it was cut from $149 to $133. And so my experience with my worker is that when they tell you something they want you to do, they press you, they punish you if you don't, even if you offer a legitimate explanation for your attitude. If it is something they want you to do, they pressure you and force you to do it, but I found out that this is illegal, that she had no right to do this. I found out from BPA, but because I didn't know Mothers Anonymous [an organization of welfare recipients], I didn't know what my rights were, I just accepted it, because I thought maybe there was a rule that I could not challenge.

Since most of the welfare recipients are women separated from their husbands, their personal and legal relationship with their men —or any men—remains a perplexing problem. Welfare laws and regulations require that the father contribute, if possible, to the support of his children. Any amounts received by the mother from her husband may be deducted from future welfare payments. If a father is adjudged capable of contributing and fails to do so, he is technically subject to prosecution and imprisonment, and *any* man "acting in the role of spouse," whatever his relationship to the AFDC mother, can legally be required to make contributions. Many county agencies conduct early-morning raids, sending representatives to the homes of welfare recipients for the purpose of detecting whether a man is present. While the law in California allows the recipient to refuse entry, mothers contend that such a refusal would endanger their eligibility.

Mrs. Richardson: One experience that I have had down there— some other mothers have had the same experience— where the fathers are contributing to the court trustee, many times you don't receive the amount from those checks that you are entitled to. I know, for a period of three months, there this money was that I was supposed to be receiving every month, because of the father's contribution, and nobody had told me about it; I didn't even know it was there, and then finally when my worker told me, then I was told instead of them mailing it out to me, I was told to go into the office. And I had to go two or three different places, three different places as a matter of fact . . . but I told them I expected to be reimbursed for transportation, which they did, in order to pick up the check, which they were supposed to mail to me. So the way I solved my own problem, I told the father, just send me my amount, and I would give him a receipt for it, and he could pay the rest to the trustee, and that way I would get the money directly.

Mrs. Smith: Of course, they are running four months behind now, but last month, in March, I got a check for $30, and he is slow about paying, so whenever they get around to order him, they prorate it so it is always a large amount, but as long as they are four months behind, I don't have that money coming in.

And a lot of time, if you have them to give you that money directly, and you have the receipt and give it to your worker, here in the past they can deduct it from your check. It all depends on the worker. A lot of time, they have the man to pay us through the court trustee, because they are so uncooperative; they will pay you one time, and then next month they don't give it to you if they get angry at you about something. They won't pay it to you, so rather than go through chance, let them pay it downtown.

Mrs. Richardson and *Mrs. Smith*: There is this "Failure to Provide" section that is used to get the fathers to contribute, but it doesn't always work out well, because last week down in Compton they have five fathers going to jail. One was determined he wasn't going to pay any money because his wife was able to get a used car. She didn't need a car to haul children to and from the doctor. He needed a new car, and she didn't even need a transportation car, so he decided that he wasn't going to pay until after he finished paying for his new car; so he was going to do about six months [in jail]. And they said if this is the only way, that's what they are going to start doing.

This is what the attitudes are once you separate from the fathers, then they don't get to dictate to you how you should live, and they punish you for it, and they won't contribute. And now my boy's father has had to stay eleven days in jail to find out that he has to contribute, and it helps. Now he is paying regularly.

Mrs. Harrison: I think that it is good for some men, but on the other hand, to have this threat of having to go to jail if he can't make his child support, this is very bad for some men, too, because some men really desire to support their offspring. I know this one case, of course this may be a rare man, but he had a situation where he separated from his wife, he wanted to support his children, but he became hostile because, first of all, she went to apply at the Bureau for assistance after they separated. Now, when she applied, she automatically has to put in this complaint for child support. So when he had been notified that this complaint had been in against him, he became very hostile, because he felt that he didn't need the DA to tell him that he has to pay child support. He planned on paying it all the time, he planned that he was going to give so much a week to her, even if he didn't give it in cash money, he would go grocery shopping and bring her something. Or bring clothes to the child, to the wife, or what have you. All right, then he decided that he wasn't going to pay, period. So then he wanted to keep the child, and they sent him to jail, and he said, "Well, feed me and clothe me, but I am not going to give her a quarter, as long as the DA has to be involved." And he rather stay in jail than to give her anything on that basis. The point is, he is not arguing about the amount. He is just hostile about the fact that they don't trust his manhood enough that he would do the right thing.

Before Congress changed the law, when me and my husband was together, he became unemployed for a long period of time, oh, like he would get a job, and in a couple of months he would get laid off, because he was the last to come and the first to go. This kind of thing. And he exhausted his unemployment [compensation]. Well, when I went to the Bureau to apply for public assistance, I wish I knew this social worker's name, but I don't remember, but she told me that I could not receive any aid as long as there was a man in my house. And following that, my husband and I had to separate, because he felt that he couldn't afford for the sake of his children to stay in the home if he couldn't find a job or keep a job, and I couldn't get any assistance if he was there. So I know that these rules have broken up a lot of homes.

Under legislation passed by Congress, welfare recipients are entitled to rent subsidies which will enable them to live in private housing otherwise unavailable to them because of economic and related factors. A pioneering effort, the program has been the target of budget cuts initiated by legislators who fear this kind of innovation. It is paradoxical, then, that the incipient implementation of this legislation was governed by the same conservative Puritan code which has underlain welfare administration for decades.

Mrs. Richardson: Well, I was told by someone working in Fair Housing [a private group] about the rent subsidy, and she told me that she thought it would be a good idea that I went to apply, since in my present budget I wouldn't be able to afford the amount of rent that would be required to adequately house myself. So I proceeded to go to the main office of City Housing and put in my application and was interviewed the same afternoon.

The lady who interviewed me . . . said that I didn't qualify for rent subsidy due to my family unit; so I asked her to explain what she meant about the family unit, and she said they were only accepting a complete family where there was a husband at the head of the family. She said, "well, this is the rule now; it might be changed shortly, but right now, this is the way it is." And she told me that she could house me in Nickerson Gardens [public housing in Watts] just any time at all. And I told her, "I think that many people in Nickerson Gardens would like to come out. This is why I was sent to you from Fair Housing." Their purpose was to help people leave the housing situation, you know, the city housing project, and to go out into more comfortable, more acceptable housing.

Well, then I talked to the first party that had handed me an application blank to fill out, and I asked her did she know when she sent me in to be interviewed by Mrs. Green that my family unit would be disqualified because of such as it is. And she said, no, she wasn't aware of that, and she asked me if I am unhappy about it, and I thought it was unfair, she referred me to the manager. She told me to speak with the manager about nine o'clock the next morning, and I proceeded to do this. Promptly at nine o'clock, I called the office and asked to speak with the manager, and he was in a conference. So the next step I took was to report back to Fair Housing my experience, and then the next step was to call my city councilman, and immediately they got on the phone. And between ten o'clock and ten-thirty, the manager himself called from Housing to tell me that my application had not been rejected, it was before him right then, he was reviewing it; and he proceeded to tell me, you know, what the rules are, how to pay the rent, and so forth.

When I checked back with Fair Housing, the same lady that referred me to the office for rent subsidy told me that she has sent in several other Colored applicants and that none of these people had been accepted to her knowledge. And I said, "Well, what reason were the applications rejected?" She said, "Well, the Housing Authority had checked with their workers, and the workers said that some of these people kept dirty houses, or they didn't pay their rent on time, or that they had illegitimate children."

The case worker is all important, and the welfare mother is literally under her dominion. Any social worker who takes her job seriously is overwhelmed by the burden of home visits, paper work, regulations, and administrative detail, for which she is grossly underpaid. Some are sympathetic and anxious to help their clients; others are officious and patronizing, or contemptuous of their lower-class charges; but all are pressured by the moral judgments implied in the legislation they administer. Since "welfare" is officially treated as a privilege and never as a right, persons eligible for benefits are often denied access to information which could bring them higher allowances. During his unsuccessful campaign for re-election in 1966, California's Governor Edmund G. Brown, a liberal, condemned a proposal for new programs to inform residents of their rights under existing welfare legislation. In June, 1967, the chief welfare administrator of California's Imperial County complained that the welfare rolls had risen in his jurisdiction because a legal assistance organization funded by the Office of Economic Opportunity was bringing eligible persons into his offices, many of whom presumably would have been otherwise ignorant of their rights. The case worker who volunteers information to his or her client may find himself on the carpet downtown for "spending the taxpayers' money" too liberally and thereby creating a potential political embarrassment.

Mrs. Harrison: We have our medical cards and we go to our dentist, when we need some dental work; so we take our cards to the local community dentist, and he has to make out some kind of a form, and send it to the County, and they have to in turn send us to another dentist, requesting him to examine our teeth to see for sure whether we need this work. Now the question that comes to my mind is "Don't they trust the integrity of our community dentist who took the same training as the other one?", and this dentist they send us to is always ninety miles away! They don't give you any extra bus fare to get over there, you know, and get back. And our dentist in our neighborhood has taken the same training, just as qualified, and yet his opinion has to be verified by a Caucasian.

Mrs. Richardson: I haven't seen a Negro state dentist either. But if you would call your worker and let he or she know that you had to go for this, they will give you $2 for transportation. . . . And when you have to go up to Bell to pick that up, they will give you extra $2 for coming out there.

Mrs. Harrison and *Mrs. Smith*: But the point is, this information is never handed down so that anyone knows about it. . . . But one thing they should do is to have all the necessary information in leaflet or flier available to the people. They don't have that now. And so much of the things are just handed down to certain people. Unless you knows somebody that knows somebody, a lot of things you miss out on, as far as you miss $2 for transportation. People don't know they are allowed to get extra money in their budget for transportation going to and from the doctor twice a week, and so many little small things that they don't know about, that they should be informed. The social workers have an attitude as "this is my money, and I am giving you something, and if you don't jump the way I want you to jump, then I don't feel you are qualified to receive this assistance," and therefore they turn you down. Now before NAPP came in, there was a lot of conflict between the workers and the clients, but now since NAPP has been in existence and we act as the liaison with the Department of Public Social Services [new name for Bureau of Public Assistance] and the clients, the attitudes are changing somewhat.[1]

---

[1] A local office of the DPSS has recently been opened in Watts, thereby moving the intake office into the ghetto itself and away from the all-white community of Bell.

Mrs. Smith: My first case worker wanted to know why I was running out to General Hospital each day. So I explained to her why. She told me she didn't like it because she wasn't going to allow this in my budget, and she said that I wouldn't receive the check next month. . . . I called Mrs. King [with the state] . . . and she called me the next week and told me she [the case worker] had been terminated, thanks to me, because . . . her supervisor found out she had done other people like this; and they had said that if more people would speak up in things like this, then they could deal more with the case worker and to change them, because in their orientation, they felt a lot of them had been told different things about when they go into a Negro home, it is always dirty and filthy, children are always nasty and hungry, there is never enough food. Then I explained to them there is never enough food because you never give us enough money to buy any food.

Mrs. Richardson: Even though they [the social workers] come out with these degrees, they are not people-oriented, for the most part, they are not socially oriented. They don't understand people very well at all.

Mrs. Smith: Now, with the social workers out at General Hospital, their attitudes, views, and concepts are altogether different. If you are not getting your maximum budget, when you go out there and you hospitalize, they would tell you that you should be getting such and such amount, call your worker; and then when you call your worker and tell her that the social worker out at General told you that you weren't getting the right amount, you should be getting this and that, and you should be allowed transportation money, the social worker right away gets insulted and tells you that the social worker at General has nothing to do with them. . . .

I think social workers out at General are dealing more with the people, and they understand their problems more, and they are trained to help the people to help themselves more. All social welfare should help the people to help themselves, and I think that they apply this concept more than the social workers that have to come to your house and make home calls. A lot of them are tired, they don't feel like driving to your house and using up all their gas, although they are reimbursed for mileage, but they don't feel that this should be a part of their job on the whole.

Mrs. Richardson, Mrs. Smith, Bullock: The big difference seems to be that a social worker coming out of the south-east office thinks of herself mainly as a policeman, and the social worker in County Hospital thinks of herself as being a *social* worker.

Mrs. Smith: The important thing is to give you a chance to explain yourself, explain your problem, to allow you the amount of money that you need to seek employment yourself or try to go back to school, and to give you money to buy your children the basic things so that they can go to school looking halfway decent so that your attitudes and views about life would change, because this they don't do. They need a manual explaining what you are allowed to have, so everybody would know what they are supposed to be getting and what not, and the people won't always be frustrated and depressed, because the mother went into a hospital, she hadn't received her check, she was going in for a gall bladder operation, she didn't care whether she lived or died. Another BPA recipient had gotten her check, and ten days later the check had not been returned, and this mother didn't have any food in her home. Her mother had to quit her job in Modesto and come down, because the case worker told this mother that he didn't give a damn what happened. Her mother had to come down and take care of these children when they could have supplied an emergency homemaker in that home. And the mother just went to the hospital, she didn't care, and this is a bad way to go into a hospital, with a bad attitude that you don't care whether you live or die. And then when I approached the worker, he said he didn't say that, he didn't know that she was going into the hospital, and he had altogether a different idea, he was going to take an emergency grocery order out to her mother that evening, and the mother has six little children at home, but her mother had to quit her job and come down here.

And then when I spoke to his supervisor and informed him that the mother had to go on general relief, because she didn't have any forms or anything to take care of herself, right away the case worker was all upset, because I had got him in trouble. So then on one hand, they tell you they don't care what happens to you, and then when you get them in a jam, they want you to be sympathetic with them; this is what I don't get. They want you to be understanding and help them to get out of trouble. As long as they're stepping on your toes, it is O.K., but don't step on their toes and get them in trouble, they want you to come on to their rescue right away.

Mrs. Williams: I've had lots of different social workers. Like Mrs. _____. When I got the [living room furniture], she asked me who

got it, and I said a friend had taken me to a furniture store and paid
cash for it for me, and I said I don't have the money to pay him.
Then she said, if they would raise those [welfare] checks, would
you pay him for the furniture? And I told her, yes, I would. She
asks me how much I'm gettin' and I say, well, I gets $110.50 every
two weeks. She asks, did I know I was gonna get that when I went
on the County. I told her I didn't, but Al [a friend] told me, "You
won't get much but you will get enough to get by."

And I told him that whatever they would give me I would appreciate it, because I didn't have no choice. And if I could really
get a job, and see how it would come out for about a week or two,
then I would call my social worker and I would tell her that I had
me a job, and I appreciate everything they did for me, and I would
offer to give 'em some of the money back. But there's no chance of
me gettin' a job because I can't get no job.

See, I need some beds, but I can't get none. 'Cause Tommy
[a son who is on NYC] gave me $20 a while ago, and I got $12 left.
Well, it would be Monday now before I get my check, and I don't
have no food in the kitchen. Well, I can't take that money and buy
no bed. I could just live with what I got, just make out with what
I got, but I have to see my *children* eating because they got to go
to school.

The administration of welfare is decentralized in what is perhaps the most complex administrative structure of any governmental program. Most of the financing comes from Federal and State
sources; the development and interpretation of standards are divided between the U.S. Department of Health, Education, and Welfare (HEW) and the State Department of Social Welfare, with the
latter bearing the heaviest responsibility; and the actual administration is entrusted in California to the counties. A large county such as Los Angeles further decentralizes its welfare operation
(both the AFDC and General Relief programs) in approximately
two dozen districts, and some districts will have smaller intake offices as well as a district office. The opportunities for variation in
day-to-day application of policies are therefore manifold, and the
welfare clients, as well as the social workers, are often aware of inconsistencies.

Mrs. Smith: Sometimes they are a little more lenient. I know this
man is not employed, he worked one or two days out of a month. . . .
They were getting $220 every two weeks. There were seven chil-

dren and two adults. And the mother called me, and she said that
she wasn't getting enough, which was true; instead of getting $440,
they were supposed to be getting $476. So I called her worker, told
the worker there was a shortage of $36. She said, "Oh, yes, I will
make it up on her next month." So they sent her an extra $36, and
in the meantime, they wanted to know if she needed any furniture.
So her living room furniture wasn't up to par, so . . . instead of sub-
mitting the regular three estimates that you used to have to give,
I sent one estimate for the living room furniture and the bunk beds
and all. She got new bunk beds, new living room furniture, new di-
nette table and a new stove.

All three: These are things that people in other areas, like Inglewood, have been getting for years. . . . The Caucasian people are
going to Barker Brothers [a high-quality furniture store] at Inglewood and places they want and getting their furniture, but I
wasn't even allowed a bed until . . . after asking, and even then I
have to work to buy the bed if I earned the $50 . . . and I didn't have
the money to buy the bed, I mean, that was the worst frustration
I have ever gone through in my life.

Mrs. Smith: The Caucasians [in Bell office] could buy and get
the strollers and all the baby clothing that they needed, but the
Negroes could not.

Mrs. Harrison: I remember with my last two children . . . I wasn't
able to get a little layette . . . a couple of blankets, two, three baby
bottles, and this kind of thing, and I couldn't get that.

Mrs. Smith: You know, I took an inventory last time I was over
in that Bell office; they have more Caucasian fathers over there
getting grocery orders and picking up checks than there are mothers. And one man told me that he has sent his wife job hunting,
and he was going to stay home with the children; she was more able
to work than he was because she weighed more than he did, and
all the children were barefoot. And he said they had asked him in
the office to cut his hair, but he refused . . . maybe this is why he
couldn't get a job, and he said as long as he could get that emergency
grocery order every week, he wasn't going to work and his wife
would. He told me that . . . over where he lived . . . there were ten fathers who were going to the BPA office every week and get their
emergency grocery order . . . but you don't see Negroes with what
they have. Now, I think this is more or less the agency's fault as a

whole, and this is one of the things that I protested against, and I think it should be ruled out, that what is good for one should be good for the other.

Like, in my case, I am allowed $16.10 a month for goat milk because my boy has eczema, doctor put me on goat milk, because I like goat milk, so I said I would try to buck the system to see if I can get it; so I told my worker the doctor was sending her a letter for next month, and she took my word, and she had them send me the money right away for the goat's milk because goat milk is sixty cents a quart. So a lot of times, you can get a pretty decent social worker, she will go along with the idea, and then a lot of times, she would ask you if you have problems. Of course, in some areas they come knock on your door to check on your house, and if your bed is made up, they want to know why it is made up today. Then that goes back to the problem of whether you should keep a nasty house, or try to buy some furniture. If you can buy the furniture, then you are taking your food money to pay for this furniture, this is the first question they want answered. Are your children eating? Then they want to check your refrigerator.

All three: They are still knocking on your door, anywhere between seven o'clock at night and seven o'clock in the morning. That is another thing that should be outlawed. . . . And then they knock, and here again is where I'm thinking you can be written in or written out, because if he knocks, true enough the law says you don't have to let him in, but if you don't let him in, you won't get no check. You know, you are always caught between the devil and the deep blue sea. . . . And there is always so much antagonism. They create emotional problems, I mean the average person on assistance is emotionally disturbed, and yet and still they want to put a father image in your home.

An unemployed father is now eligible for welfare payments under the AFDC program, but there is an important hitch. Payments may be suspended if he refuses proffered employment, regardless of the pay level. The take-home pay from a job, indeed, can be less than the amount of assistance for which he qualifies in the welfare system, but his refusal can still lead to disqualification. In the slum ghetto, most of the employment available to men is in the traditional menial and low-pay category, to which there is increasing resistance on psychological as well as economic grounds.

The functioning of the system therefore creates another disturb-
ing dilemma. In the comments below, some of the women note the
effect of these and related problems.

Mrs. Richardson: This is encouraging slave labor, you know, exploitation, because I had the same experience. They sent me on a
job, and they really gave me a headache, I had to go to a psychol-
ogist, I had to run to somebody for help. Because . . . they sent
me on a job, and they only paid $1.30 an hour, and immediately
they wanted to cut me off. . . . Then these people get a chance to
exploit you. . . . I can play an organ, and they had me demonstrat-
ing organs. They sold two organs, one $1,100 organ, one $700 organ,
and do you think they gave me a percentage? They paid me $1.55
an hour!

I think we should pay some very strict attention to the state
law where we were required to take any available job and education too, I mean, job training; for example, because you may not
be able to take a person who is a potential baker or musician or social worker and give them another job, and say that he is required
to take that job because it's available; in other words, train him
to be a mechanic when he is potentially a social worker, force him
to fit in, a square peg in a round hole, you know; this is against the
law of nature.

Mrs. Smith: There is money appropriated through BPA that where
there are no children involved, and just a single man or a single woman, a husband and wife, they can get $200 a month and go to college.
. . . I asked about this, because I wanted to go back to college, and
they told me I was getting my grant, and they couldn't give me any
more to go to school. But then when I did go out to L.A. State, I had
the supervisor and the worker at my house, wanting to know how
was I paying the tuition to go out to State, and I gave them a phone
number to call. So they called these people, and they told them that
I went to school with them, they paid my tuition, they furnished
me transportation, and my worker went so far as to trail us out there
one night to see; so she had got a brand-new wig, so she stepped
in a mud puddle. She came out, she trailed us, we saw her coming,
so I told them to go around by this little dip, and when she got out
of the car, she went right in that puddle. See, a lot of them . . . don't
take your word for what you tell them, they want to see, and . . .
I saved the checks for her to see. And they had written all over the

back that they had paid the tuition. But her point was that she didn't want me to go to school to study to be a social worker, but the worker I have now, she wanted to know when will I be able to go back to school. Now . . . they were encouraging me to go back to school.

Mrs. Harrison: One trouble with the poverty program is that . . . when the program is over, you are going to be right back where you started. You are not going to have your education, you are not going to have a job.

Mrs. Smith: And you stay right down in the poverty where you were first, so it's just really something to occupy your time for a few days and go back and sit down as you were until they think up something else to give you to do, to get you all stirred up, all enthusiastic about doing something to help yourself.

A frequent criticism directed against welfare recipients by "middle-class" Americans is that immorality and illegitimacy abound in the subsidized households. Many believe that welfare payments provide an incentive for procreation of additional illegitimate children. The fact is that a child is allowed less than $1 per day for *all* expenses: food, clothing, share of shelter and utilities, and everything else.

Mrs. Smith: One time a social worker was asking if you want a man to live in the house with you as a father image. They were also encouraging illegitimacy. And see, then they come out, they don't want you to have any more children out of wedlock to be put on welfare. What were they doing, then? Encouraging you, they wanted the man to be living there night and day.

Mrs. Richardson: And it seems that a certain segment in society is making very good plans to punish the people, women, who have illegitimate children. And . . . here is what I like to say: while I don't condone immorality, for the most part there aren't enough husbands to go around, and then too, well, a lot of people are really innocent; they don't know how it should be, and this comes from slavery. . . .

Mrs. Harrison: Back in slavery is when all the immorality, the illegitimacy came into existence. . . . The plantation owner was the one that introduced us to illegitimacy.

Mrs. Richardson: And right now, many workers would play with the recipients. I mean, this corruption, immorality is the thing of the day . . . and what I found is the one that has the most guilt is the one who is the quickest to punish someone else.

Mrs. Smith: One worker was fired from his job because he has been going with this lady for years and years, and each year she got a new car, and when she decided she was tired of him, he had a check held up, and she called him and told him to release it, and he said, "No." So she went over to the office and told them everything, and then he lost his job, because he had a wife and family.

Mrs. Harrison: You know, this business of fraternizing with one that is not your husband was introduced to us by the Caucasians. . . . This is why I want to hit the ceiling every time a Caucasian says anything to me about illegitimacy.

Watts: A View From The Outside

Late one evening in the summer of 1967, a teen-ager sat on the lawn of Jordan Downs housing project and, perhaps a little high, blew beautiful, cool jazz on a flute. Occasionally, a jet airliner roared overhead as it descended into Los Angeles International Airport several miles to the west of Watts. Its passengers, physically and culturally distant from the young flautist, may have known "Watts" only as a community in which rioting and arson had flared in 1965.

The white man's image of Watts, much like the traditional view of the African continent, is likely to be an uneven mixture of fascination and repulsion. His surface impressions are of an area characterized by quick violence, hostility to light-skinned strangers, exhibitions of sexual and physical prowess, indolence, immorality, drug addiction, and a general rejection of "middle-class" values. These impressions are rarely drawn from direct personal observation or experience, since the average white in Los Angeles County has never been in Watts. Until the summer of 1965, he probably was unaware that it existed.

Like most stereotypes, these impressions contain grains of truth. Physical violence does occur more often than in the suburban white (or higher-income Negro) communities; there are racial antagonisms, though not as deep or as pervasive as the nervous white may think; pot-smoking, extramarital sex, and other violations of standard morality are common, though there is increasing evidence that similar or greater violations in the suburbs are merely less obvious; and the frequent hustling on the streets *seems* to be a defiance of prevailing norms and mores.[1] Yet the total reality is

---

[1] See "Fighting Poverty: The View from Watts," by the editor, *Proceedings of the Nineteenth Annual Winter Meeting*, Industrial Relations Association, December 28-29, 1966, pp. 266-75.

a great deal more complex, and possibly less romantic, than the stereotypes might suggest.

If it were not for the massive public housing projects and the junkyards, the outer appearance of Watts would be almost like that of any other mid-city residential area. The residents view the community's newly acquired fame with mixed feelings. Its distorted identity as *the* riot area has brought several special programs and other benefits, and many of the youngsters now show pride in their association with Watts and a growing commitment to the community. But others, especially some of the old-timers, fiercely resent the journalistic identification of "Watts" as the ostensible location of every crime or riotous act performed in the central Negro ghetto.

Ambivalence expresses itself in varied forms. At Jordan High School football games, the students in the stands proudly give the three-fingered "W" sign that symbolizes their residence in Watts, and shout: "What has Jordan got? SOUL." The handsome youngsters in the Community Conservation Corps, a local organization funded by the federal government, march down the street to a rousing chant:

> Everywhere we go-O, People wanta know-O,
> Where do we come from? So we tell 'em:
> We're from Watts, you know,
> Mighty, Mighty Watts!

At the same time, the urge to "split" from Watts and find a more congenial environment is strong in many parts of the community, especially among the denizens of public housing. Though they still represent a minority force, the projects dominate the scene in fundamental and often controversial ways. Residents of private housing tend to resent the presence of the projects, regarding them as a source of crime, immorality, and demoralization. Ted Watkins, dynamic head of the Watts Labor Community Action Committee, probably reflects the feelings of most property owners when he denounces public housing as "piling poor people on top of poor people."[2] Many project residents would agree with the denunciation, and, other things being equal, would immediately move. But other things

---

[2] Watkins, a long-time resident of the Watts area, heads an organization sponsored by several trade unions, and funded by the federal government, for special employment, training, recreation, and consumer-education programs. The quotation is drawn from both public and private statements made by Watkins.

are not equal. Hundreds remain in public housing for all or most of their lives, unable to find comparable accommodations at a price which approximates the rental charged by the Housing Authority. A welfare recipient, for example, can rent a three-bedroom apartment in a project for about $60 a month. The apartments are not spacious, especially for the typically large family, but they are reasonably clean and adequate and the utilities are available at low cost. With private housing in short supply for a low-income Negro family, the project becomes an inevitable alternative.

The objections to public housing emerge mainly from the lack of privacy and space and the concomitant exposure of families to dangerous temptations or threats of violence. The migrant from the rural South will miss the garden space, however small; the yard and the trees; and, perhaps, the family "togetherness." In the big, impersonal city, particularly in the projects, the children may vanish from sight as they enter their mid-teens. The boys, especially, disappear into the streets for long periods, controlled more by the demands of their peers than the standards (frequently religious in origin) of their parents, or, more likely, their mothers. Lacking the presence of a father, the youngsters form alliances with one another and, almost literally, help raise one another to maturity. This sudden emergence into independence—a process identified in sociological jargon as "premature autonomy"—is a source of both strength and weakness. Many of the young people become creative, imaginative, and sensitive, but there are no clearly defined and socially acceptable goals toward which to direct these qualities. Their cleverness and charm too easily are channeled into mere hustling.

The spontaneity and independence of spirit, the search for "experience" in every form available, the interest in the immediate and the concrete rather than the impersonal and the abstract are rarely qualities which the traditionally structured school system finds congenial. The school primarily serves and appreciates a more disciplined and complaisant student. The creative youngster who is aggressive or undisciplined is less likely to survive the educational process than one who is quieter, more "cooperative," and sometimes not as intelligent. The school experience, one possible counterweight to the frustrations of the home and the street, seldom instills the sense of personal worth and potential which the ghetto youngster so desperately needs.

Despite its pervasive disadvantages, the ghetto is not without its appeal. As the Jordan youngsters affirm, it has "soul." At its best, life swings to a driving beat; the improvisations of jazz and rock fill the air; there is a warmth, an enthusiasm, a liveliness in human relationships which is rarely equaled in the staid suburbs; and a naturalness of feeling prevails in place of the inhibitions and hypocrisy of the larger society. The children are alive with exuberance, freshness, and charm, not yet defeated by the oppressiveness of their physical environment. The mother of the ghetto family, perhaps the most admirable figure of contemporary America, fights a continuous battle with the omnipresent forces which threaten the survival of her household.

In late 1968, a young adult described his feelings about the community: "The one bad thing about living in Watts is the amount of people I live around. But I know those people's ways in Watts. And I wouldn't want to learn anyone else's ways right now. The point is, I'll never be out of Watts. So you can send me to Baldwin Hills, with white people sitting on top of my house, and I wouldn't be out of Watts. I'm going to treat 'em like they deserve to be treated, and no different, just like I treat anybody in Watts, which is the way they expect to be treated, the way they deserve to be treated. And I'm not going to ever stop going into Watts. I love to look at them little black faces, running out in that street. Them little kids, I like to see 'em grow up."

In some respects Watts is a small town, almost unique in the impersonal setting of Los Angeles (once described as "seven suburbs in search of a city"). Strictly speaking, it covers a limited area, and many of the residents have attended Jordan and probably a local elementary or junior high school as well. It is not unusual for one to walk down 103rd, or 97th Street, or Compton or Wilmington Avenue and unexpectedly meet a friend or a former schoolmate, or drive down Central Avenue and be hailed by passengers in another car. The white is treated with wariness until his credentials have been established and the suspicion removed that he is a policeman, narcotics agent, probation officer, social worker, bill collector, or "missionary" bent on converting the "heathen" to the true Anglo-Saxon faith. Once the initial barrier is breached, the white will be accepted, or not accepted, as an individual (or, to be more exact, as an individual *white*).

The ambivalence is expressed in the lyrics to "Tobacco Road," a song popular in Watts in 1967, sung by blues singer Lou Rawls— himself a product of the Chicago ghetto:

I'm gonna leave and get a job,
With the help and grace of God,

Save my money and get rich, I know,
And bring it back to Tobacco Road.
Bring dynamite and a crane, blow it up and
      start all over again,
Build me a town I'll be proud to show,
But I'll keep the name Tobacco Road.
'Cause it's my home, the only life I've ever known,
I despise you because you're filthy,
But I love you because you're my home.

In other songs, such as "World of Trouble" and "Dead End
Street," [3] Rawls captures aspects of ghetto living which are readily
recognized by the youngsters: the hustler with his "processed" hair,
his big "white on white" car, and his "game"; the "hawk" (wind)
creeping into the tenement flat; the symbolic "dead end" street which
traps the youngster in frustration and poverty. Though the physical
and climatic conditions in Watts are superior to those in most other
ghettos, the hustling and the feelings of entrapment remain familiar.
The "excitement" of ghetto life is largely deceptive and illusory, for,
in fact, there is little to do in the heart of the slum ghetto. To the
customary greeting of "What's happening, brother?" the usual reply
is "Nothin'." For many years Watts did not have a movie theater;
the movies recently shown on Saturday nights at Markham Junior
High School auditorium were the result of a special post-riot under-
taking by City Councilman Tom Bradley and certain members of the
motion-picture industry. In early 1969, a new playhouse and drama
workshop was slated to open on 103rd Street. Youngsters who like
roller skating usually travel about fifteen miles to the Hollywood
Sunset Strip to a skating rink. In 1966, a new jazz spot opened on
Manchester Avenue, not far from Watts, but it took a minimum of
about $4 per person to enjoy the sounds. Even jazz—the ghetto's
indisputable contribution to American culture—remains out of the
reach of many of those who, more than any others, have created it.
      Friday and Saturday nights are "party nights." Liquor and
"grass" and music and sex provide the escapes from the harassment
and irritations of ordinary living, and, whatever the carping of over-
paid psychiatrists who live in Beverly Hills and Malibu, the catharsis
is valuable and necessary. Yet the escape is temporary and sometimes expensive and may even be a new source of trouble, since "Irvine" may show up. The conflict is virtually irreconcilable; both the
pursuit and expenditure of income will often be in areas officially

---

[3] The songs referred to have been recorded by Rawls for Capitol.

defined as illegal or illicit. Technical violations of law may be as common in the white suburbs, but this is of little comfort. Detentions on "suspicion" are commonplace in Watts, much more so than in the suburbs, and the reciprocal hostility in the community provides each antagonist with a ready rationalization for his behavior. [4]

On the other side of the coin, both the residents and "Irvine" are aware that certain offenses, notably simple assault and petty theft, are mutually excluded from the sphere of normal police action. These are considered matters for strictly private determination, subject to whatever recriminatory judgment can be applied within the community itself. There are, of course, instances where these offenses come to the attention of the police and the courts, but most of the time they remain officially unrecognized.

The more sophisticated and supposedly protective aspects of law are almost unknown in Watts. Consumer exploitation and fraud are an everyday part of commercial practice, made easier by the low educational levels and absence of usual financial resources within the community. A personal checking account is a rarity; almost all transactions are in cash, and receipts and records are scattered. The liquor stores do a thriving check-cashing business on the day welfare checks arrive, charging as much as $1 to $1.50 for each check cashed. Since checks are issued twice a month, on the first and on the sixteenth, the charges become quite high.

The few remaining stores on 103rd Street, the old commercial center which became "Charcoal Alley" during the 1965 riot, generally charge higher prices and higher interest payments on installment contracts than elsewhere in Los Angeles, partly because of factors beyond their control: high insurance rates, vandalism, poor financing, inability to maintain a volume inventory, and excessive delinquency on consumer accounts. But rumors abound that before the 1965 riot, several merchants regularly padded the accounts of their customers, trading on ignorance of arithmetic and financial matters. In most of these cases, there are now empty lots where their stores once stood.

Ironically, the poor are charged for services which the rich are offered free. The more affluent will cash their checks, even their personal checks, at a bank, department store, or grocery store without fee. The poor will sometimes be charged a non-refundable fee for the privilege of *examining* possible housing accommodations, whether for rent or sale, even though the unit may prove to be com-

[4] See Chapter V, pp. 133 - 36.

pletely unsuitable. It is equally ironical that the poor will occasionally pay for a service when a better alternative is available. The
liquor stores in Watts continue their check-cashing routine despite
the fact that the branch of the First Western Bank at 103rd and
Compton will now provide this service for many non-depositors
without charge, or at a reduced charge.[5] It is not unusual for a resident of Watts to use a private employment agency in job-hunting,
when the free, public employment service is only a few blocks away.

The pattern of consumption within the ghetto is influenced
to some degree by the discontent of the Negro poor with their role
as "second-class" citizens and consumers. They are forced by circumstance into a dependence on free or low-cost facilities, such as
public housing, county hospital, and so forth, which they tend to
regard as inferior in quality. In company with the middle class, the
poor are inclined to equate quality with price, and to be suspicious
of "bargains." Consumer studies have shown that ghetto families
remain loyal to advertised brand names in food and other products,
often rejecting the cheaper non-standard brands.[6] In spending
that part of their income which is within their control, the poor consciously avoid items which might be rated as "second class" in quality or performance. Only in this area of living is it possible to escape the demeaning second-class status which society has generally imposed upon them. Again it is ironical that the discount stores
which sell quality items to the middle class at a substantial saving are of little value to the slum ghetto resident, because they operate on a cash basis which puts them out of the reach of the poor.

This striving for a first-class status affects all age groups in
Watts, but most particularly the young people. Conversations
are often likely to focus upon cars, and comparisons among new
models are eagerly made in the fall. The youngsters talk knowledge-
ably about horsepower, compression ratios, and transmissions,
and dream of the possibility that some day they will have a car of
their own. The envy of the neighborhood is the kid who has "wheels,"
and if somehow he can manage to add a good radio (preferably with

---

[5] Welfare checks will be cashed free if the recipient is purchasing food
stamps. Otherwise, a slight charge is made, below the average charged by liquor
stores.

[6] See Kay Gannon, "Retail Food Trade in the ARA Study Area," Appendix to *Hard-Core Unemployment and Poverty in Los Angeles,* a report by the
UCLA Institute of Industrial Relations (Government Printing Office: September, 1965). Of course, it is also true that the relative absence of large chain-stores
in the poor ghetto means that many of the cheaper "house" brands are not even
available.

FM so he can pick up jazz on KBCA) and perhaps even a stereo-tape machine, his popularity is assured. To Americans unfamiliar with the distances and the public transportation deficiencies in Los Angeles, car ownership may appear to be a foolish and even incredible luxury, but in some ways it is often a deplorable necessity. The major industrial centers are, for the most part, located far from Watts, and a trip on the bus (bus*es,* to be precise, because two or three transfers are always necessary) will often require about two hours' travel time and about a dollar in cost each way. In some instances, it is literally impossible to arrive in time for the beginning day shift by using public transportation. In other cases, it is impossible to get home at the end of the night shift.[7]

Car ownership is a mixed blessing, at best. Insurance rates are prohibitive, especially for the youngsters, and many cars are completely uninsured. It is not uncommon for drivers to lack even a driver's license, or to drive with an expired or suspended license. The odds in favor of being stopped by the police are many times greater than they are in other parts of the county, and the resultant citations provoke more trouble, particularly when the fines go unpaid and warrants are issued for the arrest of the offenders. Maintenance and servicing costs are formidable, usually more than the new owners anticipated; streets and yards are dotted with the hulks of old cars in various stages of repair or deterioration. Many are tempted to obtain needed batteries and accessories by "liberating" them from other cars or from junkyards, sometimes in the middle of the night. The car, however essential it may be in some respects, is a continuing source of grief. It is noteworthy that both of the major California riots—in Los Angeles in 1965 and in San Francisco in 1966—were triggered by incidents involving automobiles.

"Irvine" is inclined to be suspicious of Negroes who drive newer or impressive-looking cars through the Watts area. The automatic assumption is that the cars must have been stolen. The young executive of a major, Negro-owned insurance company told of his

---

[7] A young graduate student at UCLA tested the Los Angeles transit system in 1965, when he rode the buses from Watts to various manufacturing sections of the county, going to Douglas Aircraft in Santa Monica and Long Beach, an automotive assembly plant in Van Nuys, and several industrial centers in the Huntington Park-South Gate-Maywood areas. He found, for example, that it was impossible to reach the Douglas plants in time for the 7:30 A.M. shift. His findings are summarized in "Some Practical Studies in Public Transportation," by Jay Carlisle, mimeographed, Institute of Industrial Relations, UCLA.

experience when he once ventured into the Watts community driving an expensive auto and wearing old clothes: he was detained
by the police and questioned at considerable length before he ap-
peased their suspicions. Of course, even when the immediate suspicion is shown to be unwarranted, it is usually possible for the
policemen to find some other reason for a citation.

The car symbolizes a major goal of the young ghetto resident—
mobility. Without wheels he is trapped, in a very real sense. He
wants to "get over," to have a pleasant home, good clothes, a car,
and respectability. The car appears to be the most attainable, at
least immediately, and for as long as it runs it gives its owner a sense
of control and freedom. Beach parties, visits to jazz spots, job in-
terviews, and scores of other experiences become possible, though
"bread" remains scarce and therefore a critical problem. Of course,
only a fraction of the lowest-income ghetto residents ever possess
a car legally, and many of them will lose possession for one reason
or another.[8] Crimes involving cars (auto theft, operating a car without the owner's consent, tampering with a vehicle, drunk-driving,
and various other traffic offenses) are second only to burglary among
all offenses committed by juveniles in Los Angeles County.[9]

Every circumstance he encounters appears to confirm the ghetto resident's belief that the major decisions affecting his life are
beyond his control. Too few are inclined to be optimistic about the
nature of their lives or their community ten or twenty years from
the present; William Armstead and Richard Townsend have observed the frequency with which the ghetto residents comment,
"It was like this when I got here an' it ain't gonna change." In a
sense, to be sure, things have changed in Watts: there are summer
parades and jazz festivals, special governmental programs, and
private job-development efforts. But it remains doubtful whether these "special" activities have fundamentally altered the life patterns of most people who live in the area.

These are generalizations which seem to cry out for documentation and it is not easy to satisfy the demand. The facts do not

---

[8] According to. the 1960 census, about twenty-seven per cent of the central
area's *workers* (the defined area includes major sections of the Negro and Mexican-American ghettos) commuted to and from work by bus or streetcar, compared to a figure of 7.5 per cent for workers in the entire Los Angeles metropolitan area. Lack of access to cars would be an even more critical problem
among the unemployed and persons completely out of the labor force.

[9] Figures are drawn from the records of the Los Angeles County Probation Department for two periods: the first six months of 1964 and the first six
months of 1966.

emerge readily or reliably from the traditional surveys and the researcher usually lives far distant from the slum. The expressions and experiences of the residents contained in the pages of this book offer some verification. Further corroboration can be gleaned from typical case histories of incidents in which the editor has been involved closely enough to observe how ghetto residents fare in their contacts with the legal system, education, health facilities, employers, and welfare. One common thread runs through all of these experiences: the Negro is the victim of a routine which entraps him even when it does not appear to be discriminatory in a direct racial sense. Let us start with law enforcement and the courts.

The relationship between many a ghetto resident and "Irvine" is one of mutual suspicion and distrust. Only occasionally does it erupt into "brutality," in the precise sense. The gratuitous beatings and shootings of suspects either on the street or in the back rooms of the precinct station sometimes occur, but these are only a part of the problem. The issue is more complex, related to the cultural biases of policemen in particular, and the police department in general, and perhaps most importantly, the *normal* functioning of the American legal system.

Four Negro youngsters from Watts, outstanding students, are riding in an old car. The police stop the car, order all of its occupants out, spread-eagle them against the sides of the car. One youngster mildly inquires into the reason for this treatment and receives a brusque response that the vehicle is suspected as a possible "get-away car" in holdups. The spontaneous gale of laughter from the kids annoys and befuddles the officers. One teen-ager explains that the car will not even start unless someone gives it a push. Several minutes later, the policemen reluctantly put away their guns and "split." No apology is offered.

A young white woman, a former teacher, is riding in a car with several young Negroes. The car is stopped by the police, and several minutes of questioning ensue. The cops obviously find it difficult to believe that her presence in such company does not reflect something immoral and illegal.

Four Negro youngsters traveling to UCLA in a car owned by one of them are detained by the West Los Angeles police one block from campus, at 10:30 in the morning on busy Westwood Boulevard, and in full view of scores of passers-by. The ostensible reason for the action is the fact that the car lacks a rear license plate, thus suggesting that it may be stolen. The legality of the car's owner-ship is demonstrable, but the suspicions of the police remain. A policeman phones Records and Identification downtown to deter-mine if any of the youngsters are wanted, using a telephone in his car. Within minutes, the car is literally surrounded by officers pour-ing out of their black-and-white cars, brandishing guns and forc-ing the youngsters to spread-eagle against the walls of a nearby bank. Bystanders are surprised and irritated, shouting to the offi-cers to let the kids alone. All four Negroes are brought to a West Los Angeles police station, where the police ransack the car in search of contraband. Seats are unscrewed, every area is examined. A war-rant is outstanding on one of the youngsters; the other three are in the clear. The youngsters point out that they are late for an ap-pointment on the UCLA campus, and an officer, obviously skeptical, phones to confirm this. Three of the youngsters are then released, without apology, the driver being ticketed for a minor mechanical defect but *not* for the missing license plate which supposedly led to the detention. They arrive on campus more than an hour late, visi-bly shaken, and convinced that the incident would never have oc-curred if their skins had been white. Their belief is undoubtedly justified.

A police car with two officers in it is parked on a Watts street. A gang of teen-agers and young adults, high on wine, descends upon the policemen suddenly and begins beating them. Residents gather around and watch. One of them moves to call for police rein-forcements, and the youngsters threaten to kill anyone who phones the police. Finally they "split" when approaching sirens are heard.

A young girl is killed in a parking lot on 103rd Street, near the new health clinic and the Jordan Downs housing project, and only a block away from Jordan High School. The police comb the sur-rounding area in search of someone who can describe the incident or identify the murderer, without avail. Many people were present in the neighborhood at 8:30 in the evening when the murder occurred, but no one seems to know anything about it except that the girl screamed. The area, close to one of the many liquor stores in Watts, is known as a trouble spot. A few days before, a white "dude" had been beaten senseless in the same neighborhood, and one of his assailants cursed bitterly when he could not remove a ring from the finger of the unconscious man. "If I had a knife, I'd cut the fuckin' finger off," he yelled.

A husband and wife are fighting a bruising battle with each other. Policemen arrive on the scene (atypically) and move to separate the combatants. The couple immediately forget their own quarrel and turn upon the officers.

The relationship between police and community is not always so abrasive, and an observer expecting this kind of excitement automatically would probably be disappointed (perhaps luckily, because otherwise he might have been the victim). Most of the time, there is merely an uneasy truce. Residents, even at a young age, learn that the symbol "E" on a car's license plate probably means "Irvine." In reality, any government-owned vehicle would have the "E," but the suspicion remains. A white driving about the area in an official University of California car, for instance, would generally be spotted as a plain-clothes cop because of the "E" on the plate. Even when such obvious identification is not available, the youngsters develop an incredible ability to spot suspicious or threatening intruders. The route taken by the cruising vehicle, the appearance of its occupants, and the way in which they observe the scene around them, all serve to identify them and what their real purpose may be. Again, the fact that Watts is somewhat like a small town makes this process easier than it would be elsewhere.

Not everyone in Watts is necessarily in this same "bag." Many older people, especially if they are home-owners, would prefer more extensive police protection, even though some of them have experienced discourteous treatment from policemen and have no reason to love the police as individuals. Most criminal acts perpetrated by Negroes are directed against other Negroes, and many residents, including most of the women, would never venture into the streets after dark. The property owners curse the projects, the migrants, and youthful gangs as sources of crime. Concerned residents petition for more and brighter street lights and a reduction in the number of liquor stores.

A Police Malpractice Complaint Center has been established by two chapters of the American Civil Liberties Union on Beach Street in Watts, designed to receive and act upon charges of police brutality or harassment. Most residents know nothing about it, and there is much skepticism about its effectiveness among those who are aware of it. There is no independent police review board in Los Angeles, and all grievances against individual policemen are handled within the police department itself. It is, of course, a rare occasion when an officer is disciplined by his fellow of-

ficers on the basis of a citizen complaint. The Complaint Center
can help build a general case in support of legislative or administrative action to reform police practices or improve the grievance
machinery, but it can seldom accomplish concrete and visible results in the specific cases brought to its attention. The process feeds
the pervasive cynicism within the community.

The resident arrested by the police must confront a strange,
impersonal, and terrifying procedure, though some have been "busted" so many times that the experience has become routine. Unless
he is lucky enough to have a steady and reasonably high income,
or influential friends, he will face the process alone and unaided.
A competent private attorney will cost several hundred dollars (a
socially conscious lawyer may charge as little as, say, $200), and
organizations such as the American Civil Liberties Union will take
the case only if there is a civil liberties aspect to it. The court will
appoint a public defender, or occasionally a private attorney with
fees fixed and paid by the court, to satisfy the constitutional requirement that a defendant must be represented by counsel. This is only
a formality, because the court-appointed counsel has neither the
time nor, in some instances, the competence to defend the accused adequately. In reality, the defendant does not have *an* attorney but, rather, a series of attorneys who show up in court on the
days on which the various hearings are scheduled.

The law requires that the detained person be released or brought
before a magistrate for formal charging and fixing of bail within
forty-eight hours of the time of arrest.[10] Chances are that the ghetto
resident will be booked at the police station, and once this is done he
has an official arrest on his record. He may be completely innocent
and further examination may result in exoneration. The paradox
of California law is that except for some arrests involving persons
under twenty-one, the arrest record can never be sealed in this circumstance; the expungement and sealing procedures, which are
limited at best, apply only to certain cases in which a hearing has
been held. The person who is a victim of "mistaken identity" must
now report an arrest on his employment application forms.

The suspect will be questioned by investigating officers, who
will be careful, presumably, to advise him of his rights to have legal

---

[10] Since the forty-eight-hours' stipulation excludes those times when the
court is not in session—which includes weekends and holidays—a person arrested after the adjournment of court on a Friday need not be charged until
the following Wednesday morning. It should be noted that in capital cases bail
may be denied.

advice and to remain silent. In the light of court rulings, a failure to inform the arrestee of his rights may result in a dismissal of the charges. The new policy has relatively little effect on the routine in the precinct station because the ghetto resident can seldom afford his own attorney and, in a surprising number of cases, he will still answer questions and make statements which may serve to incriminate him. The events in this early stage of his arrest and confinement will be critically important; they will help determine the nature and degree of the charge against him. If it is a felony, punishable by possible imprisonment, the District Attorney's office will handle the prosecution, while the City Attorney's office will receive the less serious misdemeanor cases. According to the results of early questioning and the interpretations of the District Attorney's staff, a given action could be regarded (for example) either as attempted burglary or mere trespassing.[11]

During this critical period, the suspect will usually be on his own, almost certainly if he comes from Watts. Only occasionally will there be a father at home to come to his assistance, and the mother will be so confused and intimidated that she will seldom be able to give him effective support. A youngster may count himself fortunate if any relative at all comes to the police station or the jail. Sometimes the parent will be uninterested or hostile, confiding to others and sometimes to the suspect that he might just as well stay in jail. Even if she is sympathetic, the mother may lack transportation, and may be unable to get time off from work to visit her child. Definite information is hard to obtain from the authorities, and anyone seeking such key facts as the physical location of the suspect, the exact circumstances and nature of the alleged offense, and the amount of bail to be required will find the experience baffling and frustrating. Several phone calls and visits to police facilities in various parts of the county, separated by many miles, will ordinarily be necessary to nail down the information. An unsophisticated and poorly educated person will feel helpless in the face of such bureaucratic complexity.

To make things worse, the suspect will be transferred from one jail to another several times in the first few days. A "dude" picked up in Watts will be taken to the 77th Street station, held there while he is booked and questioned, then sent downtown to

---

[11] Rarely is a lawyer present during the initial questioning. In fact, the accused could request that a public defender or a court-appointed attorney be present during the questioning, but it is unlikely that he will be sophisticated enough to make this demand.

the Hall of Justice to be formally charged and have bail fixed, transferred to the new county jail, and perhaps transferred back to the Hall of Justice jail where he will stay until bailed out, acquitted, released on probation, released at the end of his sentence, or sent to another facility. Someone trying to locate and visit the offender can spend a day or two driving throughout the Los Angeles area without catching up with him.

Most Watts residents picked up on felony charges will stay in jail. The exceptions will be juveniles without a prior record, who may be released to the custody of parents (or parent), and the minority of adults who are released without bail "on their own recognizance." Anyone age eighteen and older normally will be treated as an adult. A bail bond will cost ten per cent of the amount of bail fixed, far too much for the average slum resident to afford. The lucky one who is bailed out will be required to appear in court on at least three or four occasions, and a failure to show up at any one of them can lead to a forfeiture of bail and issuance of a bench warrant for his arrest. The courts are located in various parts of the county, the exact location determined in part by the area in which the crime occurred. If a Watts resident has been arrested for an offense taking place in West Los Angeles, he may be forced to travel all the way to the courthouse in Santa Monica, one block from the ocean, approximately a two-hour bus trip each way.

The judicial process in a felony case is complicated. A week or so after the first hearing in which he has been charged, the accused will be required to appear at a preliminary hearing to determine whether there is sufficient evidence of "probable cause" to sustain the arrest on the indicated charge. The testimony at this hearing is often decisive because it may be the only hearing in which the substance of the case is discussed. The District Attorney's office will put its major witness (or witnesses) on the stand, and the judge will decide on the basis of testimony whether the accused person should be held for trial. Sometimes the suspect is lucky: a key witness may fail to show up and may vanish from sight altogether, or, better still, may appear and undermine the prosecution's case. If a witness disappears, the suspect will be released but will remain subject to rearrest if the "victim" subsequently reappears. Some potential witnesses will be fearful about having to put a finger on the suspect, anticipating retaliation from his friends or relatives.

During this hearing, the ghetto resident will be "represented" by someone from the Public Defender's office. The suspect's consultation with his assigned counsel will consist, at most, of a few hurried words shortly before the hearing, or perhaps during the hearing itself. He has never met his counsel before, and may never meet him again. The public defender is carrying an armload of documents, has trouble recalling his "client's" name, and seems to make little effort to dig deeply into the case. He has had access to the District Attorney's files in the case, but it is unlikely that he has had time to study them carefully. Nor has he had occasion to obtain additional facts from the accused, from witnesses, or from other sources. To the accused, the hearing possibly represents the difference between freedom and years in prison; to the public defender, it is just another case, to be handled as routinely as possible.

If the judge rules that the evidence justifies a trial and that the defendant's legal rights have been observed, a date will be set for the arraignment, at which time the accused will enter his plea. This next hearing may be in another courtroom, and for the Watts resident the location is likely to be the county courthouse in Torrance, a middle-class white community which is about twenty-five minutes away from Watts by car, and about an hour and a quarter away by bus. The plea is another critical step in the process, but again the defendant is left virtually on his own. Unless he is unusually persistent and sophisticated, or has interested friends, he probably will not see his new counsel from the Public Defender's office until the morning of the scheduled arraignment, and then perhaps for only a few seconds.

The observer sitting in the courtroom, or standing in the hall just outside, is impressed by the scene. Scores of criminal cases are on the court's docket for the morning session, and the accused is never precisely certain when he will be called to appear. Defendants, witnesses, attorneys, and marshals mill around in apparent confusion, awaiting the appearance of the judge. These defendants are the lucky ones, those who are not yet behind bars. The less fortunate arrive in police vans outside, straight from the county jail. When their moment comes, they will be paraded into the courtroom. Their faces, even their names, are unknown to the men who are to be their lawyers. Every once in a while, a public defender will huddle with his charge, and a brief conversation will take place. "Conversation" is perhaps not an apt term because the accused usually says little. The defender is probably discussing the plea, and suggesting the course he prefers. The response is likely to be a nod of the head, or a shrug of the shoulders. The expression on the defendant's face will range from deep concern to apparent boredom and disgust.

In these proceedings, everything seems to depend on the transcript of the preliminary hearing which is now in the possession of the offices of the District Attorney and the Public Defender. The routine procedure recommended by the defender in many felony cases, it would appear, is to waive a jury trial and submit the case to the judge, for decision based on the transcript of the preliminary hearing and the probation report. The defendant, of course, is not bound to accept such advice, but the defender will probably explain that it is the best alternative available. He may assure a robbery suspect that, by waiving a jury trial, he *may* be able to bargain with the prosecution and judge for a county jail- instead of a state prison-sentence.[12] If the bargain is refused, the waiver agreement can be withdrawn and a trial scheduled. The defendant must give his answer quickly, and he has had no opportunity even to think about it. He cannot tell whether or not this is really the best "deal" he can expect, but it is likely that he will accept the defender's advice. There appears to be little else he can do.

The effect of this process, in many cases, is to transfer the decision, almost routinely, to the probation officer and the judge. The judge will defer his sentencing until the probation report has been submitted to him, and its contents will often have a critical influence on the result. The probation officer, another vastly overworked official, will put together the facts on the defendant's prior arrest record, if any; his employment and school status; his family and home background; and his impressions of the character and personality of the accused. The judgment in this case will depend on three factors: the transcript of the preliminary hearing, the probation report, and the judge's personal attitudes toward the nature of the crime committed. Judges vary considerably in their conceptions of the relative severity of various criminal offenses: some will be especially hard on narcotics offenders, others on robbers, still others on sex offenders, and so on. Unless he has a particularly strong bias in one direction or another, the judge will probably be guided by the probation report in determining the harshness or leniency of his sentence.[13] At no point in this complicated process, except in the preliminary hearing, has any testimony been taken on the crime

---

[12] The term of confinement in the county jail is shorter, the facility is more accessible to potential visitors, and the prisoner *may* qualify for a daytime work-release program. All of this reasoning, of course, is based on the assumption that the accused will plead "guilty."

[13] This, of course, refers to the judge's discretion in accepting a reduction in charge and in granting or refusing probation; the law itself stipulates minimum and maximum sentences for given offenses.

itself. The defendant has been "represented" at that hearing by a defender whom he had never met before and who was only partially familiar with the details of the case.

To an outsider, and certainly to a Watts resident, it would appear that the judicial process ultimately serves the convenience of the courts rather than the interests of the defendant. Some of the young people even suspect, wrongly, that the private information they give to the public defender will find its way to the District Attorney's office, and they have little respect for either the competence or the integrity of the men selected to represent them. They often believe that the chief purpose of the defender is to get the case out of his hands and into the hands of the probation officer and the judge, as quickly as possible.

A competent and knowledgeable private attorney will maneuver to persuade the District Attorney's office to reduce the charges against his client, in return for a strictly unofficial agreement to plead guilty to the lesser charge. This process, technically identified as "plea bargaining," has no officially recognized status within the judicial system and, indeed, is formally disavowed by the client in court at the time of the change of plea and the sentencing. It is, nevertheless, an integral part of the practice of criminal law, constituting a means by which the attorney can exploit the prosecution's and court's dislike for costly and time-consuming jury trials to the advantage of his client. This assumes, of course, that the defendant has been guilty of *some* violation of law; if he asserts complete innocence, or if the State's case appears weak, the responsible attorney will demand a full trial and seek an acquittal or dismissal of charges. The Watts resident sometimes refuses to believe that the Public Defender's Office is genuinely independent of the District Attorney's office. If the suspicion were justified, it would call into question the willingness and ability of the defender to bargain hard with the District Attorney's staff. Clearly, even with the best of motivation, the defender has little time for bargaining and maneuvering.

The overriding fact emerging from this complex process is that the accused now has a criminal record, unless he has been unusually lucky or has had a sophisticated attorney. He must, at best, henceforth affirm that he has been arrested on a criminal charge, and it is uncertain whether a potential employer will take the trouble to inquire into all the conditions related to and subsequent to the arrest. There are legal provisions for the expungement and/or sealing of records, as we have noted, but they are restricted to certain types of cases (principally, offenses committed by persons under twenty-one) and not generally known or understood. This has special significance for the ghetto youngster, who may have become involved with the law because he was "hustling." The "hustler" seeks an income, all or part of it, outside the law, by crimes ranging from gambling to theft and robbery. Many slum residents will hustle, at some time or another, largely because this has been a traditional source of income, and often the only one which appears to be available. Once caught, the hustler may eventually be compelled to adopt such practices as a permanent mode of living and source of "bread." Unless he can somehow arrange for erasure of the record, he may be barred from legitimate employment in firms or agencies which hesitate to hire persons with "criminal" records.

It is now an accepted fact that the penalties of the law fall most heavily upon particular groups: the poor, the ethnic minorities, and the politically unpopular. The observer in the Torrance courtroom does not need to be reminded of this fact, for a perpetual stream of Negroes and Mexican-Americans flows through the room. The Anglos seem a minority, conspicuous by their relative absence. Since the Torrance court serves a large section of the south central ghetto, it is not surprising that many Negroes are present among the accused. Yet the court's jurisdiction covers an extensive lily-white area in the southwestern part of the county, and other courts also draw disproportionate numbers of minority persons. Many of the defendants are young people, in their late 'teens or early twenties. For some it is their first encounter with the judicial system, but for others it has become almost a way of life.

The presence of minorities in the courtroom is an ostensible basis for the statement that Negroes (and Mexican-Americans) have less respect for law than do other ethnic groups. This statement, like so many others relative to minorities, reflects a circularity of reasoning which approaches tautology. The law, in its normal "nondiscriminatory" operation, automatically penalizes and entraps the minority poor. What constitutes crime in any society is a matter of social definition, and the activities of the more affluent and powerful are less likely to be classified as unlawful than are those of the poor and powerless. In its 1967 report, the President's Commission on Law Enforcement and Administration of Justice, chaired by the Attorney General, noted the pervasiveness of undetected and unpunished white-collar crime.[14] The illegal actions of the middle-class professional or businessman will less frequently

---

[14] *The Challenge of Crime in a Free Society* (U.S. Government Printing Office, 1967), pp. 31-34, 47-49, 51.

be penalized, partly because this group's influence on the lawmaking process itself is strong, and partly because the enforcement of law is more timid and less harsh in their areas of the community. The wealthier can afford high-level legal counsel, which both protects them from technical violations of the law and helps them avoid punishment if accused.

These are not the only factors which burden the poor in their relations with the legal system. The law of averages itself operates to their disfavor and disadvantage because the likelihood of a police interrogation is many times greater in the poor areas, especially black ones, than it is in those of the rich. The representatives of the law-enforcement agencies are not shy in admitting this; indeed, the practice is defended as a logical and necessary part of law enforcement. Inasmuch as the south central ghetto is a high crime-rate area, the police are more inclined to conduct a "field investigation" in any instance where they suspect illegal activity. The investigations may result in more arrests, thus boosting the official crime-rate index.

Sometimes a seemingly minor or superficial factor can trigger an investigation: the sight of a man unpacking something from the trunk of a car (this, in fact, incited an incident in 1962 which led to a police raid on a "Black Muslim" mosque in Los Angeles and the death of several blacks); the absence of a license plate; a normal infraction of a traffic law (the so-called "Deadwyler case" in 1966 centered on a death which resulted when a police officer *with drawn gun* approached the Negro driver of a car that had been stopped for speeding and possible drunk-driving). Investigations and raids are occasionally based on tips from anonymous informers, which, not infrequently, are erroneous. When the Mayor of Los Angeles in mid-1967 issued a somewhat guarded and obscure apology for a police raid triggered by such incorrect information, his statement was a precedent-shattering event.

When Negroes (especially young Negroes) venture outside the ghetto, the preconceptions of the police will again lead to questioning and detention. In many of the white sections of the county, the sight of a Negro walking the street will immediately excite suspicion, unless it can be presumed that he or she is a domestic servant.[15] Negro youngsters driving in an all-white area will often

---

[15] In fairness it should be added that in some wealthy sections, *anyone* seen walking the streets at night will be suspected, since it is assumed that all those who belong in the neighborhood will be riding in a car. The son of a United States Supreme Court Justice was once accosted by the police in a high-

be stopped for questioning, unless they are accompanied by a white adult. The Watts Negro will sometimes be hesitant about traveling in white areas. Of course, the average white will experience the same hesitancy about traveling in Watts, but there is a crucial difference. He looks upon the police as protectors, whereas the Negro regards them as enemies.

The policeman is not without his own case. Some of the residents, especially among the teen-agers and young adults, hate and distrust all policemen, even those who may be performing their duties without prejudice. The mere sight of a police car will arouse hostility in the breast of many a Negro in Watts. Some suspects will automatically scream "brutality" whenever they are questioned or detained, regardless of their treatment. Violence is quicker to erupt in Watts than in the white areas, and the police are correspondingly more jittery. Even correct and reasonable police behavior does not necessarily produce rapport: the two California Highway Patrolmen who arrested the Fryes in the minor traffic incident which triggered the August, 1965 riot apparently behaved impeccably in their initial handling of the inebriated youngsters.[16]

Nor can it be denied that irrespective of the quality of police practices, more "crime" will be committed in the slum ghetto. It hardly requires documentation to assert that the poor man is more likely to steal or rob than the rich man; or that, for the reasons suggested elsewhere, "hustling" in the legally actionable sense is more likely to occur in Watts than in Beverly Hills (a recent investigation of rigged card games at the Friars Club in Beverly Hills is a fascinating but fortuitous exception); or that an environment full of rage and violence will produce more murders and assaults. Even the relatively better housing conditions in the Los Angeles ghetto cannot eliminate the frustration and bitterness which a sense of social and economic entrapment engenders. When alcohol and pills are added to this brew, an explosion may be inevitable. An unemployed youngster who is physically powerful, unafraid to risk death, and "high" on wine or drugs is a formidable adversary.

The critical point in relation to the law-enforcement process is that most participants behave in a manner which seems logical and reasonable—and even inevitable—from their respective viewpoints. Though there is conscious discrimination in some in-

---

income area of the county, on precisely this basis, and his principled refusal to identify himself led to a brief stay in jail.

[16] See Robert Conot's excellent treatment of the 1965 riot, *Rivers of Blood, Years of Darkness* (New York: Bantam Books, 1967), pp. 3 - 29.

stances, few are genuinely aware that alternatives may exist.[17] The youngster who hates the cops, the cop who fears the kids, the attorney or public defender who functions in the assembly line of justice, the prosecutor who embodies "law and order," and the judge who dispenses an Olympian equity to all, are rarely corrupt or malicious villains. They live in accordance with a system and a procedure which alternately serves and entraps, depending on their own standing within a complex bureaucratic hierarchy. They perform a function which seems predetermined and predestined and very little amenable to any kind of personal choice.

The first encounter with bureaucratic routine occurs when the ghetto youngster enters school, and the pattern he finds there is likely to recur through his lifetime. In theory, the educational process provides an important "socializing" experience, by which the young person acquires the awareness, skill, and knowledge needed to function in the world outside the ghetto. Yet the school is, in a sense, an isolated outpost, an unreal place based on premises about life which are foreign to the youngsters trapped in its routine.

More than half of the young people of Watts will never complete high school.[18] Among those who do, a high percentage will receive only the form, not the substance, of an education. Their diplomas are a reward for good behavior rather than for superior achievement. Their reading, literary, and mathematical skills will be several levels below the twelfth grade, and the high school graduate may find that he is no more successful in the labor market than

---

[17] The behavior of Los Angeles policemen in the middle of 1969, as observed directly by the editor, serves as an appalling reminder that deep-rooted racial prejudice and personal viciousness remain characteristics of many police officers. I can cite scores of examples of harassment, gratuitous beatings and shootings, and bigotry perpetrated by the Los Angeles Police Department over the past few months alone, directed against persons of all ages and ethnic backgrounds but mainly against black and brown youngsters. The viciousness seems to be more intense since the defeat in May of Thomas Bradley, a Negro city councilman who was a candidate for Mayor, by the incumbent Mayor— who exploited the "law and order" issue. The most frightening aspect of the situation, however, is the extent to which the prevailing system can protect, and even encourage, the individual policemen responsible for such practices.

[18] The estimate is based on a study of the class of Summer, 1966, which showed that 650 had entered the B10 grade and only 301 had graduated. Though officials argue that some of the missing will receive their diplomas at other schools, at night school, or in the summer, the figures do not take account of those who drop out either in junior high school or in the interim *between* junior and senior high. Hence, it seems likely that the fifty per cent figure remains substantially correct.

his friend, who dropped out. When his experience is communicated to his younger associates, the motivation to stay in school becomes even weaker.

Probably a majority of the *graduates* of Jordan High School will, at some time, enter a junior college, college, or university, but it is uncertain how many will complete a higher education or even survive the first semester or quarter. Traditionally, the eligible students have been counseled toward a junior college in the central or southern area of Los Angeles, with the brightest of the youngsters encouraged to enter one of the smaller four-year colleges such as Whittier, Occidental, Redlands, Pepperdine, and Pomona. High school counselors appeared to accept the premise that a youngster from the ghetto would be more at ease and better adjusted in a small college than in a university. The opportunities were limited because these are some of the most expensive schools in the Southern California area, and only a scholarship winner could possibly hope to attend.

A growing concern with minority problems nationwide, plus the 1965 riot, has brought major changes. Colleges and universities, including many outside of California, actively compete for the bright students at Jordan, offering more scholarships, in relation to enrollment, than at most of the white schools in the district. The University of California at Los Angeles (UCLA) administers an Upward Bound program for selected Jordan students, housing them on campus during the summer and bringing them back for special Saturday sessions during the regular school year. The youngsters attend classes, lectures, concerts, and programs set up especially for them, and receive a unique exposure to the college environment. By the time they have completed their Upward Bound experience, they have gained additional insight and motivation to push them toward higher education. But even before the Upward Bound projects were initiated under the antipoverty program of the Federal government, the Watts community and Jordan High School could boast of a graduate who became a Rhodes Scholar, the first Negro to be selected from the Western United States; and, together with another black from the East, in the same year, the first from anywhere in the country since the selection of Alain Locke in 1907.

Yet these programs, like so many others directed toward the residents of a ghetto, fail to affect the vast majority of people in the community. The youngsters selected are the ones who are regarded as qualified or potentially qualifiable, some of whom would have "gotten over" without the added support of special programs.

A pupil who is out of favor with the local school administration, or is considered to be excessively unconventional and undisciplined, is less likely to be recommended for admission. Many school administrators are obsessed with matters of "image," and perpetually worried about how their students will be received and observed by the middle class. Such concerns make the school bureaucrats even more timid than usual—an extraordinary achievement in itself.

Certain of the high school youngsters are sufficiently independent and unorthodox so that they spontaneously resent the unimaginative routine of school. Already made suspicious by experiences outside the classroom, they resist the imposition of authority and standards which appear to be without reason. The authorities and the rebels are constantly at war over such noneducational issues as haircuts, dress, language, and scores of other things. For months, the ghetto schools in Los Angeles fought bitterly against the "natural" hair-do adopted by many of the youngsters, both boys and girls. The "natural," considered African in appearance, violated the established tenet that Negro youngsters should look as much as possible like whites. Administrators preferred a shorter hair style for the boys, a straightened and more conventional style for the girls. Some of the schools have reluctantly surrendered on this profound issue, but their preferences remain clear. The kid with the "natural" is not a likely designée to represent the school at a conference in San Fernando Valley or West Los Angeles.

Of course, the administrators have genuine problems on more rational grounds. The slum-ghetto school is a trading post for drugs and narcotics of all types, though relatively few of the youngsters venture beyond the milder forms, such as marijuana and pills. Some of the kids earn their pocket money in school by retailing drugs to fellow students, and not a few make this their major source of income, during and after their school days, until "Irvine" finally catches up with them. Many of the youngsters are "high" on drugs or alcohol during school hours, or carry knives and guns. Sometimes this state of affairs erupts in violence, but more often the bitter and bored kids simply go to sleep. They are little concerned with what goes on in the classroom (if anything), and the school is delighted if and when they decide to drop out. In all likelihood they will be officially listed as "dropouts," and when the occasion demands, school spokesmen will loudly deplore the "dropout problem." An outsider might get the impression that the school is desperately fighting to retain those who leave, but the reality is frequently quite different. The administrators would be horrified if the alienated youngsters were to reappear in the admissions office.

As a rule, the girls fare better than the boys; a smaller proportion will drop out, though pregnancies become a problem in many
instances. They tend to make better grades than the boys, are quieter and more disciplined, do their homework, and spend less time
on the streets. The result, in part, is that the pre-eminent role of
the Negro *woman* is further strengthened, since she may be better educated than the Negro man. There is still another reason for
her relatively stronger position: she has probably managed to avoid
conflict with the school authorities and the law, while the "dude"
will have some sort of stain on his record. Even were she to become
a prostitute, her chances of avoiding detection by the police would
be better than the corresponding chances of the male hustler. Her
prospects for either getting a job or going on welfare are consequent-
ly more favorable than are those of the man.

The schools have their own methods of dealing with unaccept-
able or recalcitrant students. The law in California makes it difficult to remove a youngster from the school system before he reaches
the age of sixteen, but he may be suspended for several days, transferred to another school for "social adjustment," sent to a special
school for those with serious behavioral problems, or, occasionally,
referred to the juvenile courts for punitive action. The unwanted
youngster will rarely be formally expelled, because this is a complicated procedure requiring action by the Board of Education itself.
The school can make it clear to him, however, that his departure
would be welcome.

As a result, a constant flow of pupils enters and leaves the ghetto school. The kid transferring for "social adjustment" reasons is
supposedly departing his home school because his relations with the
faculty and administration there have deteriorated to an intolerable
level, and a new school environment, distant from the wayward
companions and other influences contributing to his lack of adjustment, will give him a chance to start anew. His transfer, typically,
is initiated by his home-school administration, and his destination
is invariably another segregated school elsewhere in the ghetto.

It is unlikely that the premise behind the "social adjustment"
transfer has ever been fully tested. Clearly, the environment of one
ghetto school is not significantly different from that of another,
and the irony is that the school to which the youngster goes will
already contain many others who have transferred for the same
reason. Thus he will encounter at least as many "bad companions"
in the new school as in the old. The real function of the adjustment
transfer appears to be to demoralize the obstinate rebel and persuade him either to drop out, when he can, or to accept the author-

ity of the administrators and teachers. Otherwise, he will face a series of transfers and accompanying conflicts with a succession of officials.

It would be misleading to suggest that a ghetto school, such as Jordan, is characterized only by discord and discontent. A high percentage of the pupils, certainly of those who survive the full three years, could not be classified as members of the "hard core." The rituals of secondary education—football and basketball games, rallies, dances, ceremonies, concerts, and so forth—are performed with at least as much enthusiasm as in the suburban white schools. For many youngsters, especially those who have managed to distinguish themselves athletically or socially, the school experience may remain a cherished oasis in an otherwise frustrating existence. They will stay loyal to Jordan, even while recognizing the weaknesses in the educational process itself.

The perceptive youngster detects and resents the inferiority of the education to which he is exposed. The more creative and imaginative he is, the more he is likely to come into conflict with the school bureaucracy. He has a low tolerance for boredom and routine, the very qualities which most often characterize the school system. One youngster comments: "They [the teachers] feel we don't want to learn, so they don't teach us what we should learn; they teach us what they want us to learn. A lot of students can't stand school; they are rebellious." Kenneth B. Clark describes the self-fulfilling prophecy of the educators:[19]

> Children who are treated as if they are uneducable almost invariably become uneducable. This is educational atrophy. It is generally known that if an arm or a leg is bound so that it cannot be used, eventually it becomes unusable. The same is true of intelligence.
>
> Children themselves are not fooled by the various euphemisms educators use to disguise educational snobbery. From the earliest grades a child knows when he has been assigned to a level that is considered less than adequate. . . . It all adds up to the fact that they are not being taught; and not being taught, they fail. They have a sense of personal humiliation and unworthiness. They react negatively and hostilely and aggressively to the educational process. They hate teachers, they hate schools, they hate anything that seems to impose upon them this denigration, because they are not respected as human beings, because they are sacrificed in a machinery of efficiency

[19] Kenneth B. Clark, *Dark Ghetto* (New York: Harper & Row, 1965), p. 128.

and expendability, because their dignity and potential as human beings are being obscured and ignored in terms of educationally irrelevant factors—their manners, their speech, their dress, or their apparent disinterest.

Teachers are neither universally loved nor universally hated in the ghetto school. The youngsters are quick to perceive differences in competence, interest, and motivation among their instructors, and their judgments are refreshingly free from prejudice. A sensitive white teacher will be rated high, an insensitive Negro low. As Clark suggests, the young people seek respect as individuals, and will respond to anyone who gives it to them. Their expressed attitudes toward Negro teachers, policemen, and social workers, among others, demonstrate convincingly that color does not automatically determine the degree of rapport. Indeed, perhaps the most abrasive relationship is that between a middle-class Negro teacher or administrator and a lower-class "street-wise" Negro pupil. Nor are the youngsters any more tolerant of incompetence in a Negro than in a white. Their discontent will not be assuaged *simply* by placing Negroes in the classroom and the administrative offices. They seek greater community control, but they are well aware that this goal is not reached by adding Negroes to the staff of a white-dominated school.

Of course, other things being equal, a Negro will find it easier to communicate with the pupils than will a white. Aside from this consideration, it is obviously important that the Negro youngster be exposed to the sight of competent and resourceful Negroes in "non-traditional" positions, especially so if the career models are men. Other things, however, are rarely equal. As some of the youngsters observe, several of the Negro teachers and administrators are placed in the ghetto school merely because they are black, not because of special competence on their part. Watts pupils sometimes express the opinion, rightly or wrongly, that the better and more qualified Negro teachers are eventually transferred to schools outside the low-income ghetto, leaving their own schools with the less qualified. Even when high percentages of teachers and lower-level administrators are Negro, oftentimes they will serve under a white principal, thus diluting and perhaps negating the positive impact of their presence. The sight of a white principal directing Negro teachers may only confirm a suspicion that the whites still run the show. To balance this, a Negro, former principal of Jordan High School, has become an area superintendent, with a jurisdiction covering many predominantly white schools, as well as the segregated Negro schools in south central Los Angeles. However, most students are little aware of him. It is also true, as we have seen in an earlier chapter, that community pressures in 1968 and 1969 were generating major staff and administrative changes in the area.

The major problem faced by a well-motivated and dedicated teacher is that the primary interests of the teen-ager may lie out-side the classroom. Unless he can observe some demonstrable rele-vance of educational subject matter to his own present and future life pattern, he will regard classroom attendance as an annoyance. The Anglo middle-class youngster may be equally disenchanted by the academic routine, but he is made aware by his surroundings and by parental example and prodding that it must be accepted and mastered. The ghetto youngster has no corresponding oppor-tunity to be impressed by the relevance of the classroom material, particularly in the more abstract and intangible fields such as the humanities and the social sciences.

Most heads of Negro families—in this case, the women—are conscious of the importance of education. Whatever truth there may once have been in the statement that Negroes do not value education highly, it has no current validity in Watts. Most mothers do their best to support their children in the struggle for a high school diploma, often making valiant sacrifices in pursuit of this goal. The effort is wearing because the majority of people in the housing projects are on "welfare" and no provision is made for school supplies, extra clothing, and the various fees which schools continue to charge for items ranging from gym clothes to dances. In some instances, of course, family and general economic pressures force youngsters into the labor market prematurely, but the mothers usually strain to keep their children in school as long as possible.

The difficulty in the relationship of the youngsters to the edu-cational system lies elsewhere. The traditional school structure is not oriented to serve a youngster from a non-middle-class back-ground, and the Watts youngsters often (but *not* invariably) find their interests and needs more readily satisfied outside the school. Particularly in the later teens, one's status among peers, as defined in sexual and other terms, provides powerful competition for the more conventional academic status as defined by the teachers and ad-ministrators. The high achiever will sometimes be derided as "square" or "lame" by his peers, and there is a generally communi-cated expectation, shared by many teachers, that only a minimum standard of education is to be maintained.

Much of this is hardly unique to the minority ghetto or to the predominantly Negro school. The Anglo youngster is subject to many of the same pressures, and his own confrontation with the complex emotional problems of the teens is likewise unsettling. We have noted that there are counter-pressures in his environment which reinforce the motivation to achieve in school and even to proceed into college. On the other hand, the Negro youngster from the slum ghetto is likely to endure a special problem which relatively few of the Anglo youngsters will encounter. Since most of the Watts young people are raised in broken homes, and thereby exposed to what is essentially a matriarchal family structure, the need to demonstrate one's manhood and masculinity is particularly acute among the "dudes." Every challenge must be met, every sign of weakness or softness erased. If an excessive interest in education, homework, and studies becomes identified as unmasculine, the peer pressures against it will be overwhelming. The white teen-ager is less likely to confront these special constraints.

Another problem endemic to the poverty ghetto is the relative lack of sophistication concerning the requirements of an adequate education. Parents will recognize the practical importance of being "educated" in a modern technological society, but they have no basis for judging the quality of the schooling offered to their children, or the specific conditions which are essential to its effectiveness. This is particularly true, of course, for the migrants from Southern states where the qualitative standards of Negro education are especially low. Regular homework, the preparation of term papers and essays, the use of library resources, and other ingredients of a genuine educational experience will be little known or perhaps foreign to those who are themselves the product of an inferior education.

Whatever the level of sophistication, the home conditions in Watts are rarely conducive to maximum efficiency in the use of time and talent for study. Families are typically large; space is limited; the younger children will disturb the older; books and reference materials are scarce; and the distractions of TV, intrafamily quarrels, sex play, and so on are omnipresent.

The male teen-agers, in particular, may begin to "con" their parents with respect to such questions as the regularity of their school attendance, the amount of assigned homework, and the quality of their performance at school. A mother will often be unaware of the fact that her son has been skipping classes or failing to do his homework until she receives notification from the vice-principal's office of his potential (or actual) suspension or of some other disciplinary action. Even when she becomes aware, it is difficult to apply the discipline and the control which the Anglo parents can usually exert. She does not have the support of a man in the household, and by this time the counter-influences of the street may have become insuperable.

The early entrance into independence and autonomy creates obvious disadvantages for many young people in the ghetto, but it also has balancing compensations which the inflexible bureaucracy of the school rarely recognizes or builds upon. Forced to rely upon their own ingenuity for survival and uninhibited by traditional conceptions of form, they can become creative and innovative in many fields: language, art, music, drama, ceramics, and even poetry and literature. One of the most tragic sights in the ghetto is that of an intelligent and articulate youngster who can barely read or write. In his own way, and in his own jargon, he can express remarkable insights and spontaneous aesthetic talent. But the schools are slaves to tradition and form, resistant to deviations from an established norm.

Again, the bureaucracy rewards caution and conformity, and penalizes innovation and risk-taking. A teacher or administrator who experiments with radical departures from conventional methods may find himself (or herself) at odds with other teachers or administrators who have both a temperamental and philosophical attachment to the *status quo*. Not too long ago, a couple of teachers in a ghetto junior high school introduced some new approaches to the teaching of history in their classes, preparing skits for presentation by members of the class. By dramatizing certain incidents of history, they could enlist latent acting skills of students in the interest of learning. Though the experiment appeared successful from the viewpoint of the students themselves, the experimenters received a frigid reception from other professionals within the school. One teacher eventually abandoned teaching in the Los Angeles schools.

Textbooks and other materials are notably unimaginative in helping students achieve a positive self-image. Only in 1967 did the State Board of Education finally adopt a new American History text for use in California junior high schools, which gives recognition to the role of minorities in the building of American society.[20] The book is controversial, and not all schools use it. Though

---

[20] The book is *Land of the Free*, by historians John Caughey, John Hope Franklin and Ernest May. (Los Angeles: Ward Ritchie Press, 1965.) The adoption by the State Board of Education took place only after the authors agreed to undertake certain revisions.

Negro history has now been introduced into ghetto schools, it remains essentially an annex to an otherwise conventional structure. The youngsters note that, at best, it encompasses the contributions of a few outstanding Negroes— such as George Washington Carver— who have been "recognized" by whites.

The same lack of sensitivity pervades other parts of the school program. Though school concerts, on special occasions, offer the music of composers like Duke Ellington and W. C. Handy, as well as William Grant Still, the standard song books give little or no attention to the types of music which could immediately appeal to youngsters of the ghetto. Ironically, the song books retain the "traditional American" pieces which are sometimes associated with slavery or with minstrel shows and other forms of entertainment in which racial stereotypes are commonly projected. An imaginative educational program would first build rapport with young people by making use of those materials which are meaningful to them and within their experience. While even a casual observer could detect the importance of "soul" music to a ghetto youngster, the formal school program functions as if it never existed. The most obvious bridges to empathy and understanding remain uncrossed.

The more conventional teachers and administrators offer impressive excuses for the failure of schools to educate the ghetto youngsters: excessive class size, weakness in the home environment, unavailability of funds for improved facilities, disciplinary problems which impede the educational process and undermine teacher morale, entrance of many youngsters who have been subjected to ineffective education in other states, and constant turnover among pupils and staff. Every excuse is justified, as far as it goes. In 1965, the Governor's Commission to Investigate the Los Angeles Riot (the so-called "McCone Commission") recommended that class size in the south central ghetto area, within elementary and junior high schools, be reduced from the present average of thirty-three to a maximum of twenty-two, and that a permanent pre-school program be established for disadvantaged youngsters at the age of three, concentrating on language skills.[21] It criticized the almost complete absence of libraries and hot-lunch facilities in south central schools, a gap which has since been partially filled. Yet, in most instances the deficiencies serve only as a rationalization for bureaucratic inaction, rather than as a basis for aggressive reform movements.

---

[21] See *Violence in the City—An End or a Beginning,* December 2, 1965, pp. 60 - 61.

School officials are uniquely defensive in the face of comments and recommendations which could be interpreted as critical of prevailing practices. In 1962 and 1963, the editor and an associate made studies of various school policies which had resulted in and encouraged the removal of many pupils, while obscuring the real reasons for their departure. The existence of such policies was obvious to and informally acknowledged by teachers and administrators, but for months the official reception to the published studies was hostile. A subsequent examination of dropouts from Jordan High School, conducted within the school system, confirmed that there is little correlation between the stated and the genuine reasons for "dropping out."[22]

In their contacts with the public schools, as elsewhere, the ghetto residents must confront bureaucratic inertia and a massive attachment to traditionalism. Many teachers regard only a few of their pupils as being genuinely "educable," within the framework of prevailing educational techniques. A teen-ager comments, "Teachers don't teach; they only give out assignments." There is, of course, a wide range of teaching ability and motivation within the schools, and some teachers will make an extra effort to reach and stimulate even the "hard core" among their students. They are exceptions: most of the teachers will "split" from the community at the end of the teaching day, after having performed only the routine of education. Their relationship with the sharp but irreverent "dudes" is not likely to be friendly.

His entrapment in the mindless bureaucratic routine of the school will convince many a teen-ager of something which will haunt him throughout his lifetime: that his destiny is controlled and perhaps predetermined by forces which he is powerless to overcome. The so-called "Coleman report," a massive statistical study of minority-group education, confirms the critical role played by anomie in affecting the achievement level of Negro youngsters. Testing the effect of a number of variables upon the achievement of Negro and white students, the study finds that Negroes are most clearly affected by their sense of whether or not they can realistically con-

---

[22] See Robert Singleton and Paul Bullock, "Some Problems in Minority-Group Education in the Los Angeles Public Schools," *The Journal of Negro Education*, Spring, 1963, pp. 137-45. The study of Jordan High dropouts was part of the "Back to School Pilot Project," conducted with Federal financing in 1963, unpublished, and available only in mimeographed form. The study found, for instance, that many boys officially listed as dropouts because of "lack of interest" actually departed because of an "unsatisfactory school situation."

trol their environment and their destiny. In the words of the report,[23]

> it appears that children from advantaged groups assume that
> the environment will respond if they are able enough to affect
> it; children from disadvantaged groups do not make this as-
> sumption, but in many cases assume that nothing they will
> do can affect the environment—it will give benefits or with-
> hold them but not as a consequence of their own action.

In the Watts area, most of the experiences of young persons
tend to reinforce the impression that luck and chance are more decisive than planning in determining their future. The whims and culturally influenced preferences of school administrators, teachers,
policemen, social workers, and employers remain controlling. At
Jordan, in the mid-1960's, an outstanding athlete was more likely
to make a "good" adjustment to school than one who was equally
bright but less talented in this special direction. An accent or a hair-
do can affect one's social or economic status, sometimes in unpredictable ways. Instead of offering the youngster a positive self-image
and a sense of control over his environment, the school is inclined to
achieve precisely the opposite effect. The "hard core" youngster
begins to drift through life, his direction and destination influenced
mainly by whim, accident, and impulse.

Except for a group of social scientists (and, recently, a few politicians) who espouse a guaranteed family income in some form, most
of the governmental and private policy-makers appear to favor job
creation as the foremost, if not the ultimate, solution to the economic
problems of ghettos such as Watts. The residents echo this sentiment enthusiastically and frequently. The most common complaint,
exceeding even the bitter recriminations against "Irvine," is that
jobs are unavailable and that Negro families in the slum ghetto
cannot earn enough income from legitimate sources to maintain
themselves above the poverty level.
The complaint of the residents clashes sharply with a prevailing belief elsewhere in the community that the opportunities for
Negroes have expanded many times over in the last few years.[24]

---

[23] James S. Coleman, et al., *Equality of Educational Opportunity* (U.S.
Department of Health, Education, and Welfare, 1966), pp. 320 - 21.
[24] See, for example, the results of a nationwide poll conducted by Louis
Harris for *Newsweek* magazine, summarized in William Brink and Louis Harris,
Black and White (New York: Simon and Schuster, 1966), esp. pp. 127 - 29.

So strong is this conviction in some sections of the white population that racial discrimination in the labor market is regarded as a thing of the past, a historical item which has no relevance to present conditions. The expressed grievances of Negroes are dismissed as the presumably face-saving excuses of those who cannot compete for existing jobs on the basis of skills and aptitudes.

White incredulity in the face of claims of discrimination has undoubtedly been strengthened by the pervasiveness of legislation and administrative orders specifically requiring equality of opportunity in employment. Virtually all states with significant minority populations, outside the South, have enacted fair employment practices measures; the California law went into effect in 1959, about fourteen years after the passage of the first state law in New York. Title VII of the Civil Rights Act of 1964 established a Federal commission (the Equal Employment Opportunity Commission) to apply and enforce the same principle nationally. Executive orders have further extended it to government agencies and private contractors doing business with the government, and most of the country's prominent firms have signed up in the special Plans for Progress program, thereby pledging themselves to affirmative action in recruitment of minorities for job openings. In the Los Angeles area, both city and county ordinances deal with "human relations" questions in general and with specific application to employment. The observer would glean the impression that few aspects of the labor-market problem remain unaffected by public policy.

The statistics, drawn from censuses and surveys, offer a somewhat confusing, but nevertheless revealing picture. The total Negro community has made economic progess in absolute terms, but the white population has progressed too. Therefore, a gap remains, with its continuing potential for frustration. Most Americans judge their employment success not merely in relation to some past level of money income, but, more realistically, in relation to what they consider the level at which they *should* be situated, a consideration heavily influenced by the norms projected by TV and the other mass media. Domestically, as well as internationally, a revolution of rising expectations is gaining momentum.[25]

---

[25] A special report, prepared by the Bureau of Labor Statistics and the Census Bureau, and released by the White House in early November, 1967, notes that Negro families have made some progress in average incomes relative to those of white families during the 1960's, but that the average Negro family still receives only fifty-eight per cent of the income obtained by the average white. It should be added that many official documents use "nonwhite" as equiv-

Perhaps of greater relevance is the new statistical evidence of a phenomenon which has long been obvious to any sophisticated observer of the American Negro community. The word itself — *community* — hides the complexity of the problem, for in fact there are several, quite distinct segments of the Negro population, each of which has progressed (or retrogressed) at a different pace. A recent White House report emphasized a major source of difficulty: "What is most troubling is that in many of the worst slum areas of America, life is not getting better for Negroes—it is getting worse."[26] The resident of public housing in Watts, or of the tenements of Chicago or Cleveland, was well aware of this critical piece of information years before the news reached the Washington economists and the White House staff.

In the Los Angeles area even a stranger could not fail to note the vast gulf between the "good" and the "bad" housing within the central Negro ghetto, if he were to venture from its western to its eastern boundary. There is no complete consistency of pattern, but, in general, the quality of housing tends to deteriorate as one moves eastward. The housing on the western edge, in the Crenshaw-La Brea area, reflects a middle-income community, and the still integrated Baldwin Hills neighborhoods contain some of the most attractive and impressive houses in Los Angeles. The ghetto to the east of Crenshaw but west of the Harbor Freeway, nearly all of it within the "curfew zone" designated in the final stage of the 1965 riot, is less attractive as a rule, but definitely no slum. This is not predominantly a community of professionals, but rather of the employed working class or, perhaps, the lower middle class. Their living conditions do not represent the "American dream,'" but they are several notches above the poverty line. As the traveler crosses the freeway, going east, the impressions become more mixed. Reasonably well-maintained blocks of single-family dwellings are interspersed with aging and dilapidated housing, though, as we have noted previously, the exterior appearance only occasionally suggests a "slum" as an Easterner familiar with Harlem in New York or Woodlawn in Chicago might tend to define it. The dissimilarities within the ghetto are, nevertheless, striking.

---

alent to "Negro," though the former term also covers Orientals who normally enjoy significantly higher living standards than do Negroes. This overstates the progress of Negroes, a distortion of little significance nationally, but important in California where the Japanese and Chinese populations are substantial.

[26] *Ibid.*

Of course, the resident of a Negro ghetto shares certain problems with his "soul brothers," whatever the quality of his housing. In most instances he will remain within the confines of a ghetto, his spatial mobility being considerably restricted. He may live relatively well, but his options in relation to location are markedly fewer than those available to a white with a similar income. Largely because the so-called neighborhood school remains integral to the American public school system, the school attended by his children will probably be inferior in educational rating to the average school in a white area, though again the differences *within* the ghetto are noticeable. And any black person, whatever his income, can suffer indignities from a policeman, salesman, or real estate agent, among others.

Despite these mutual experiences, the various communities within the larger ghetto exist virtually as independent economic and (to a considerable extent) cultural entities. On balance, a street-wise youngster from a low-income Watts family stands a somewhat better chance of being invited to the home of a socially conscious white in the western or northern Los Angeles area, than to the home of a Negro professional in the Crenshaw neighborhood. While there has been recent evidence of a tendency among the black intellectuals to re-identify themselves with the masses (Stokely Carmichael is an example of one intellectual who deliberately changed his speech patterns and other characteristics so as to make himself more acceptable to nonintellectuals), the divergences remain wide. If a "middle-class" Negro ventures into "Watts" at all, in most instances the residents suspect that his motivation is political or mercenary.

Civil rights legislation, even in the employment field, has had little impact in the low-income ghetto. If a movement were initiated to repeal the California FEP legislation, the opposition to it would undoubtedly be intense in the middle-class Negro areas. The voters in the low-income Negro neighborhoods would also voice their opposition, primarily because they would readily detect the racist nature of such a campaign; but the piece of legislation under attack would have little or no practical meaning to them. A surprisingly high proportion of slum dwellers, technically eligible to register and vote, would probably stay home. Thurgood Marshall and Roy Wilkins remain heroes to much of the middle class; but the residents of Watts, especially the young people, are less enthusiastic—assuming that they even recognize the names.

These differences reflect, in part, the changing nature of the labor market in general and discrimination in particular. Liberalized public policy has removed several of the traditional barriers to the employment of "qualified" Negroes in positions commensurate with their actual educational and skill levels, thus benefiting the middle class, or those who would immediately join the middle class if they were paid in accordance with their qualifications.[27] The experience of the Negro with a college degree, possibly a Ph.D., working as a mailman or porter, not uncommon in the days of *overt* and *identifiable* racial discrimination, is seldom observed today outside the South. Negroes with advanced degrees in such fields as engineering, research, data processing, public administration, and other technical areas often enjoy a seller's market for their services, at least in government or the major corporations.[28] But the Negro without these specialized qualifications is in a much different "bag," as the typical resident of Watts will quickly attest. The laws, court cases, demonstrations, and so forth have hardly touched his problems. Indeed, he may be worse off, partly because the general level of skill required in industry has risen and partly because employers have discovered more subtle ways to discriminate.

There is, in consequence, a wide "perceptions gap" within the ghetto itself and between the Negro and white communities as a whole. The low-income Negro perceives no progress, or he may even detect retrogression; the middle-class Negro perceives advances in some fields but not in others; and the average white apparently is convinced that Negroes, as a group, have advanced fast and far over recent decades, perhaps faster and farther than he would have preferred. The low-income Negro may believe that riots call attention to his critical economic plight, but it appears more likely that the whites regard them only as expressions of lawlessness.[29] The appearances of Negroes in nontraditional roles, however token they

---

[27] For evidence, see, *e.g.*, Paul Norgren and Samuel Hill, *Toward Fair Employment* (New York: Columbia University Press, 1964). I would emphasize that racial discrimination remains severe in the skilled trades, many sales and clerical occupations, and several other fields, and probably in smaller firms generally, except for traditional jobs. There also remain vestiges of salary differentials, promotional barriers, and other forms of direct or subtle discrimination.

[28] There is one qualification to this generalization. The graduates of certain "Negro colleges" in the deep South, characterized by inferior educational standards, may still fail to meet prevailing requirements.

[29] Differences between white and Negro attitudes on the effect of the 1965 Los Angeles riot are described in T. M. Tomlinson and David O. Sears, "Negro Attitudes toward the Riot," and Richard T. Morris and Vincent Jeffries, "The White Reaction Study," both reports issued by the UCLA Institute of Government and Public Affairs as part of the Los Angeles Riot Study. See also Brink and Harris, *op. cit.*, pp. 120-24.

may be, serve to persuade many whites that any Negro with talent and skill can succeed in today's labor market. From their limited viewpoint, Negro poverty is a reflection of personal weakness or inferiority, not of discrimination.

If this correctly describes the dominant attitudes of Negroes and whites at the time of the 1965 Los Angeles riot, the gap is almost certainly wider and deeper today. The communications media have bombarded the community with reports and information suggesting that job openings and placements, training slots, rehabilitation programs, make-work projects, and other benefits have multiplied in the Watts area since the summer of 1965. The training programs are ubiquitous, but in total they involve only a few thousand trainees at a time. Unless there happens to be a facility in their immediate neighborhoods, most of the unemployed or underemployed youngsters in the south central ghetto will be unaware of their existence. The general public is led to believe that a massive program of retraining has been launched in the ghetto, but in reality the various projects enroll only a small fraction of the area's eligible population.[30]

Controversy still rages around the activities of the Management Council for Merit Employment, Training & Research, a nonprofit organization of businessmen formed soon after the 1965 riot by H. C. "Chad" McClellan, a former paint-company executive who had once served as an Undersecretary of Commerce in the Eisenhower Administration. McClellan, like his friend John McCone, is imbued with a sincere passion for public service and a concern with the social responsibilities of business. Yet, by philosophy and temperament he remains essentially conservative, reasonably at ease with an "achievement-oriented" middle-class Negro, but distant from the cynical and rugged denizens of the slum ghetto.

Anxious to involve local businessmen in a private and voluntary effort to expand job opportunities for Negroes, McClellan persuaded a large number of executives to join him in accelerating the recruitment and placement of unemployed persons from the riot area. Working closely with staff members of the California Department of Employment, McClellan and his associates asked several hundred businesses to keep a monthly tab on the number of new hires from the south central area of Los Angeles, presumably coterminous

---

[30] The final report of the McCone Commission stated that as of May 1, 1967, 4,696 persons were enrolled in vocational training programs, exclusive of regular adult-school courses and NYC-CCC community work through the Watts Labor Community Action Committee; this figure is for the entire Watts and south central area of Los Angeles.

with the boundaries of the major rioting. The Council subsequently reported that the cooperating firms had made approximately 18,000 job placements from the curfew area between the late summer of 1965 and the fall of 1966. The figure was so impressive, especially in relation to the various estimates of unemployment in the area (a special census in November, 1965, found less than 12,000 unemployed in roughly the same area), that it immediately aroused skepticism. While defending the basic accuracy of the figure itself, the Council has carefully avoided the issuance of supplemental or updated figures. It commissioned a USC professor of business administration to study a sampling of the initial placements, who reached generally favorable conclusions as to the pay level, duration, and quality of the employment generated and the employees hired. Despite this, neither McClellan nor the author of the study would claim that the conclusions necessarily apply to the total figure. The data are sparse: the placement figure is based wholly upon the brief reports of cooperating firms; no differentiation is made between part- and full-time jobs, or between long- and short-term; no reliable information is available on the normal hiring patterns and turnover rates of the member firms, so that it is impossible to evaluate how much the placement of Negroes from the area has actually increased, if at all; and the reports are not monitored so as to assure that the figures refer *only* to Negroes from a uniformly defined area.[31]

All such reports are met with deep cynicism within Watts. Confronted with the statement that at least 18,000 job placements from his part of the community had already been made in a one-year period, the youngster will eye the speaker incredulously and respond, "You must be jivin', man!" He is especially skeptical if the Department of Employment is reportedly involved, knowing by long experience that "there's no action behind it." If he is "hard core," someone who is functionally illiterate, has a police record, or unsatisfactory work experience, he has probably submitted an endless number of applications without result. Or perhaps his self-doubt, alienation, and cynicism have become so deep that he has virtually abandoned the search for legitimate employment, relying on the gains from "hustling" to keep himself alive. If so, he will inevitably encounter the police, perhaps several times, and his prospects for imprisonment or premature death are depressingly high.

---

[31] The findings of the USC study are reported in "Experience of Los Angeles Employers with Minority Group Employees," by William H. Reynolds, Report to Management, No. 16, Graduate School of Business Administration, University of Southern California, March, 1967.

Largely because many ghetto residents are suspicious of census-takers, and strangers in general, they are missed in the official population counts. If they are involved in an illegal activity of any kind, they will vanish from view completely whenever a pollster or researcher appears. The census totals of population and unemployment in the Watts area, therefore, are invariably far below the estimates made by residents and researchers alike; in 1965, for instance, the McCone Commission report estimated unemployment at about 25,000, more than double the figure produced by the special census in November of that year.

The unemployed, however defined, constitute only one segment of the critical economic problem in a low-income ghetto. Many of those in the poverty bracket are outside the labor market, for reasons related to age, health, or their status as female heads of families with small children. Some are engaged in illegal or illicit practices (drug peddling, theft, robbery, prostitution, pimping, gambling) which produce an irregular and unpredictable income. Technically they are "self-employed," in a kind of subeconomy which partially serves certain felt needs that society has outlawed on moral grounds. It is unlikely that the small, "independent businessmen" in the subeconomy will ever be counted and categorized in the census.

Employment, as such, does not automatically end the poverty of a ghetto resident. In Watts, as in other sections of the nation, a high proportion of the poverty-stricken are already employed full-time.[32] The traditional "Negro" jobs pay low wages, and many are being automated out of existence. The youngster with an NYC job, paying $1.40 an hour for a thirty-two-hour week, or the adult with a NAPP job, paying $4,000 a year full-time, are counted among the employed, along with those who are experienced aircraft workers, professional employees, or secretaries. Yet these are specially created government jobs, subject to the vagaries of annual funding and roughly comparable to the WPA or NYA jobs during the 1930's. They are lumped together with all other jobs in the usual employment figures cited, but obviously they provide neither the income,

---

[32] A special report issued by the U.S. Department of Labor in the summer of 1967 guessed that subemployment (defined as the unemployed, the underemployed, and the fully employed who fail to earn sufficient income to bring them above the poverty line) amounted to about thirty-four per cent in the South Central area of Los Angeles. For national figures, see the latest available annual report of the President's Council of Economic Advisers, usually issued in January of each year.

the security, nor the promotional opportunity which permanent
employment would hopefully assure.

The special jobs, however, serve a highly valuable function,
because in most instances they are the only ones readily available
to persons in the "hard-core" category. Despite publicity and pro-
nouncements to the contrary, private industry and public agencies
have not substantially revised their hiring standards to expedite
the recruitment of job applicants with low educational levels, prison records, lack of experience, poor test performance, language difficulties, and "negative" work attitudes or characteristics. Again,
the ponderous bureaucracies of both public and private enterprise
move slowly and reluctantly.

In theory, the Employment Service (a part of the State Department of Employment, but financed by the federal government) is the
initial channel through which the Watts resident can be introduced
to regular employment, special training, or participation in one of
the antipoverty programs. Until the 1965 riot, the offices of the
Service were located beyond the perimeter of Watts, sometimes
in predominantly white and therefore hostile areas, but one concrete result of the riot has been to stimulate the location of facilities in the Watts community. Ironically, the incorrect journalistic identification of "Watts" as the locus of rioting has made it a
particularly popular area for new programs and new public construction. Even some ventures which lie outside the boundaries of Watts,
such as Aerojet-General's Watts Manufacturing Company, have
appropriated the community's name for its public relations value.

The resident who is immediately qualified for an available job
(and, therefore, not greatly in need of the services of the Department of Employment in the first place) will be referred without delay,
but nearly everyone else will be mired in an infinitely complicated
bureaucratic process. The applicant may be lucky enough to qualify reasonably quickly for an on-the-job training slot in one of the
major companies which receive government funds for such purposes,
but this is a long shot. The slots are limited in supply and only open
at certain times of the year, and the normal hiring standards apply
for all other jobs. The remaining alternatives are referrals to a training program, such as the Watts Skill Center, the Community Skill
Center in Gardena, the Transportation Opportunity Program run
by the Teamsters Union in Pico Rivera, or a special employment
project such as the Neighborhood Youth Corps (NYC) or the Concentrated Employment Program for adults. Many of these are useful and well-run programs, but the opportunities are limited, trans-

portation may be difficult and costly, and some interviewers may
still tend to screen out persons who are not regarded as employable,
such as those with a narcotics (i.e., marijuana) record. Whatever
the quality of the training, many of the applicants will be instinc-
tively skeptical about its potential value to them. Having seen little evidence that persons in their category actually obtain permanent and well-paid jobs as a result of such training, they may tend to
be mainly interested in the weekly training allowances. The chances
are strong that they will not enroll at all or will drop out before com-
pleting the program. Even if they survive the training, they may
then seek out another training program.

As in the case of law enforcement, the judicial process, and
the schools, it is difficult to identify a personal villain in the employment field. There are employers and agencies which continue to
discriminate on direct racial grounds, but this does not appear to
be the primary problem in any of the situations we have examined.
The observer notes, in fact, that a high proportion of the professional
employees in the various public agencies are Negroes. Among the
firms cooperating with the Management Council, many of them
government contractors, most are classified as "equal-opportu-
nity employers" and their reputations for maintaining merit employment are reasonably good. It is precisely this fact which illustrates
the complexity of the problem confronting the "hard-core" ghetto resident. He can be barred from employment through the normal routine of public and private enterprise, without a trace of discrimination in the legally actionable sense.

There are exceptions. Aerojet-General, a major aerospace firm,
has established the Watts Manufacturing Company near Watts,
and the usual hiring stipulations have been dropped. Police records
and absence of a high school diploma constitute no automatic bar
to employment. A number of enlightened executives and administrators in the Los Angeles area have begun a review of standard
personnel tests and other traditional impediments to employment
of the minority poor. Programs such as those sponsored by the Watts
Labor Community Action Committee and the Teamsters Union
regularly enroll the "hard core." Yet, as of late 1968, these remain
minor points of infiltration into an otherwise immovable bureaucratic structure.

The problems are subtly interrelated. The school bureaucracies and the law enforcement bureaucracies initially entrap the ghetto resident, and the results of that entrapment are then grist for
the mill of the employment bureaucracy. Inadequate education and

the police record are perhaps the foremost reasons for disqualification of the Watts resident from suitable work. One routine feeds,
and feeds upon, the other. The consequence will be that many will
ultimately be trapped in the most complex bureaucracy of all: public welfare.

The welfare system represents the ultimate triumph of bureaucratic routine. The life of the welfare recipient is regulated in almost every detail by the dictates and directives of the case worker,
the Department of Public Social Services (formerly the Bureau of
Public Assistance), the State Board of Social Welfare, the Department of Health, Education, and Welfare, the State Legislature,
and the Congress. Everything from the basic food-and-clothing
allowance for the children to the relationship of a woman to her
friends becomes a proper subject for inquiry.

As we have noted, the administration of the public welfare system is an especially complex and multifaceted one. The division between Federal, state and local responsibility leaves room for vast
inconsistencies in policy among the states and the counties. Per-
vading the administrative structure is a Puritan morality which
asserts the right—indeed, the duty—of the state to regulate the
private morals as well as the economic resources of all those dependent upon welfare assistance.

Essentially it is the AFDC (Aid to Families with Dependent
Children) program which governs the lives of mothers in Watts.
There are many other programs blanketed under the general definition of "welfare"—Old Age Security, Aid to the Blind, Aid to the
Needy Disabled, General Relief, and special medical services, among
others—but none approaches the magnitude or impact of AFDC in
the low-income ghetto.[33] The AFDC allowances are given primarily
to the female heads of households with children under the age of
eighteen, though California is one of the approximately two dozen
states which permit payments to families headed by an unemployed
man. For reasons indicated previously, the latter provision remains
secondary in importance, and desertion, divorce, death, incapacity or
imprisonment, or other grounds for absence of a male breadwinner,
continue as the major conditions qualifying a family for relief.

Before 1968, the poor family migrating to California could not
qualify for "welfare" under the AFDC program until it had been in

---

[33] In the county as a whole, the other programs, taken together, are more
expensive than AFDC.

the state for at least a year. Under the influence of a court ruling, California rescinded the one-year residency requirement in 1968, but it undoubtedly will be reinstated if and when the courts permit. Under a California law, needy families must wait at least three months after the desertion of the father, or a separation not accompanied by a divorce suit, before they are eligible for AFDC relief, regardless of their length of residence in the state.[34] There are many who smugly assume that "generous" welfare benefits attract hordes of potential freeloaders to California, but, in truth, the average AFDC family in Los Angeles County has resided there for fourteen years. The family stays on the AFDC rolls for fifteen months, on the average.

The "generosity" of California's welfare allowances is highly relative. Compared with those granted in Mississippi or Alabama, they seem impressive, but closer examination demonstrates the shallowness of such comparisons. In Los Angeles County, a mother with three children under age eighteen will receive an average of $221 a month, or $2,652 a year. The poverty standard now used by the Federal government, based on studies by the Social Security Administration, sets the line at an annual income of $3,335 for a family of four. The Bureau of Labor Statistics, in early 1969, issued a new calculation of a "moderate" budget for a city worker's family of four and fixed the level at $9,076 a year; its lower budget amounted to $5,915. By any definition, the welfare recipient's family is hardly wallowing in luxury in the high-cost Los Angeles area.

This is only the beginning of the story. The children may be dropped from the monthly budget when they reach eighteen, even though they may still be unemployed and living at home. The mother with *five* children in the household, only three of them under eighteen, may receive only $221 a month. In practice, the children may be kept on the budget after reaching eighteen, particularly if they are attending school or are about to do so; but sooner or later they will be dropped.

An income from any source other than "welfare," including gifts of some value, will be examined with extra care and suspicion, if and when it is detected. Of course, the absent father remains legally responsible for the support of his children even while he is out of the household, and the Department of Public Social Services will try to pressure him into making payments if he is able to do so. If he fails to pay voluntarily and resists the demands of the DPSS,

---

[34] Legal-assistance organizations have recently brought suit challenging the legality of many of these restrictions.

the District Attorney's office will be informed. While in theory the
man can be prosecuted and jailed for failing to provide support,
in practice this happens only in a minority of cases. Some of the
men will vanish from sight, possibly "splitting" the jurisdiction
of the local authorities. Others will make irregular efforts to pay,
or will send gifts to the children, but their chances for decent employment are already slim and a great many will end up in jail for one
reason or another. Whatever their reasons, they will rarely be reliable
providers.

The welfare system offers little incentive for the maintenance or
restoration of family life. On balance, it still remains easier for the
family to qualify for aid if the father is absent. If and when he makes
payments for support, they will be deducted from the usual welfare allowance, so that the family is no better off than before. The
relationship between father and mother may be so abrasive that
they prefer to remain separated, and the welfare of the children may
actually be served better by this arrangement. Certainly their exposure to violent parental struggles can be an embittering experience,
which may very well influence their own attitude toward family
life.

Under any circumstances, the major burden of supporting and
raising the children in an AFDC family rests on the mother. Technically, she is required to report any income or important gifts received by anyone in the household, but the extent to which this
is enforced will depend largely upon the case worker. Some workers
will inquire into the origins of any new piece of furniture or clothing
observed in the house, while others will be considerably more liberal
in their attitude. If there appears to be a major acquisition, however,
it will almost certainly be investigated. The worker may want to
know whether it is a gift from the father or from a boy friend, and
whether any other gifts have been obtained from the same source.
The value of a gift or contribution can be deducted from the regular
allowance, but again the policies vary.

If there is a new couch in the living room, or a new refrigerator
in the kitchen, or a new bed in the bedroom, the questions may begin:
"Where did you get them?" "How did you get the money to purchase
them?" "Do you have a boy friend?" "What is the giver's relationship
to you?" "Does he visit here often, or sleep with you?" "How can you
afford to buy things that aren't provided for in the budget?"

Though it would seem that the only relevant issue is financial,
much of the questioning will focus on the sex of the donor, if one is
discovered. The mother may be able to show that the item was pur-
chased out of the welfare allowance, but this is contrary to the pre-

sumptions of the DPSS. The budget is fashioned to meet the rock-bottom needs of the *children.* If extra expenditures are made by the mother, it is presumed that the money came from some other source or that she is scrimping on the regular items in the budget. When the "other source" is a man, the questioning becomes more intense. Apparently it would be simpler if the donor were female, and no question of a possible sexual relationship could be raised.

The welfare agency is deeply concerned about the possibility that a man, either the supposedly absent father or a boy friend, is sneaking back into the household. If there is a "man acting in the role of spouse," regardless of his relationship to the mother, he is legally liable for the support of the children. A woman who makes occasional contributions to the household would not be similarly responsible. In some areas, the authorities have arranged early-morning "raids" on welfare homes, designed to detect the presence of an unauthorized male.

"Morality" and economics thus become intertwined. It is not clear whether the woman is entitled to have sexual intercourse with a man, aside from the question of whether she receives anything tangible from him. Presumably the sexual act indicates that the man is indeed serving in the role of spouse, but it is uncertain whether the absence of proof of intercourse excuses him from legal responsibility. The relationship of the woman with any man is clouded, however platonic it may be.

If the husband, or any member of the household unit, is contributing money, the welfare allowance will probably be adjusted downward. In the past, as some economists have noted, this often constituted a hundred per cent tax on any earnings received by a member of an AFDC family. Unless the *net* income of the worker were above the amount of the allowance, the family could not measurably benefit from his or her employment. This put the older children in a peculiar position: as long as they remained in the household, their income must cover a part, or all, of the budget normally provided by the DPSS when they are classified as dependents.[35]

---

[35] A complicated formula governs the amount of income, earned by a child in an AFDC household, which must be deducted from the welfare allowance. Whether the mother benefits from his or her employment depends on the age of the child, the size of contributions made toward room and board and other items, the amount of savings accumulated by the youngster, and other factors.

As I have noted before, the 1967 Social Security amendments liberalize these policies somewhat, so that the AFDC household may retain the first $30 of monthly earnings without reduction in allowance and one-third of the combined net earnings of nonstudent members above that amount. A part- or full-time student will be able to retain all of his earnings.

Prevailing mores obligate the father and the older, able-bodied children to help support the household. The principle is clear-cut, from a popular viewpoint: taxpayers must not be required to assume the responsibilities which properly belong to the father or to another "responsible relative." The same taxpayers, however, have directly or indirectly created the disabilities which prevent Negro men from fulfilling those "responsibilities." Every burden borne by the low-income Negro household—from involuntary ghettoization to inadequate or inferior education, from poor housing to the family disintegration and illegitimacy directly associated with slavery and the social denigration of the Negro male—is a product of white society.

Contrary to some impressions that cheating is widespread among welfare recipients, precisely the reverse situation prevails. An audit of family welfare cases in California has detected intentional fraud in less than one per cent of the cases. Thousands of persons, eligible for welfare aid in one form or another, never receive it. Many welfare recipients never obtain the full benefits to which they are legally entitled, or they may be unreasonably disqualified from assistance.

Every potential expenditure, other than rent, food, and standard items, is subject to negotiation with the case worker and to his or her arbitrary decision. What about beds and bedding for the children? A washing machine? A stove? Bus fare for a teen-age son so that he can look for work? The AFDC mother is caught in a dilemma, whichever way she turns. Suppose the washer breaks down: should she wash all the clothes in the kitchen sink, with perhaps five or six children in the household? Should she try to get the defective washer repaired? Should she try to purchase another washer? If there are repairs, she must borrow the necessary money or take it out of the budget intended for something else, or possibly bargain with the case worker for some extra money.

The case worker may be sympathetic, but she too is trapped within a rather inflexible system. She can either "play it safe" and stick closely to the rules and precedents, or she can take chances and stick her neck out. In the latter circumstance, she will probably come into conflict with her superiors at some point, for the Department itself is under pressure from the Board of Supervisors. The Supervisors must bargain with the taxpayers, the State Board of Social Welfare, and the State Legislature, and the complex chain continues. Whatever his personal sentiments, no one in the welfare system will feel that he exerts meaningful control over the end result.

The empathetic and innovative case worker or administrator

is crushed by the sheer weight of the bureaucracy. The worker has sixty cases every month to deal with, and, whatever her own inclinations, she is forced to establish and maintain a routine into which the AFDC mothers are absorbed. If he has an uncompromising social conscience, the welfare administrator probably will not survive. Frustration will drive him elsewhere. Everywhere the fundamental law of bureaucracy can be seen in operation: responsibility is so diffused that "passing the buck" is easy and inevitable.

The physical and mental health of the members of the AFDC family is governed by the same principles and the same routine. The so-called "Medi-Cal" plan, which extends state-financed medical and hospital benefits to welfare recipients and indigents, remains the focus of controversy. Enacted under the previous Democratic administration of Governor Edmund G. Brown, it is a major target for cutbacks under the Republican administration of Governor Ronald Reagan. While the controversy rages, the average AFDC mother in Watts continues to be heavily dependent upon governmental facilities and the interpretations of rights made by a hierarchy of officials ranging from the case worker to the governor and members of the State Legislature. Traditionally, the County Hospital and the public health clinics have been the major source of critical medical services provided to the poor, and though the role of the private doctor has now expanded, the public facilities remain overcrowded with the patients from Watts and other low-income areas.

The County Hospital is about thirteen miles from Watts, and transportation for a sick person is a perpetual problem. Several bus transfers on inadequate public transit are tiring at best—and costly; for anyone who is ill or injured, the arduous bus journey is almost intolerable. Even if a car or ambulance is available, the trip can be taxing, and the inevitable period of waiting after arriving at the hospital will increase the tension and disability. A sick or injured person from Watts can get emergency treatment at, say, St. Francis Hospital in Lynwood, a private Catholic institution, but he will be referred to County (General) Hospital for more extensive or intensive treatment, unless he has the funds to cover the usual charges at St. Francis or some other private facility. The projected county hospital for the south central area is still a year or two away.

The welfare recipient can now take her children to a private doctor for regular medical treatment, and the allowable charges will be paid by the government. If she or her children require a major operation, it may be performed either in a private hospital or County, depending upon the nature of the operation and the interpretations of the regulations. County Hospital is not popular with the mothers of Watts, aside from the distance; the hours of waiting, the red tape, and the apparent routineness and superficiality of attention, the abundant rumors of poor care or incompetence make the prospective patient fearful and resentful. Even during the campaign for construction of a new county facility in South Los Angeles, some residents with whom I talked expressed doubt about the worth of another county hospital, and if they supported the proposal it was on the assumption that the new hospital would not simply be a duplication of the old. Meanwhile, the new clinic run by the USC Medical School hires local residents as neighborhood workers and struggles to achieve a genuine foothold in the community.

My observations suggest that the dominant reaction to health-and-welfare policies parallels the response to the other aspects of life affecting the ghetto resident. The youngster and adult alike are conscious of and continually reminded of a "second-class" status: the worst jobs are reserved for Negroes; the least and worst education is granted to Negroes; "due process of law" is least applicable to Negroes; and the poorest health care is available for Negroes. In minor compensation for these basic social deficiencies, society provides welfare allowances which are inherently demeaning and subject to the whims of hostile or inflexible bureaucrats. And, in an astounding display of arrogance, the whites themselves assume the role of the "exploited" and grieve that the Negroes are taking advantage of the taxpayers' beneficence.

Concerning Watts, the phrase which comes to mind is the familiar proverb: "The more things change, the more they stay the same." Watts has changed, and Watts is still the same. The form has been transformed, but the substance has not. Every problem has been solved, except the really important and difficult ones.

Everyone is searching for the perfect answer: something which is reasonably cheap, politically feasible, technically acceptable, and not very risky. This is chimerical, but the delusion persists. The answer, if there is one, lies in unexplored and dangerous territory, where the risks are great and the rewards uncertain. In the short run, it seems easier to initiate a few studies and conferences, spend some more (but, proportionately, not very much) money on palliatives, and trust that a solution will eventually emerge from the *mélange*.

The problem, in large part, is that "we" are dealing with "them."

The people on either side of the desk in the personnel office, or the Employment Service office, or welfare office, are different people, whatever their race or national origin may be. The "dude" on one side has "made it" in the highly stratified and organized society of contemporary America; the other remains on the outside. Each looks at the other, and thinks consciously or subconsciously, "Baby, if you were more like me, we could come to an understanding, and everything would be up tight."

Of course, in a sense they are both right, and therein lies the dilemma. We live in a society which values homogeneity and conformity, whatever it professes to believe, and we are dealing with heterogeneity. There are variations within the ghetto, between the ghetto and the larger community, and even within that larger community itself. Yet, ultimately, the price of access to success is still the capacity to merge one's individuality into the standardized pattern of an impersonal system.

If there is a justification for a white man like myself to write about the problems of black people, it lies in the duality of the world through which the problems must be approached. The Negro trapped in a ghetto lives in the midst of a society fashioned by others to serve their own needs and interests. The larger community defines the "role" of the Negro, and then condemns the Negro for playing the role, or finds a rationale for its attitudes in the resultant stereotyping of the black person. The Negro is caught in a "no-man's land": he lacks access to the full opportunities in the white sector, and is unable to achieve a cultural and economic autonomy of his own. His destiny is shaped by forces beyond his control, and only a profound change in the thinking of the white community can release him from the constraints upon the development of his potential as an individual.

A major hangup among whites is that so few of them recognize the creative potential of the low-income, non-middle-class ghetto resident. Even the white liberals, whose liberalism so often is a kind of group status symbol and an adjunct to their intellectualism, may bring with them an attitude of *noblesse oblige*. They want and seek to do "the right thing" in relation to the plight of the American Negro, but they may or may not have an empathy with the ghettoized Negro in the flesh. The Negro, expecially the resident of a slum ghetto, is perpetually treated as a problem that must be overcome, rather than as a valuable resource that has remained chained.

As long as this attitude pervades the community's approach to the genuinely complex problems suffered by blacks in the central city, there will be frustration, bitterness, and conflict. There are endless varieties of programs which will "work," provided they are financed and administered with imagination and boldness. No program, however perfect technically, will succeed if it proceeds from a premise which rejects the worth of those to whom presumably it is addressed.

The proposal for a "guaranteed family income" or "negative income tax," popular with several liberals and at least one outstanding conservative spokesman, contains this built-in defect. It is a much fairer and more efficient substitute for the complex and capricious welfare bureaucracy which now prevails, but it will neither solve the problem of poverty in its most critical form, nor assuage the discontent of those who feel unrecognized and exploited. Indeed, one implication is that poor people are inherently or inevitably unproductive and must be subsidized by society. It is undeniable that some of the poor, for reasons of health, age, family status, or mental capacity, *are* unsuited for any kind of productive employment, but this assumption does not apply to the vast majority of unemployed or underemployed residents of the ghetto. Unless it is accompanied by major structural reform of the entire economic system, the guaranteed income will ultimately be viewed as demeaning, just as "welfare" is.

The last thing the ghetto youngster needs is another reminder from the larger society that he is regarded as unproductive or unworthy. The schools, the police, the agencies, and the other social institutions have already conveyed this canard only too well. Every time the youngster says "nigger"—and it is often—he reflects, consciously or unconsciously, the judgment which society has imposed.[36] He is likely to be cynical about almost everything, including his own future in a system which has traditionally rejected him. It is this cynicism which every program in the ghetto must take into account if it is to have any impact at all. Otherwise, it will never even

---

[36] Perhaps there is an alternative psychological interpretation of this language. Some of the black residents of the ghetto now reverse the moral and ethical implications of certain words traditionally used by whites in an invidious sense. For example, "bad" can come to mean "good." In further rebellion against white standards, the youngster might attach a meaning to the term "nigger" which is wholly different from the usual implication.

Possibly the worst consequence of racism is the self-doubt and self-hate it has generated among black people. Mrs. Williams, for example, reports that one of her sons has been taunted by *Negro* administrators and fellow students at his school, because of the darkness of his skin.

partially involve those who are most alienated from the prevailing system.

This is why the "Black Nationalists" are in possession of a profound truth. Whites may deride what they regard as the simplicity and apparent racism of the slogan "Black is Beautiful," but it is a useful antidote to the common implication that "black is bad." The English language tends to use "black" as a synonym for "evil."[37] If blacks and whites are to live and work together productively, they must mutually reject the invidiousness not simply of such language, but of the images on which it is based.

For the Negro who refuses (or is unable) to become a white in everything but color—and there are skin lighteners to deal with that problem—the dominant white society provides two practical alternatives: (1) entrapment in unemployment, or welfare, or the traditional employment which offers an income below the poverty line; and (2) pursuance of a livelihood in areas officially designated as unlawful or immoral. With his cynicism toward the "token" anti-poverty programs, it is easy and almost natural for the hard-core ghetto resident to drift into and remain in "hustling" for his principal source of income. Though the white bigots will volubly condemn "hustlers," it is probable that many of them welcome the practice, because "hustling" offers an inexpensive rationalization for bigotry and a ready exculpation from their own responsibilities. The situation parallels, on a larger scale, the oft-cited experience of the underpaid and exploited (but "faithful," of course) domestic servant in a white household who occasionally purloins some silverware or other minor items. Her white employer, never seriously harmed by the thefts, will thereby find it easier to argue the "moral inferiority" of Negroes and to justify the low wages paid. The employer, indeed, can even assume an air of generosity rejected or betrayed, just as the average citizen who blocks the entrance of Negroes into "his" neighborhood, "his" schools, and "his" jobs can become loudly indignant about "all those Colored people" taking advantage of his "generous" welfare allowances.

Anyone who doubts the potential creativity of the hard-core ghetto youngster should take a closer look at the activities of the street hustler. Claude Brown and Arthur Dunmeyer have pointed out, correctly, that in another context the "dude" who runs a num-

---

[37] A few examples: "blackmail," "blacklist," "blacken," "black-hearted," "a black day."

bers game could be regarded as a mathematical wizard.[38] An unemployed person in a slum ghetto must use an uneasy combination of daring, imagination, calculation, and charm in order to survive at all. If no moral judgments were made and the usual criteria of a free-market economy were applied exclusively, his entrepreneurial skill might be rewarded instead of punished. Parallels in white society are again enlightening. At least one fortune in American business has derived from the originally illegal sale of alcohol; the man who was simply a high-level hustler (racketeer) one year was to become a highly respected businessman the next. A change in social morality and law had made the difference.

The attractiveness of street-corner hustling is difficult to understand outside the ghetto, because it is risky, uncertain and irregular in reward, and without a future. Yet these very qualities may give it an appeal to youngsters who, in the context both of history and their contemporary experience, find the middle-class career ladder meaningless and irrelevant. A job as a box-boy in a grocery store or as a service-station attendant holds no psychological problems for the middle-class, or even the rich, youngster. His acceptance of low-level work is temporary and uncommitting; this is no career, merely a means of financing a car or a surfboard or extra expenses. Indeed, his employment serves in a sense to demonstrate his manhood, the "character" and ambition which the middle-class culture prizes perhaps more highly than any other quality. Eventually he will wear a white collar and enter a trade or profession befitting his status in society. The route will probably be made easier by his father and other relatives and associates who have the right connections and know the right people.

No such alternative appears to be available to the Watts youngster, unless he stands high in his graduating class at Jordan and qualifies for attractive scholarships. The low-level job is no temporary or transitory phenomenon: indeed, it is archetypical of the "Negro" job in this country. Acceptance of such work does not demonstrate his manhood; in a sense, it denies it. He has no expectation, and no reason to expect, that he will soon follow a career path that leads progressively upward into the professions. There is no father at home to give him guidance and smooth his way into a respectable and decent-paying job.

---

[38] Testimony of Brown and Dunmeyer before the Ribicoff Committee, "Federal Role in Urban Affairs," Hearings before the Subcommittee on Executive Reorganization, U.S. Senate Committee on Government Operations, 89th Congress, 2nd Session, Part 5, August 29, 1966, pp. 1101, 1111.

Working at the kind of "slave" or "gig" most immediately available to him does not necessarily enhance his prestige or status within his peer group. Hustling seems to challenge his creativeness, intelligence, and ingenuity far more than a routine job would, and if it is risky, the risk itself may serve to prove his manhood. In this context, he has much in common with the speculator in the white community, the respected citizen who plays the stock market, drills for oil, gambles in real estate, or otherwise takes big risks for big stakes. Neither the ghetto hustler nor the white "businessman" is career-minded; the route through the various levels of a career, with its regular increments in salary and status, is not for them. Their temperaments are more suited to the irregular and uncertain, but perhaps more exciting, ups and downs of a gambler's life.

There are, of course, critical differences. The white speculator functions within a legal and social framework which sanctions and rewards his activities. The oil driller, for example, will pay far less income tax on his profits than will the steady, unspeculating middle-class careerist, thanks to the oil-depletion allowance. The risk-taker in the ghetto finds a contrary situation: the law is hostile and punitive. To be sure, he reports none of his hustling income to the Internal Revenue Service and he is not bothered by paycheck deductions. This is some advantage, and many youngsters deeply resent and suspect those deductions whenever they may work at a job. But the net effect is negative: his considerable entrepreneurial risk-taking talents lead not to a seat on the Stock Exchange but to a cell in County Jail.

The difficulty with hustling, aside from its illegality and the consequences thereof, is that it can reinforce a defeatism and cynicism about genuine opportunities for development of personal capacities in useful and socially acceptable ways. The alienated youngster, in particular, can become so bitter that he distrusts the motivation of virtually everyone. It is interesting that two of the public figures who seem to be most popular in Watts—John F. Kennedy and Malcolm X—both were assassinated. The fact of their assassination may tend to serve as proof of their sincerity: "They must really have been doing something if they were running that much danger." The resident is likely to explain the murders in terms of his own feelings. Though the now-official explanations are that Kennedy was killed by an emotionally unbalanced leftist and Malcolm X by a Muslim angered by his criticisms of Elijah Muhammad, the ghetto resident (and a great many outside the ghetto) may be

more inclined to think that their activities in behalf of the rights
of black people had something to do with the assassinations.

Obviously this degree of skepticism can become both self-rein-
forcing and self-defeating. The youngster who automatically antic-
ipates rejection, and acts on that basis, is more likely to be rejected.
A deeply wounded person will reflexively assume that everyone
else is trying to con him, and that he must "take" before he is "tak-
en." The resultant behavior will simply confirm the preconceptions of
some whites that the hard-core ghetto residents are inherently hustlers, and not to be trusted.

What is needed, in part, is a restructuring of the economy in
ways which will allow for the full expression and development of
talent in whatever form it occurs, regardless of the current (and
perhaps ephemeral) condition of the private "competitive" labor
market. It is tragic, in both social and personal terms, to compel
a potentially first-rate musician, artist, or actor to become a third-
rate mechanic, or perhaps even a hustler, in order to survive. At
the very least, every youngster, in or out of the ghetto, should have
the educational opportunity and economic support he needs during that critical period in the late teens and early twenties when he
is searching for his own identity and his role in the larger society.
This implies the existence of an educational system which is relevant
to his needs as an individual, and a public or private subsidy which
will be sufficient to relieve his more urgent economic pressures.

One imaginative approach, "New Careers," is a hopeful first
step. Creating new jobs in human services—medical care, education, recreation, social work, law enforcement—could put many
a ghetto resident on the first rung of a career ladder leading ultimately into the professions. A re-examination of conventional procedures that have a dubious relationship to performance on the job—
standard written tests, rigid educational or credential requirements,
stipulations regarding criminal records—could open the door to
tens of thousands who may have a potential which has never been
explored. The ghetto resident would at last have a practical alternative to entrapment in a "dead-end" job or hustling.

The development of "community" institutions is another route
that deserves exploration. The cooperative, community-oriented
corporation, integral to Robert Mason's concept of socio-economic
communalism discussed in an earlier chapter, and the citizens' board
attached to the local schools, as suggested by Paul Williams, are
means by which the community can experience the power and re-

sponsibility and, to some degree, the independence which it has systematically been denied. It would be foolish to pretend that these "solutions" do not themselves raise complex problems, or that it is ever possible for a "community" to achieve that total independence which is implied in some of the more extreme statements of the Nationalist position. But every meaningful experiment entails risk and the chance of failure. The only certainty we can depend on is the knowledge that the traditional approach has failed completely and finally.

The first priority, I think, is to improve the quality of teaching and law enforcement in the ghetto areas. And this suggests, more than anything else, a better quality of *teacher* and of *policeman;* no physical improvement, no reduction in class size, no revision of textbooks or curriculum, no "community relations" program, and no change in patrolling technique can offset the negative influence of an ill-equipped, insensitive, or prejudiced teacher or police officer. The tragedy now is that these professions, holding a strategic and critical position in the structure of the community, attract a type of personality which, frequently, is precisely the reverse of what is needed. It is frightening to contemplate, for example, that the *rookie* policeman is regarded by the kids, and obviously with good reason, as their major enemy. This can only mean that the police academies still attract and graduate many who are temperamentally and professionally unsuited for the role they should perform in the community. Even more frightening is the awareness that ghetto youngsters can now identify with and relate to only a small proportion of their teachers and counselors. Apparently the sensitive, dedicated, flexible, and insightful person needed in this function is, all too often, not attracted to or does not survive in a teaching role within the ghetto.

There is, as I have said, no easy answer to any of these problems. Nothing less than a fundamental change in the thinking of the white majority, and the infusion of innovation and flexibility into a bureaucratic society characterized by the opposite qualities, is required as a condition for progress. No white can really "understand" what being black means in contemporary America, but at least he can ask himself honestly whether he would change the color of his skin in the context of the existing society. He can ask himself whether, in a *black*-dominated society, he would willingly accept for himself and for his children the kind of schooling, the kind of "law and order," the kind of employment, and the kind of welfare which the whites now offer the blacks.

If he is honest in his self-appraisal, perhaps he will begin to understand why the slum ghetto youngster seeks escape in pot and pills. Perhaps he will even begin to know why people sometimes burn and loot and try to die. And perhaps his understanding will be the first critical step in the process of saving both whites and blacks from the "fire next time."

A Note on Language

The language of the ghetto youngster is, to put it mildly, always picturesque and imaginative. Used as a code among peers and a mark of membership in the "club," slang is an ever-changing instrument of communication. Some of the words eventually find their way into more general circulation, such as *split* (leave) or *dig* (like or understand). A few of the slang terms mean one thing in Westwood (Anglo territory) and another in Watts: *up tight*, for instance, usually means "angry" or "nervous" on the West side, and "everything is O.K." in the Watts area. However, in the ghetto, some slang words change meaning quickly, or can mean two different or perhaps contradictory things at the same time. A term in wide circulation one year can be obsolete the next. Undoubtedly this is one way by which the youngsters can prevent "nonmembers" from breaking the code too readily. I am told that there is an amazing similarity in ghetto slang among the cities of the country, though there are cases where a particular term will have a strictly local or regional significance. I have asked a few of the Watts youngsters to define some of the slang words in most frequent use as of early 1969, but I emphasize that by the time these words appear in print many of the following terms will have disappeared or their meaning will have changed.

Bad: This is a word which has both the usual connotation and a second one which is unique to the ghetto. When a "dude" says, "It's a bad scene," he means it in the typical and generally accepted sense. But when he refers to, say, a jazz group and describes it as "bad," this is high praise, and implies that the group is "together," "funky" (lots of "soul"), and "cookin'." The meaning intended is,

274

again, perfectly clear to the youngsters at all times and confusing to anyone else.

Bag: general term, meaning one's "thing," anything that interests or motivates someone or represents a usual activity. *Trick bag* describes a hustler's frequent routine—the verbal or other tricks he uses to get money or achieve other goals.

Blood: Same as *Brother* or *Sister*.

Box: radio or record player.

Brother or *Sister*: a fellow black person.

Cold: ungenerous, unfeeling, unfriendly. This can refer either to a person or an action: "He's a cold dude," or "That's pretty cold." It sometimes refers to a tough "cat" who often pulls a knife or beats up neighborhood people. But "cold," in certain limited senses, can also have a favorable connotation. As one youngster explains, "When I say, 'That's a cold-blooded automobile,' that means I want this car and I'm gonna get it." The youngsters can use "cold" in a number of different ways, with subtle shadings of meaning, but they always know by the context and voice inflection precisely what meaning is intended at the moment.

Cook: usually used in connection with jazz, or some form of musical improvisation in which the musicians are in a good (or, as above, "bad") groove. Synonymous with *work* or *work out*. The implication is that the group is "doing its thing," and "righteously taking care of business."

Cool: one of many terms indicating approval. "Cool" can refer to a person or an action: one can say, for instance, "That's a cool dude," or "it's cool." In all cases, it is a synonym for *up tight, together, groovy*. It has some of the implications of Marshall McLuhan's usage of the term, but is somewhat broader and less specialized.

Dude: male, usually a young man, generally synonymous with *cat*. The female counterpart is *broad*.

Gas: a noun, e.g., "it's a gas, man," which can mean either a very good or a very bad experience with someone or something.

Groove: to have a good time, usually implying dancing, partying, listening to jazz or rock.

Groovy: synonymous with *cool, mellow,* and *up tight*.

Honkie or *Honky*: a white person, usually used in an unfavorable sense. Synonymous with *Whitey*. In common use in 1967 and early 1968, but apparently not so much used in late 1968 and early 1969. Some of the militant youngsters now use the term *pig* instead, referring either to whites in general or, specifically, to white policemen.

House nigger and *Field nigger*: phrases drawn from the terminology used in slave plantation days, which then distinguished between the (more favored) servants inside the master's house and the slaves laboring in the fields. "House nigger" has an unfavorable, and "field nigger" a favorable connotation at this time. As one youngster explains the difference: "When the boss is sick, the house nigger says, 'Yes, boss, when you sick, we sick,' and the field nigger prays he will die because that's one less motherfucker."

Irvine or *Chico*: the police or a policeman. Commonly used in Los Angeles in 1966 and 1967, much less common in 1968 and 1969.

Jive: to lie or "mess around." Often used in the form of "jivin'," as in "The dude's jivin'," meaning that the young man is lying or "running a game."

Mellow: another synonym for *cool, groovy,* and *up tight.*

Right on or *Go ahead on*: a general expression of approval or encouragement. The youngsters add "on" to many standard terms, just for added emphasis.

Rip off: to steal. As in, "Someone ripped off my box" (Someone stole my radio).

Shine on: to ignore. Can refer either to a person or a thing: "I shined him on" (I ignored him) or "I shined it on" (I ignored it).

Slave or *Gig*: a job.

Soul: black, or expressing the feeling or personality of black people.

Taking care of business: on one's job. Also used in the more general sense of "doing what you are supposed to do."

Together: same as *Groovy.*

Trip: can be used either as a noun or a verb. "To trip" often means to get "high," on pills, "grass," alcohol, or whatever, but sometimes it merely means "having a good time," or digging the "sounds" with extra enthusiasm, or playing a game on someone.

Up tight: another youngster explains this term: "I feel like I'm ready, I'm up tight, it's cool. Like some cat would ask me: 'Man, how're you doing at school?' I say, 'it's up tight.' In other words, I got a fair average, I am moving through there with no problems, and it's not a strain, and everything is together. The black people use 'up tight' in many ways. Because I can tell my buddy, somebody said they were going to kick his ass. He might say, 'It's up tight.' And if I had any sense, I would know already that he *knows* someone is going to kick his ass. See, it's all by the phase of the conversation where you are communicating." Here is one example where the slang has almost a diametrically opposite meaning in the white community. However, the ghetto youngster will sometimes add to the confusion by using the term in the "white" sense: he may say, "The dude got up tight," meaning the "dude" got angry or nervous or defensive. Normally, when he uses it in reference to a thing or a situation, it means that everything is "together." Occasionally it is used as part of a longer expression: "up tight, out of sight." These words, incidentally, were the title of a popular song written and sung a few years ago by Little Stevie Wonder, a rock singer.

Chuck and *Jerry* give a general interpretation of ghetto language: See, in slang you find a word to fit his [the other guy's] conversation. We two know what we are saying, what we mean. It has meaning to us because we didn't get it out of a dictionary, which had a meaning to a society that does not want us included in it, so we have to find something to do and talk about, to get along with each other.

When you were young, you know how you used to talk to your friends without your mother knowing what you were talking about. It's the same thing. We are using the language that we don't want our mothers and fathers and other people to understand.

It all depends on your awareness of each other. When we have things in common, we'll relate to each other, and also to other people *when we want to.*

Of course, we know the whites have their language too. There comes a time when you got to speak your language, and there comes a time when you got to speak his. We have two languages.

The Contributors

Most of the names below are fictitious, but the brief biographical information is correct in essence. In several instances, I have changed or obscured details in order more effectively to conceal identities. It has also been necessary to omit the biographies of many participants, either because we considered it unwise to include them or because I simply did not have the information needed. In perhaps a dozen cases, the "interviewing" was done in the community by residents themselves, or the tapes were recorded by local persons whose names I did not even know. The ages given are approximate, as of the end of 1967.

"Al": About thirty years of age, he is a friend of "Chuck," "Tommy," and their mother. Not much is known about his further history.

"Bill": Eighteen years of age, he was born in the East but came to California when he was very young. He lives with his parents, and several brothers and sisters, in a house in Watts. He was transferred among various schools in the south central area until he dropped out (or was forced out). For a number of offenses committed when he was a juvenile, he was given probation. He has been irregularly employed since leaving school, but is now working with a project funded by the federal government.

"Chuck": Twenty years of age, he was born in the deep South, educated in the elementary schools there, and came to California with his parents, and three younger brothers, when he was about nine years old. He lives with his mother and four brothers in a housing project, and graduated from high school in the mid-1960's. For one offense he was given straight probation, which was in effect until

recently. He has been unemployed most of the time since leaving school, but has had occasional short-term jobs. He writes: "During the first two or three years [in California] things were booming for my family, and later things was all going bad. Later things began to boom and my father was injured on his job permently. This is when poverty became the cause of my family's defeat. My schooling here in California is not different from that in my home town. . . ." Then, when he entered high school, "things, people and surroundings changed. People seemed to sense a mass corruption but at this time it was not known. Large number of people began to talk of what is known today as Black Power. . . ."

"*Dick*": About twenty-one years of age, he was born in the Los Angeles area and attended local schools. Most of the time he has lived with parents and relatives in a duplex in Watts, and now is enrolled at a junior college. He feuded often with the administrators in high school, and was the target of various disciplinary actions. He finally acquired his diploma through junior-college attendance.

"*Fred*": About twenty years of age, he was born in Texas but attended junior and senior high schools in Watts, graduating in the mid-1960's. Until 1968, he lived with his parents and other relatives in a housing project, but then moved to an apartment toward the west side of the ghetto. Like the other youngsters, his employment has been intermittent and irregular, but as of early 1969 he was working in a market.

"*George*": About nineteen years of age, he was born in the Los Angeles area and attended the Watts-area schools, graduating from high school in the late 1960's. Until 1969, he lived with relatives in a house in Watts, but recently entered military service. He has worked intermittently since leaving school, but has been unemployed much of the time.

"*Henry*": Twenty years of age, he was born in Louisiana and migrated to California when he was nine years old. He attended junior and senior high schools in Watts, and graduated from high school in the mid-1960's. He has occasionally worked on a short-term job and in an antipoverty program, but most of the time he has been unemployed. He was on probation for several months, but entered military service in 1969.

"*Herbert*": About twenty years of age, he was born in Texas but came to Watts with his family while still quite young. He lives in a housing project with his mother and a large family, including three younger brothers and five sisters. He, too, is on probation.

He graduated from high school in the mid-1960's, and has been intermittently employed in local antipoverty programs since leaving school.

"Jerry": About twenty-four years of age, he was born in the deep South but came to Watts while still a small child. His parents owned some small houses in Watts, one of which they occupied, but they later separated and when I first met him, "Jerry" was living in a housing project with his mother and other relatives. Somewhat later, he married and moved into another project. He attended the Watts-area schools, graduating from high school in the early 1960's, and subsequently attended a junior college for a while. As a result of several run-ins with the law, he is now on probation. He has worked irregularly since leaving school, though he has recently been employed in a job financed by federal funds.

"Sam": Nineteen years of age, he was born in the deep South and came to California with his mother, brothers and sisters, when he was ten or eleven years old. He has three younger brothers and three sisters, all of whom live in a small house in Watts. He attended Watts schools through the eleventh grade, when he dropped out. He also has been on probation, but required to serve six months in jail as a condition. He has been unemployed most of the time since leaving school, but was intermittently enrolled in training or other antipoverty programs from early 1967 to early 1969.

"Shirley": One of Mrs. Fitzgerald's teen-age daughters, she attended South Gate High School, a predominantly white school located just to the east of Watts in a segregated, white, middle-class community.

"Steve": About twenty years of age, he was born in Texas but came to Watts at the age of nine. He attended the area schools and graduated from high school in the mid-1960's. He worked occasionally in antipoverty programs after leaving school, and later enrolled in a junior college. He, too, has been on probation.

"Tommy": About nineteen years of age, he is "Chuck's" younger brother. He graduated from high school in the late 1960's, and has recently been employed by an antipoverty program.

"Wally": Almost twenty-one years of age, he was born in the Watts area and attended the local schools, graduating in the mid-1960's. He worked in the recreation field for a time, and then attended a junior college. His employment has been intermittent.

"Mrs. Andrews": An older woman, age unknown, she lives

in the Watts area and her children all have attended the local schools. In 1968, she was attending classes in a junior college in the area.

"Mrs. Brown": The mother of "Fred's" girl friend, and a long-time Watts resident, she jotted down her comments in response to a suggestion by "Fred."

"Mrs. Farrington": Another older woman and long-time resident, she too was interviewed by a young adult.

"Mrs. Fitzgerald": An older woman, and long-time resident of the Watts area, in the late 1960's she was the president of a PTA in a local school. Her children were enrolled in area schools.

"Mrs. Gray" and *"Mrs. Osborne"*: Both older women, and residents of the Watts area, they have children in the local schools. They were interviewed by a young adult in the community.

"Mrs. Harrison": About forty years of age, she was born in Seattle, Washington, and came to the Watts area in 1955. She completed high school, and has been employed in several projects funded by the federal government. She has six children and for much of her life, since the departure of her husband, she has received welfare allowances. Now, however, she is employed by one of the training programs, after a stint with the Neighborhood Adult Participation Project.

"Mr. Martin": An older man, approximately forty, he has been active in past years in various antidiscrimination activities, though he is not an official of any organization.

"Mrs. Richardson": Separated from her husband, and the mother of six children, she has received AFDC allowances for several years. She was born in the South, but has lived in California for over twenty-five years and has attended some college here, in addition to working occasionally at a variety of jobs. She lives just west of the area designated as Watts, in a private house. Her age is approximately fifty.

"Mrs. Smith": Also separated, with two children who are minors, she too has received AFDC allowances. Born and raised in the South, she has lived in Watts for about fifteen years, and in 1967-68 worked with the Neighborhood Adult Participation Project. In addition, in 1967 she was enrolled in college classes, studying social work. She is in her middle forties.

"Miss Stanley": About twenty-eight years of age, she was born in Los Angeles and attended area schools at the elementary, secondary, and college levels. For several years she lived with her parents in Los Angeles, and served in a number of capacities within

several of the antipoverty and community-development projects. She later joined the staff of a large Eastern university.

"Mrs. Williams": The mother of "Chuck" and "Tommy," she was born in Louisiana and was married at the age of twelve. A resident of public housing, she has relied on welfare allowances since her husband deserted the family several years ago.

Robert Mason: Born in Bearden, Arkansas, in 1948, Mason came to Watts in 1952. He attended the local schools, lived for a time in the Nickerson Gardens housing project, and became one of the Markham Junior High students who developed what was later to become the Student Committee for Improvement in Watts (SCFIW). A graduate of Jordan High School in 1966, his record as a top scholar and basketball player brought him forty-three different scholarship offers from colleges and universities (including that of a National Merit Scholarship). He chose a scholarship at Seattle University, but switched in January, 1968, to the Santa Barbara campus of the University of California. Largely as a result of his increasing involvement in the black movement and his interest in community action, he is re-examining his original goal of a business career.

He credits a black teacher at Jordan High, and Stokely Carmichael, with whom he came into contact at Seattle, as major influences upon his thinking and his participation in community action. Other, less personal, influences have been Harold Cruse (Author of *The Crisis of the Negro Intellectual,* a book highly regarded by many of the black students); Malcolm X; Eldridge Cleaver; and Jomo Kenyatta.

In 1969, he was one of eight Santa Barbara black students, all of them active in the Black Students Union, who were arrested on a "conspiracy" charge when police officers literally crashed through an apartment door early in the morning, without a search warrant and with only the excuse that they had been asked to evict the tenant. The landlord denied under oath that any such eviction order had ever been requested or issued. In the course of their illegal entry, the officers smashed windows, broke locks, and ransacked the premises.

Richard Townsend: "My father served in the Navy during World War II. Before that he had worked in a coal mine somewhere in Alabama where he had his back broken. After he had returned from service in the Navy, he married my mother. My mother, just like my father, was born in Alabama. She was raised in Lowndes County, Alabama, near Selma, and had attended Selma University before she married.

"I was born in 1948 in Birmingham, Alabama, the son of Ocie and Rosie Townsend. Eleven months later I left for California with my grandmother, who I lived with until my parents followed.

"At five I started kindergarten at George Washington Elementary School in Compton. I went to George Washington up through the fifth grade. At this time my parents separated and my mother moved to the area near Broadway and Florence. This is when I began to attend Manchester Avenue School and a little later 68th Street school. This is when I can recall a radical change in my school performance.

"We moved to Watts in 1960. I lived in the Jordan Downs [housing project] and attended Markham Junior High for three years. I then went on to Jordan High School and moved to another apartment in the Jordan Downs, where just my mother and I woud would live until I began college.

"My activities with the Student Committee for Improvement in Watts began in junior high school. The meetings and discussions that we held in Sue Welsh's classroom, after school, began to make us all aware of the conditions of our community. (Note: Sue Welsh was a teacher who later became a Teen Post director and advisor to SCFIW.)"

Paul Williams: "I was born in Los Angeles, April 25, 1948, in General Hospital. I lived on 32nd Street some of the time that I grew up. I began school at Dolores Mission on First Street and I lived in the Aliso Village [housing project]. I stayed there until I was nine years old, went to Catholic grade school from one to third grade, [and then] I went to Utah Street School. At the age of ten, I moved out in Watts. I lived in Watts to the present day, went to 92nd Street School, Markham Junior High School, Jordan High School, and Harbor College.

"The time of living in Watts was the most significant of my history. I learned in what way I was suppressed; I learned which way I was being psychologically defeated. I learned quite a bit of myself, the reality of economics and politics. Economically we was considered low-income; I might have a middle-class value but I know exactly where I am as far as being low-class.

"My education was not well-rounded: [weak] in verbal communications, I mean in reading and writing, I was quite deprived of that education. But to survive in this society that suppresses the poor, I've maintained a good bit of consciousness of my situation to where I was involved in trying to change it.

"But as I grew, I began to get very pessimistic in the changes that I was trying to obtain. The things that I was involved in always included white people. I was developed into an integrationist. In junior high school and high school I played sports—football, track, and anything I could to occupy my mind—a lot of constructive things, instead of turning off into something that's destructive and not doing nothing worth while. At the same time I'm trying to get away from it, every day I have to live with it since it is a part of the community.

"But I found, going to Harbor College, I was going away, trying to get away from black people, as I found quite a few black students doing the same thing. And when I got out there I came to a lot of realities, a lot of good ones and some not so good.

"My major was business, [but] I couldn't dig business at all, because before that I worked at Douglas Aircraft for a year and I was very unhappy with the job that I had. I wanted to advance on, so I went back to college. I [had] stayed out of school for a year, and when I got to Harbor I found out that communications between people were necessary. From whatever perspective you look at, communications was necessary."

(Note: Having graduated from Harbor (Junior) College in mid-1969, Paul Williams was admitted to UCLA in the fall quarter, as a social science major.)

Sometimes I wish I could grow a lot faster and mature a lot faster so I can help produce the right and not the wrong, help produce for man as much as I can. Sometimes living in Watts brings me to the point where I'm just a drop in the ocean, an ocean that is dirty. As I mature older and older, I come to see that being twenty-one years old is just a young, young man lost in a big, big world of people. And these people to me are animals: very primitive, very unconcerned in this society because of the mentality of individualism that has arisen. I find that man is supposed to be a social animal, but he's not. He's not a social animal because, for one thing, he's not concerned with his group or his society or his world, or the people that live in it, primarily. He is concerned basically about a lot of modern technology, the machine.

And sometimes I feel like I even don't want to live in Watts, because Watts is in the United States, the United States is in the Western hemisphere, and the Western hemisphere is part of the Western philosophy, and the Western philosophy is doomed to die. Watts is a container of filth and ignorance, because it was created by the white man. There're containers all over the country, of black people, and they hold and suppress the people that are in them. The filth and ignorance that's in the community is fermenting, to where it's exploding out of the container, and this chemical of filth in the black community is going to emerge and going to destroy itself along with the country, just to prove that black people's minds haven't been robbed, they can't live in this country where they are second, they can't live in a society where they're unhappy.

Some of these thoughts might be abstract and unheard of to white people, but I'm talking directly to you, because the first thing I see is that you're wrong, you're dirty, dirty wrong. As I relate to you, you can believe that I'm watching you consistently, watching you because you should be watching the fools that run this society, and control things, and suppress people, and you're not doing anything about it. White people are so hung up in maintaining their society or maintaining what they have. Yes, you should watch the ones that control your society, you should do something about the people who are poor, you should be doing something about the black people who've been psychologically defeated. And once they come to the reality that you are the problem, like I have learned that white people are the problem, they are going to destroy you.

Paul Williams

About the Author

Paul Bullock was born in Pasadena, California, in 1924. He attended Occidental College in Los Angeles where he majored in Economics, taking his B.A. and M.A. in that field. From 1948 to 1950, he took further graduate work, specializing in Labor Economics and Industrial Relations. In 1953, he joined the staff of the UCLA Institute of Industrial Relations as a Research Assistant. He is at present an Associate Research Economist with the Institute, specializing in manpower economics, particularly the employment and educational problems of minority groups in the Los Angeles area. In February, 1969, he became the director of the Pico-Union Project, one of two major urban-action programs undertaken by the University in the area.

Mr. Bullock has written or co-authored articles for *The New Republic, Frontier, Dissent, California Management Review, Journal of Negro Education,* and *Industrial Relations.* A study of minority unemployment and underemployment, supervised by him from 1963 to 1965, had its findings released in *Hard-Core Unemployment and Poverty in Los Angeles,* published by the Government Printing Office.